The
Glorious Gospel

The Original Design, Identity & Destiny

SELLAPPAN PALANIAPPAN

ANISSA P. ZUCKER

Summary

In The Glorious Gospel: The Original Design, Identity & Destiny, readers are taken on an extraordinary journey through the eternal purpose of God, from creation to redemption, to the ultimate union of heaven and earth. This gospel is not just the story of salvation; it's the breathtaking revelation of who God is, who we are in Him, and the glorious destiny that awaits all creation. Rooted in deep theological truths and saturated with scriptural insights, the book unpacks the grand narrative of God's love, grace, and plan for all things.

The journey begins with the eternal God—Father, Son, and Holy Spirit—existing in perfect love and unity. In the first part, the book explores God's original design in creating humanity for divine family, destined to share in His life and glory. But this design was disrupted by the Fall, as human beings chose religion over relationship and intimacy with God, leading to an identity crisis and corruption of the human design.

But the disruption wasn't the end. In the heart of the book, we see God's response through the vicarious humanity of Christ. The incarnation—the Son of God becoming man—ushers in the ultimate solution to restore humanity to its intended purpose. Through Christ's perfect life, sacrificial death, triumphant resurrection, and glorious ascension, all of creation is included in God's redemptive work. This part vividly explains how Jesus' life and work restored the human identity, redeeming all that was lost.

Moving forward, the new creation reality takes center stage. The book shows how, through the Holy Spirit, believers are empowered to live from perfect union and oneness with Christ, walking in grace, and fulfilling the call to manifest heaven on earth. This new life as sons and daughters of God reflects God's original intent—a people filled with His life, revealing His glory.

The final sections paint a breathtaking picture of creation's ultimate restoration. With the unveiling of mature sons, creation responds to God's eternal plan, yearning for the day when all things are renewed. The new earth becomes a place of unimaginable beauty and harmony, as heaven and earth are united. Love's final victory is the defeat of sin, death, and evil, ushering in a future where God's glory fills all things, and His love reigns forever.

As the book reaches its crescendo, it points toward the eternal purpose fulfilled—a future that goes beyond glory. The new creation will be a place of infinite discovery, adventure, and unbroken communion with God. Eternity will be an ever-expanding journey into God's love and wisdom, where believers live in perfect fellowship, exploring the wonders of His renewed universe.

In The Glorious Gospel, readers will discover the profound truth that God's plan for humanity goes far beyond mere salvation. It is the unfolding of His eternal purpose, a story of identity, destiny, and the ultimate union of heaven and earth. Through this compelling narrative, readers are invited to see the gospel not just as a rescue from sin, but as the revelation of their true identity and the glorious future they are destined for in Christ.

Acknowledgements

The completion of **The Glorious Gospel: The Original Design, Identity & Destiny** has been a remarkable journey, and I am deeply grateful for the various sources of support, inspiration, and tools that made this work possible.

First and foremost, we thank God for the revelation of His glorious inheritance, which has unfolded so beautifully throughout this book. Every word is a reflection of His eternal love and grace, and our prayer is that this book will help others see the majesty of His plan for all creation.

Special thanks go to The Passion Translation (TPT) for its fresh and deeply moving rendering of the Scriptures. The TPT's focus on the heart of God's love and grace has profoundly influenced the tone and direction of this book. Additionally, other Bible translations such as the Mirror Bible, New International Version (NIV), New Living Translation (NLT), and English Standard Version (ESV) provided crucial scriptural foundations, helping us present these truths with both clarity and theological integrity.

We are also grateful for the assistance of Claude, an advanced AI assistant, whose help with editing, refining ideas, and providing feedback proved invaluable throughout the writing process. While maintaining the authentic voice and message of the book, this technological tool helped bring greater clarity and coherence to the presentation of these eternal truths.

We want to acknowledge Tommy Miller, Chris Blackeby, Greg Lilley, Don Keithley, Damon Thompson, Mike Parsons, Jamie Englehart, Malcolm Smith, John Crowder, Baxter Kruger, Paul Young, Gil and Adena, Liz Wright, Phelim Doherty, Nanci Coen, Justin Abraham, and many others who have been very influential in shaping our understanding of our inheritance in Christ. Their teachings, writings, and ministries have deeply impacted our spiritual journey, and their insights have helped illuminate the profound truths of God's eternal purpose. We also extend our thanks to the wider community of scholars, theologians, and authors whose works have contributed to our understanding. Though many have not been referenced directly, their insights have shaped our thinking and fuelled our passion for sharing these glorious revelations.

Special thanks to Anna Teo for generously taking your precious time to review, provide feedback, edit, and proofread the manuscript multiple times. Your swift and excellent service is deeply appreciated. This manuscript could not have been completed without your willing and generous support, and labor of love.
Finally, to our readers—thank you for embarking on this journey with us. Our hope is that this book will stir your heart, challenge your understanding, and ultimately lead you deeper into the revelation of God's love and your identity in Him. It is for you, the seekers and disciples of Christ, that this work was written, and we pray it will encourage you to walk boldly into your destiny.
To God be the glory, now and forever.

Table of Contents

PART 1

The Eternal Purpose

Chapter 1

The Triune God: Love, Light, and Life

Before anything came into existence—before the stars shone, before the first breath of humanity—there was God. But God was not alone. The essence of the Christian faith rests on the mystery of the Trinity: Father, Son, and Holy Spirit, coexisting eternally in perfect harmony. This reality defies human logic, for God is one in essence, yet three distinct persons. It is not a mathematical problem to be solved but a divine mystery to be embraced.

The Trinity reveals something profound about the nature of God: at the heart of His being is relationship. God is not solitary, distant, or disconnected. Instead, He is eternally communal, and this community is founded on love, light, and life. Each person of the Godhead—Father, Son, and Holy Spirit—lives in perfect union, and this union is the foundation of all that is good, true, and beautiful. Understanding the triune nature of God is the starting point for comprehending the rest of the gospel.

God Is Love: The Eternal Fellowship

The Apostle John declares boldly, "God is love" (1 John 4:8, TPT). This is not a casual statement or a passing remark. It is a revelation that unlocks the very essence of who God is. Love is not merely an attribute of God; it is His identity. And because God is a Trinity, His love is relational. For love to exist, there must be a beloved. In

God, the Father eternally loves the Son, the Son eternally loves the Father, and this love is expressed through the Holy Spirit. Thus, within God's own being, there is a perfect, self-giving love that has no beginning and no end.

In John 17:24 (TPT), Jesus speaks of this love when He prays, "Father, I ask that you allow everyone that you have given to me to be with me where I am! Then they will see my full glory—the very splendor you have placed upon me because you have loved me even before the beginning of time." Before the creation of the world, before time itself, the Father loved the Son. This love is not like human love, which is often conditional or based on merit. It is a pure, selfless love that flows from the heart of God and defines His very existence.

This eternal fellowship of love between the Father, Son, and Spirit is not only the basis for creation but also the foundation for understanding why God created at all. God did not create the world because He needed something or someone to love. He was not lonely or incomplete. Instead, His love was so full and overflowing that it could not be contained. Out of the abundance of His love, God created the world to share this divine fellowship with His creation.

This is why love is at the center of the gospel. It is not merely a message of salvation from sin, but an invitation to enter into the very love that exists within the Trinity. When we are saved, we are not just forgiven of our sins—we are drawn into the eternal relationship of love that exists between the Father, Son, and Spirit.

Visual 1.1 presents images (symbols) illustrating the Trinity, the relationship between Father, Son, and Holy

Spirit, their union and oneness, as well as their unity and distinction. However, images cannot fully describe or express the inexorable, infinite, and transcendent nature of God.

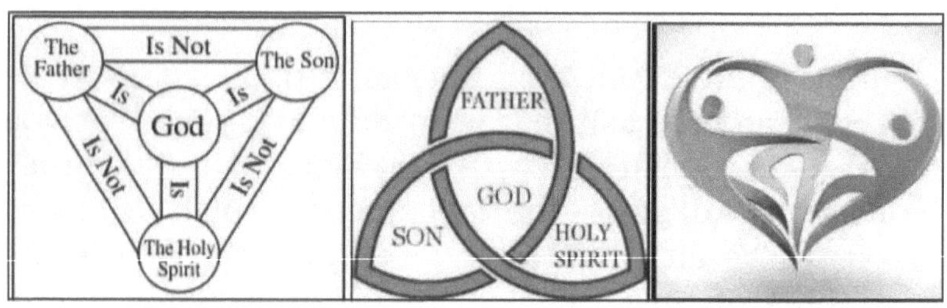

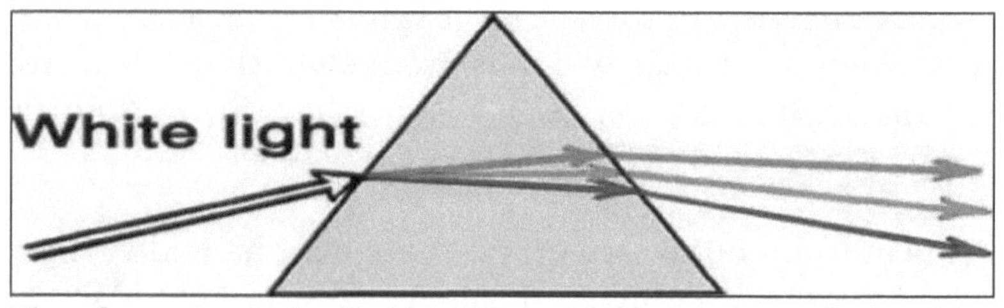

Visual 1.1: Symbols used to illustrate the Trinity, relationship between Father, Son, and Holy Spirit, their union and oneness, as well as their unity and distinction.
(**Source:** image of A symbolic representation of the Trinity, emphasizing the flow of love between the Father, Son, and Holy Spirit - Search)

As we explore the depth of this divine love and fellowship, it becomes clear that separation from God is a misconception. The Sidebar highlights how our union with God is foundational to our identity and existence.

Sidebar: No Separation - The Union of God and Humanity

The idea of separation between God and humanity is a misunderstanding. While sin has caused alienation in humanity's mind (Colossians 1:21,

Isaiah 59:2), God has never turned away from us. From the very beginning, when Adam sinned, it was God who sought him out, demonstrating His desire to remain close. This separation exists only in our perception, not in reality.

In John 14 and 17, Jesus describes a profound union, saying, "I am in the Father, and you are in Me, and I am in you." This divine relationship is not one of distance, but of oneness and inclusion. Acts 17:28 affirms this, declaring that "in Him we live, move, and have our being." God is not a distant deity, but One who is fully present within us, sustaining and filling all things.

The apostle Paul expresses this reality in Galatians 1:16, when he says that God "revealed His Son in me," emphasizing the inner presence of Christ. As believers, we are the temple of God; His Spirit dwells in us continually. God is not in some far-off place, waiting for us to reach Him. He is closer than we can imagine, residing in our hearts, fully engaged with our lives here and now.

This intimate union means that God is not a distant future hope, but a present reality. Any belief that God is "not here, not now, not me" is a misconception. God's nearness, as both Creator and Redeemer, assures us that He is always with us, dwelling in us as a source of love, strength, and purpose. The truth of our union with Him means we are never separated, but fully embraced in His presence.

God Is Light: The Purity of His Being

While love forms the core of God's relational nature, light reveals the purity and holiness of His being. In 1 John 1:5 (TPT), we read, "God is pure light. You will never find even a trace of darkness in him." This declaration speaks to God's absolute perfection and the absence of anything sinful, evil, or impure in His nature. God's light is not merely physical brightness but a spiritual truth that reveals, clarifies, and makes all things visible. Where there is light, there can be no shadow, no deceit, no hidden agendas.

The imagery of light is used throughout Scripture to represent God's holiness and righteousness. In the Old Testament, when Moses encountered God on Mount Sinai, the light of God's glory was so overwhelming that Moses had to veil his face (Exodus 34:29-35). Similarly, the prophet Isaiah, when he saw a vision of the Lord in His heavenly throne room, was overcome by the brilliance of God's holiness, crying out, "Woe is me! For I am lost; for I am a man of unclean lips" (Isaiah 6:5, ESV). The light of God exposes all things, and in His presence, no imperfection can remain hidden.

In the New Testament, Jesus describes Himself as "the Light of the world" (John 8:12, TPT). This is a profound statement that reveals not only Jesus' divinity but also His role in illuminating the truth of God. To see Jesus is to see the Father, and to walk in His light is to live in the truth. When we embrace Jesus, the light of God enters our lives, dispelling the darkness of sin, confusion, and fear.

Moreover, God's light is life-giving. In the very beginning, God spoke, "Let there be light" (Genesis 1:3, TPT), and light burst forth, bringing life to creation. The connection between light and life is central to understanding the gospel. Jesus came not only to shine a light on our sin but to bring us into the fullness of life. In John 1:4 (TPT), it says, "Eternal Life is in him, and this life gives light to all humanity." The light of God is not just a guide; it is the source of life itself.

God Is Life: The Source of All Existence

If love is the heart of God and light is His purity, then life is His gift to all creation. The Triune God is the source of all life, both physical and spiritual. From the opening chapters of Genesis, where God breathes life into Adam (Genesis 2:7), to the Gospel of John, where Jesus declares, "I have come to give you everything in abundance, more than you expect—life in its fullness until you overflow!" (John 10:10, TPT), the message is clear: God is the giver of life, and in Him, life finds its ultimate meaning and fulfilment.

The life that God offers is not merely survival or existence. It is a quality of life that is marked by fullness, abundance, and joy. This life is not constrained by the limitations of the natural world, for it is rooted in the eternal nature of God Himself. To partake in God's life is to enter into the very life of the Trinity—a life that is vibrant, dynamic, and eternal.

In Jesus, the life of God is made available to all humanity. As the eternal Word made flesh, Jesus embodies the life of God and makes it accessible to us. Through His death, resurrection and ascension, Jesus opens the way for us to enter into the fullness of life that the Father, Son, and Spirit share. This is why Jesus can say, "I am the resurrection and the life. Anyone who believes in me will live, even after dying" (John 11:25, TPT). The life that Jesus offers is not confined to this world but extends into eternity.

The resurrection of Jesus is the ultimate demonstration of God's life-giving power. Death, which had reigned over humanity since the fall, was defeated once and for all. In Christ, we are not only forgiven of our sins but are also given the gift of eternal life. This life is not something we must wait for in the future; it begins the moment we place our faith in Christ and are born again into the family of God.

Visual 1.2 depicts Jesus as the light of the world, shining into the darkness and bringing life to all creation.

Visual 1.2: Jesus, the light of the world, shining into the darkness, bringing life to all creation.
(**Source:** image of Jesus, the light of the world, shining into the darkness, bringing life to all creation - Search)

The Trinity's Role in Creation

Understanding the triune nature of God helps us grasp the depth of creation itself. When we read the creation narrative in Genesis, we see all three persons of the Trinity at work. God the Father speaks, the Word (Jesus) brings creation into being, and the Spirit hovers over the waters, sustaining life (Genesis 1:1-3, TPT). The creation of the universe was not an isolated act by one part of the Godhead but a collaborative work of love and power between the Father, Son, and Spirit.

In Colossians 1:16-17 (TPT), Paul writes of Jesus, "For through the Son, everything was created, both in the heavenly realm and on the earth, all that is seen and all that is unseen... Everything exists through him and for him. He existed before anything was made, and now everything finds completion in him." Creation, then, is not only from God but for God, designed to reflect His glory, His love, and His life.

Creation was also an act of purpose. God did not create out of need, as though He lacked something, but out of an overflow of love. The world was made to reflect His goodness, and humanity, created in His image, was destined to live in intimate relationship with the triune God. This purpose was disrupted by sin, but as we will see in later chapters, God's love and life would not be thwarted by the fall. From the beginning, God's plan was to restore humanity and all creation through the redemptive work of Jesus.

Conclusion: Participating in the Divine Life

The Triune God—Father, Son, and Holy Spirit—calls us into the very fellowship that existed before the foundation of the world. The love, light, and life that flow between the persons of the Trinity is now made available to us through Jesus Christ. This is not a distant, abstract idea, but an invitation to live in communion with God Himself. Through the incarnation of Christ, the light of God has come into the world, and through His death, resurrection and ascension, the life of God has been given to all who believe.

Paul writes in 2 Corinthians 4:6 (TPT), "For God, who said, 'Let brilliant light shine out of darkness,' is the one who has cascaded his light into us—the brilliant dawning light of the glorious knowledge of God as we gaze into the face of Jesus Christ." To gaze upon Jesus is to see the fullness of God's love, light, and life. It is through Christ that we are brought into the eternal fellowship of the Trinity, where we are no longer strangers but beloved sons and daughters.

The beauty of the gospel is that we are not merely forgiven of our sins and left to figure out life on our own. Rather, we are invited into the very life of God Himself. We are called to share in the same love that the Father has for the Son and that the Son has for the Father. We are given the light of Christ to guide us and the life of the Spirit to sustain us. This is the fullness of the gospel, and it is the destiny for which we were created.

As we move forward in this book, we will explore how humanity was designed to live in this divine relationship, how sin disrupted that design, and how God, in His love, has been working to restore us to our true identity and purpose. The gospel is the story of God's unrelenting love—a love that began before time and will continue into eternity.

Chapter 2

Created for Divine Family

Humanity's story begins not in isolation but in relationship. From the very outset, God's intention was to create a family—a people who would live in communion with Him, reflecting His love and sharing His life. This divine family is not a result of human achievement or effort, but a gift rooted in God's eternal purpose. Before the foundation of the world, God had already set His heart on humanity, desiring to bring us into His life and love. This chapter explores the profound reality that humanity was not an afterthought but central to God's plan, created to participate in the divine family, a family that mirrors the eternal fellowship of the Father, Son, and Holy Spirit.

In the Image of God: A Reflection of the Divine

The creation of humanity is a unique event in the narrative of Genesis. While all other creatures were spoken into existence, God takes a more personal approach when creating humanity. Genesis 1:26 (TPT) declares, "Let us make man in our image, after our likeness." The plural "us" hints at the triune nature of God—Father, Son, and Holy Spirit—working together in unity. This collaborative, intentional act reveals that humanity was made to be a reflection of God Himself. We are not like the animals or the rest of creation; we bear the very image of the Creator.

But what does it mean to be created in the image of God? It means that humanity, unlike any other part of creation, is designed to mirror the relational nature of God. Just as the Father, Son, and Holy Spirit exist in perfect love and unity, so too is humanity created for relationship—with God and with one another. We are created to be a reflection of the love that flows within the Trinity, embodying that same love in our relationships. Being made in God's image also means that we carry a unique dignity and worth. Every human being, regardless of race, gender, or status, is marked by the divine imprint. As Psalm 8:5 (TPT) reflects, "You've made him [humanity] only a little lower than Elohim, crowned like kings and queens with glory and magnificence!"

This divine image also bestows upon us a role and a purpose. Genesis 1:28 (TPT) continues, "God blessed them and said, 'Be fruitful and multiply. Fill the earth and govern it. Reign over the fish in the sea, the birds in the sky, and all the animals that scurry along the ground.'" Humanity was created not just to exist but to reign, to steward creation in partnership with God. This stewardship reflects God's own rulership over the universe, and our call to govern creation is an extension of His authority, a sign of the intimate relationship between God and humanity.

Visual 2.1 depicts Adam and Eve in the Garden, reflecting the image of God and exercising their dominion over creation.

Visual 2.1: Adam and Eve in the Garden, reflecting the image of God and their dominion over creation.
(**Source:** <u>image of depiction of Adam and Eve in the Garden, reflecting the image of God and their dominion over creation - Search</u>)

As we consider our identity as part of God's divine family, it's essential to understand what it means to be created as sons and daughters of God. The Sidebar expands on how this identity shapes our relationship with our Creator.

Sidebar: Sons of God: Our Identity in Creation

From the very beginning, God conceived humanity in His heart, designing us to reflect His image and likeness. In Genesis 1:26, God declared His intention, saying, "Let us make man in our image, after our likeness," blessing humanity to be fruitful, multiply, and have dominion. This conception in God's mind came before our physical formation, marking humanity as uniquely designed for relationship with Him.

God physically formed Adam in Genesis 2, breathing life into him and creating a being that embodied both the dust of the earth and the breath of God. Eve was then drawn from Adam's side, symbolizing the future relationship of Christ and the Church—the Bride taken from the life of the Bridegroom, signifying union and shared purpose.

Just as all creation reproduces after its kind, God also brought forth humanity after His kind—to bear His image and share in His nature. Adam brought sin and death through disobedience, and his fallen nature was passed down through humanity. But Jesus, the "last Adam," took the consequences of sin upon Himself on the cross, dying the death that humanity deserved. His resurrection marked the beginning of a new humanity; as He rose, we rose with Him, born from above and now identified not with the earthly Adam but with Christ, the heavenly Man.

We are "rock hewn from the Rock" (Isaiah 51:1), sharing in Jesus' life and nature. Where Adam was of the earth, Jesus is from above, and we, too, are born of the Spirit, transformed by His life within us. Jesus is the "firstborn" (Colossians 1:15) and monogenes (unique Son) in all creation, having preeminence, yet we are included in His divine life. This identity transcends human species; we are sons and daughters of God, a divine class of beings who share in the life, authority, and relationship that Jesus has with the Father through the Spirit.

As sons and daughters of God, we are invited to co-reign with Christ, included in His eternal relationship with the Father. Our identity is not merely as human beings but as members of a divine family, empowered to live out God's purposes on earth. Through Christ, we inherit His authority, presence, and life, carrying out our calling to reflect God's glory and love to all creation.

God's Eternal Purpose: A Family of Sons and Daughters

Before time began, God's heart was set on creating a family. Ephesians 1:4-5 (TPT) unveils this glorious truth: "And he chose us to be his very own, joining us to himself even before he laid the foundation of the universe! Because of his great love, he ordained us, so that we would be seen as holy in his eyes with an unstained innocence." Humanity was not an afterthought or a response to the fall. From the very beginning, God's purpose was to bring us into His family, to adopt us as His sons and daughters (placing us in the position of mature sons, like the younger prodigal son).

This adoption is not a mere legal status; it is an invitation into the very life of the Trinity. We are invited to share in the same relationship that the Son has with the Father—a relationship of intimacy, love, and belonging. When Jesus teaches His disciples to pray, He begins with "Our Father" (Matthew 6:9, TPT), inviting us to address God in the same intimate way that He does. This is the heart of the gospel: that through Christ, we are brought into the family of God, not as outsiders or servants, but as beloved children.

Understanding 'adoption' as used in Scripture highlights our placement as mature sons and daughters in God's family. The Sidebar further clarifies how this adoption is a call to live out the fullness of our identity in Christ.

The Apostle Paul emphasizes this in Romans 8:15 (TPT): "And you did not receive the 'spirit of religious duty,' leading you back into the fear of never being good enough. But you have received the 'Spirit of full acceptance,' enfolding you into the family of God. And you will never feel orphaned, for as he rises up within us, our spirits join him in saying the words of tender affection, 'Beloved Father!'" This is the transformative power of the gospel—God has not only forgiven our sins but has brought us into His family, giving us a new identity as His children. This family relationship is at the core of God's eternal plan for humanity.

In Christ, this divine family is not limited by natural descent or ethnic boundaries. Galatians 3:28 (TPT) declares, "And we no longer see each other in our former state—Jew or non-Jew, rich or poor, male or female— because we're all one through our union with Jesus

Christ." The family of God transcends human divisions, uniting us as brothers and sisters in Christ. This is the fulfilment of God's original design: a diverse family, united in love, reflecting the image of the triune God.

Visual 2.2 illustrates that all nations and peoples are included in the one family in Christ, reflecting God's eternal purpose.

Visual 2.2: All nations and peoples are included in the one family in Christ, reflecting God's eternal purpose.

Living as God's Image-Bearers: The Call to Reflect His Glory

To be made in the image of God is to be called to reflect His glory. But this reflection is not something we can achieve through our own efforts. It is a gift of grace, a transformation that occurs as we live in relationship with God. 2 Corinthians 3:18 (TPT) describes this process: "We can all draw close to him with the veil removed from our faces. And with no veil, we all become like mirrors who brightly reflect the glory of the Lord Jesus. We are being transfigured into his very image as we move from one brighter level of glory to another. And this glorious transfiguration comes from the Lord, who is the Spirit."

Our purpose as image-bearers is to reflect God's love, light, and life to the world. This means that we are called to live in such a way that others see God through us. Jesus said in Matthew 5:14-16 (TPT), "Your lives light up the world. Let others see your light from a distance, for how can you hide a city that stands on a hilltop? So don't hide your light! Let it shine brightly before others, so that your commendable works will shine as light upon them, and then they will give their praise to your Father in heaven." As we live out our calling as sons and daughters of God, we become beacons of His glory, drawing others to Him.

This call to reflect God's glory also involves our role as stewards of creation. In the beginning, God entrusted humanity with the care and governance of the earth. This stewardship reflects our identity as image-bearers, called to rule with the same love and care that God demonstrates toward us. When we care for creation, we reflect God's heart for the world He made. When we treat others with love, kindness, and respect, we reflect the relational nature of God. This is the high calling of being made in the image of God.

But this calling is not a burden. It is an invitation to participate in God's work in the world. As we live in communion with Him, we are empowered by His Spirit to fulfil our purpose. The Spirit, who hovered over the waters at creation, now dwells within us, transforming us into the likeness of Christ and enabling us to live as God's image-bearers in the world.

Conclusion: Created for Communion

Humanity's purpose is not found in isolation or self-sufficiency but in communion with God and one another. We were created to be part of a divine family, to share in the love, light, and life of the Trinity. This family is not something we earn or achieve; it is a gift of grace, rooted in God's eternal plan. Through Christ, we are brought into this family, adopted as sons and daughters, and called to reflect the image of God in the world.

As we continue in this journey through the gospel story, we will explore how this divine family relationship was disrupted by sin and how God, in His love, has been working to restore humanity to its original purpose. But here, at the beginning, we see the foundation: we are created for communion with God, to live as His beloved children, and to reflect His glory to all creation.

Chapter 3

The Pre-existent Christ and Humanity

Before time began, before the creation of the world, Christ existed. This profound truth is central to understanding the gospel and the eternal purpose of God for humanity. The pre-existence of Christ reveals that the plan for human salvation and restoration was not an afterthought or a reaction to the fall. Instead, it was part of God's eternal design. In Christ, we see not only the Savior who redeems humanity from sin but also the One in whom humanity was always meant to find its identity and purpose. This chapter explores the significance of Christ's pre-existence and what it means for humanity's original design and ultimate destiny.

The Pre-existence of Christ: A Cosmic Reality

The opening words of John's Gospel make a bold declaration: "In the beginning, the Living Expression was already there. And the Living Expression was with God, yet fully God" (John 1:1, TPT). This "Living Expression" refers to Christ, the eternal Word of God. Before anything else existed—before the foundations of the earth were laid—Christ was there, existing in perfect unity with the Father and the Spirit. He is the eternal Son, not created but begotten, co-equal with the Father and the Spirit in glory, power, and majesty.

The significance of Christ's pre-existence cannot be overstated. It tells us that Christ is not merely a historical figure who appeared in time; He is the eternal Logos, through whom all things were made. As Colossians 1:16-17 (TPT) explains, "For through the Son, everything was created, both in the heavenly realm and on the earth, all that is seen and all that is unseen... He existed before anything was made, and now everything finds completion in him." This means that Christ is not only the Savior but also the Creator. He is the one in whom the entire cosmos finds its origin, purpose, and meaning.

Christ's pre-existence also reveals the deep love and intention behind creation. The world was not created out of randomness or necessity but out of the overflowing love of God. In and through Christ, the triune God decided to bring forth creation as an expression of divine love and goodness. And at the center of this creation was humanity, made in the image of God and destined to share in the eternal fellowship of the Father, Son, and Spirit.

Humanity's Creation in Christ

The pre-existence of Christ shapes the way we understand the creation of humanity. Genesis 1:26 (TPT) tells us that God said, "Let us make man in our image, after our likeness." The "us" in this passage points to the triune God—Father, Son, and Holy Spirit—working together in the act of creation. Humanity was not created in isolation but in Christ, the eternal Son. Christ was the blueprint, the model after which humanity was made.

This truth is echoed in Ephesians 1:4 (TPT), which says, "And he chose us to be his very own, joining us to himself even before he laid the foundation of the universe!" This profound statement reveals that God's plan for humanity was established before creation itself. In Christ, humanity was chosen and predestined to be part of the divine family. Our existence is not an accident; we were created to be united with Christ, to share in His divine life and glory.

Being created in the image of God means that we were designed to reflect Christ, the perfect image of the Father. Christ is not only the revelation of who God is but also the revelation of who humanity is meant to be. When we look at Christ, we see the perfect human, the One who fully embodies what it means to live in union with God. He is the fulfilment of humanity's original purpose and design.

Visual 3.1 depicts Christ as the pre-existent Word, the creator of the heavens and the earth, standing at the center of creation.

The Incarnation as the Unveiling of God's Plan

While Christ's pre-existence affirms His eternal nature, His incarnation—the moment when He took on human flesh—is the clearest expression of God's eternal plan for humanity. The incarnation is not merely a reaction to sin; it is the ultimate revelation of God's desire to unite humanity with Himself. In John 1:14 (TPT), we read, "The Living Expression became a man and lived among us! And we gazed upon his glory, the glory of the One and Only who came from the Father overflowing with tender mercy and truth!"

The incarnation reveals that the Son of God did not come to earth simply to rescue us from sin, though that was certainly part of His mission. More fundamentally, He came to restore humanity to its original design and purpose. By taking on human nature, Christ sanctified humanity, becoming the perfect bridge between God and man. In Him, the divine and the human are united, showing us that God's plan has always been to bring humanity into the fullness of His divine life.

This is why theologians speak of Christ as the "Second [Last] Adam" (Romans 5:12-19, TPT). Where the first Adam failed, bringing sin and death into the world, Christ, the Second Adam, succeeded, bringing life and restoration. Through His life, death, and resurrection, Christ reversed the effects of the fall, restoring humanity to its original place in God's plan. But more than that, He elevated humanity to a new level, bringing us into the very life of the Trinity. In Christ, we are no longer separated from God; we are united with Him, sharing in His glory and love.

Visual 3.2 portrays the nativity scene, capturing the moment when the incarnate Christ stepped into human history, bringing God's presence into the world in the form of a newborn child.

Visual 3.2: The Incarnation, with Christ stepping into human history.
(**Source:** image of Incarnation, with Christ stepping into human history, bridging heaven and earth - Search Images)

Christ and the Ultimate Destiny of Humanity

The pre-existence of Christ also points us to the ultimate destiny of humanity. If Christ is the beginning—the One in whom all things were created—He is also the end, the One in whom all things will be fulfilled. As Paul writes in Ephesians 1:10 (TPT), "And because of God's unfailing purpose, this detailed plan will reign supreme through every period of time until the fulfilment of all the ages finally reaches its climax—when God makes all things new in all of heaven and earth through Jesus Christ."

Christ is the Alpha and the Omega, the beginning and the end (Revelation 22:13). Our destiny is not a mystery; it is to be united with Christ, sharing in His eternal life and glory. In Him, we find our true identity, our purpose, and our fulfilment. All of history is moving toward this ultimate goal—the full revelation of Christ and the restoration of all things in Him.

This is the hope of the gospel. It is not merely the hope of personal salvation but the hope of cosmic renewal. In Christ, the entire creation will be redeemed and restored, and humanity will take its rightful place as sons and daughters of God, reigning with Him in glory. As Paul writes in Romans 8:19-21 (TPT), "The entire universe is standing on tiptoe, yearning to see the unveiling of God's glorious sons and daughters! For against its will, the universe itself has had to endure the empty futility resulting from the consequences of human sin. But now, with eager expectation, all creation longs for freedom from its slavery to decay and to experience with us the wonderful freedom coming to God's children."

Christ's pre-existence, therefore, not only reveals the origins of humanity but also its destiny. In Him, we were created, and in Him, we will find our ultimate fulfilment. The gospel is the story of God's eternal plan to unite all things in Christ, bringing humanity into the fullness of His life and love.

As we recognize Christ's eternal role and His work on our behalf, it's crucial to understand that His work is fully complete. The Sidebar explains how we are invited to live in the fullness of His finished work.

The "finished work of Christ" on the cross encompasses the entirety of His life, death, resurrection, and ascension. Jesus did not accomplish part of the work and leave the rest for us to complete. Rather, He finished it fully (John 19:30), providing complete reconciliation, forgiveness, acceptance, and justification for all humanity. Through His work, we are invited to enter into this finished reality, not by our own efforts, but by simply receiving His gift of grace.

This finished work means that salvation is by grace alone. We don't "add to" Christ's work or strive to complete it ourselves. Instead, we receive and live out what He has already done, stepping into the new life He has given. As we embrace this truth, we begin to experience the fullness of life in Christ, knowing that we are already forgiven, accepted, and justified—not by our works, but by His grace.

In Christ, we are invited to rest in His finished work, rather than striving to earn what He has already provided. This truth frees us from the pressure of "finishing the race" ourselves. It is God's grace that empowers us, and His Spirit that enables us to live in alignment with His purpose. Our journey is not about achieving salvation, but about living out the reality of the gift we have received.

Conclusion: The Centrality of Christ in the Story of Humanity

As we reflect on the pre-existence of Christ, we begin to see that the story of humanity is, at its core, the story of Christ. From the very beginning, humanity was created in Him, through Him, and for Him. The incarnation is the unveiling of God's eternal plan, the moment when Christ stepped into human history to reveal our true identity and destiny. And the end of the story—the ultimate fulfilment of all things—will be found in Christ, when all creation is brought into perfect union with Him.

The gospel is not just a message about individual salvation. It is the story of God's eternal purpose for humanity, a purpose that began before time and will continue into eternity. In Christ, we find our beginning, our purpose, and our end. He is the pre-existent Word, the One in whom all things hold together (Colossians 1:17), and the One in whom all things will be made new.

As we continue our journey through the gospel story, we will see how Christ's incarnation, life, death, and resurrection are the fulfilment of God's plan to bring humanity into the fullness of His divine life. The pre-existence of Christ reminds us that God's love for humanity is eternal, and in Christ, we are invited to share in that love, both now and forever.

Chapter 4

Angels and the First Creation

Angels, often described as mysterious and majestic beings, play a significant role in the divine narrative. Before humanity's (physical) creation, angels were brought into existence as part of God's first creation, tasked with specific roles and purposes in relation to God's plan. Understanding the role of angels helps us grasp the broader context of creation and the cosmic reality that frames the gospel story. This chapter will explore the creation of angels, their purpose in God's design, and how they fit into the larger story of God's eternal purpose for humanity and all creation.

The Creation of Angels: Heavenly Beings with Purpose

Long before the creation of humanity, God created a host of spiritual beings known as angels. These beings were formed to serve, worship, and carry out the will of God. Angels are described throughout Scripture as powerful messengers and warriors of the divine, dwelling in the heavenly realms and standing in the presence of God. In Colossians 1:16 (TPT), Paul writes, "For through the Son everything was created, both in the heavenly realm and on the earth, all that is seen and all that is unseen, every seat of power, realm of government, principality, and authority—it was all created through him and for his purpose."

Angels were created through Christ and for Christ, just as humanity was. Their existence serves a higher purpose, to be instruments of God's divine will and to participate in His work. In the book of Job, we catch a glimpse of the joy and excitement that surrounded the creation of the world, not only for God but also for the angels. In Job 38:4-7 (TPT), God says, "Where were you when I laid the foundation of the earth? Tell me, if you have understanding... when the morning stars sang together, and all the sons of God shouted for joy?" Here, the "morning stars" and "sons of God" refer to the angels, who rejoiced as they witnessed the unfolding of God's creative work.

Angels, unlike humans, do not bear the image of God and possess a different kind of free will. While they have the capacity to choose—evident in the rebellion of Lucifer and his followers—their choices operate within a unique framework compared to humanity's. They were created with specific roles and duties, primarily to serve God and minister to His creation. Hebrews 1:14 (TPT) tells us, 'What role, then, do the angels have? The angels are spirit-messengers sent by God to serve those who are going to be saved.' Their existence is deeply connected to God's plan of salvation for humanity, and they play a supportive role in ensuring the unfolding of God's purposes.

As we explore the purpose and roles of angels in creation, it's helpful to understand how they interact with humanity. The Sidebar highlights the distinct yet complementary roles of angels and humans in God's design.

Angels and humans were created with distinct, purposeful roles in God's creation. Unlike humans, angels are not a race; they don't marry or produce offspring. Each angel is individually created and designed for specific functions within God's kingdom. The different orders of angels include seraphim, cherubim, principalities, and the seven spirits of God, each with unique responsibilities—whether in worship, guidance, or governance.

When angels fulfil their purpose, they experience joy, much like humans do when aligned with God's will. Angels act as spiritual governors, assisting and guiding humanity toward maturity as sons and daughters of God. Hebrews 1:14 calls angels "ministering spirits sent to serve those who will inherit salvation." They served Jesus in the wilderness after His fast and play an active role in the lives of believers, helping us fulfil God's purposes.

As coheirs with Christ, we are called to cooperate with angels to accomplish God's will on earth. God delegates certain tasks to angels, rather than doing everything Himself, highlighting the collaborative nature of His creation. In our maturity, we are empowered to do "greater things," yet it is always Christ within us who accomplishes this work.

Angels fulfil God's purposes in creation, while humans, uniquely made in God's image, are designed for intimate fellowship with Him and given authority over creation. Our relationship with

The Heavenly Host: Worshipers of the Divine

One of the most prominent roles of angels is worship. Throughout Scripture, angels are portrayed as worshipers, constantly glorifying God and declaring His holiness. Isaiah's vision of the throne room of God in Isaiah 6 gives us a vivid picture of angelic worship: "In the year that King Uzziah died, I saw the Lord sitting upon a throne, high and lifted up... Above him stood the seraphim... And one called to another and said: 'Holy, holy, holy is the Lord of hosts; the whole earth is full of his glory!'" (Isaiah 6:1-3, TPT). The angels stand in awe of God's majesty and holiness, continually offering praise and adoration.

The book of Revelation also gives us a glimpse into the heavenly realm, where angels surround the throne of God, singing hymns of worship and bowing before Him. Revelation 5:11-12 (TPT) describes this scene: "Then I looked, and I heard the voices of myriads of angels in the circle around the throne, as well as the voices of the living creatures and the elders—myriads upon myriads, and as many as thousands upon thousands! And they all cried out with a loud voice: 'Worthy is the Lamb who was slaughtered to receive great power and might, wealth and wisdom, honor, glory, and praise!'"

In their worship, angels remind us of the glory and majesty of God. They model the proper response to God's holiness—one of awe, reverence, and adoration. Their constant praise also serves as a reminder that all of creation is ultimately meant to glorify God. Humanity, as part of this creation, is also called to participate in this eternal worship. The angels, though distinct from humanity, are part of the broader family of God's creation, united in their purpose to glorify the Creator.

Visual 4.1 illustrates angels worshiping around the throne of God. The book of Revelation describes this scene, showing the four living creatures, twenty-four elders, and countless angels gathered in worship before Him (Revelation 5:11-14).

Visual 4.1: Angels worshiping around the throne of God. (**Source:** <u>image of angels worshiping around the throne of God - Search Images</u>)

Angels and Humanity: Guardians and Messengers

In addition to their role in worship, angels are often depicted in Scripture as messengers and protectors of humanity. Throughout the biblical narrative, we see angels acting as intermediaries between God and His people, delivering messages, providing guidance, and offering protection. One of the most famous instances of angelic intervention occurs in Luke 1:26-31 (TPT), when the angel Gabriel appears to Mary to announce the birth of Jesus: "During the sixth month of Elizabeth's pregnancy, the angel Gabriel was sent from God's presence to an unmarried girl named Mary, living in Nazareth, a village in Galilee. She was engaged to a man named Joseph... Gabriel appeared to her and said, 'Rejoice, beloved young woman, for the Lord is with you, and you are anointed with great favor... You will become pregnant with a baby boy, and you are to name him Jesus.'"

In this passage, Gabriel serves as a divine messenger, delivering one of the most important announcements in history—the birth of the Savior. This is just one example of how angels act as God's intermediaries, conveying His will and ensuring that His plan is carried out in the world.

Angels also serve as protectors and guardians of God's people. In Psalm 91:11 (TPT), we are promised, "God sends angels with special orders to protect you wherever you go, defending you from all harm." This role as protectors is seen in various parts of Scripture, including the story of Daniel in the lions' den, where an angel shuts the mouths of the lions, ensuring Daniel's safety (Daniel 6:22, TPT).

These protective and messenger roles highlight the deep connection between angels and humanity. Although angels are spiritual beings who dwell in the heavenly realms, they are actively involved in the affairs of human beings, working behind the scenes to fulfil God's purposes. Angels are not to be worshiped, as they themselves are created beings, but they serve as instruments of God's will, revealing His care and protection for His people.

In God's heavenly assembly, often referred to as the Divine Council, we see a remarkable example of collaborative decision-making involving both God and His spiritual beings. The Sidebar provides insight into this unique council and its role in divine governance.

Sidebar: The Divine Council - God's Heavenly Assembly

Scripture introduces a fascinating concept known as the Divine Council—a heavenly assembly where God gathers with angelic beings, and, on occasion, even humans, to make significant decisions. Psalm 82 and Psalm 89 portray God presiding over this assembly, exercising justice and delegating authority. In Daniel 4, we see that "the decision by the watchers" resulted in Nebuchadnezzar's humbling, indicating that angels may play an active role in guiding the course of events.

1 Kings 22 provides a unique example of this process, where God allows the members of His council to contribute to the outcome of Israel's battle. When asked for suggestions, a spirit steps forward with a plan, and God permits it to be carried out, even though the decision leads to a negative outcome for King Ahab. This instance reflects God's inclusive leadership within the council, allowing His created beings to participate in His purposes, sometimes going along with their choices even if they may not align perfectly with His ideal.

Occasionally, humans are included in this council. Figures like Enoch and, through prophetic visions, prophets such as Isaiah and Ezekiel, are brought into God's presence and invited to witness or contribute to divine decisions. This council model, with God as the ultimate chair, suggests that God values the input and engagement of His creation in governance and extends this authority to His trusted servants.

Through the Divine Council, God not only leads but invites others to share in His decision-making process, reflecting a relationship of trust and participation within His heavenly family. This interaction also foreshadows our own role as believers, called to eventually co-reign with Christ as sons and daughters in God's kingdom.

The Rebellion: Fallen Angels and the Cosmic Conflict

Not all angels remained faithful to God. Scripture reveals that a portion of the angelic host, led by Lucifer, rebelled against God's authority. Lucifer, described as a beautiful and powerful angel, became filled with pride and sought to exalt himself above God. Isaiah 14:12-14 (TPT) recounts Lucifer's fall: "How you have fallen from heaven, morning star, son of the dawn! You have been cast down to the earth... You said in your heart, 'I will ascend to the heavens; I will raise my throne above the stars of God... I will make myself like the Most High.'"

This rebellion led to a cosmic conflict between the forces of good and evil, a battle that continues to play out throughout human history. The fallen angels, now distinct from demons (who are earth-bound spirits of deceased hybrid giants), are actively opposed to God's plan and seek to corrupt humanity, drawing people away from their Creator. Revelation 12:7-9 (TPT) describes this spiritual battle: "Then a terrible war broke out in heaven. Michael and his angels fought against the great dragon... The great dragon was thrown down—once and for all. He was the serpent, the ancient snake called the devil, and Satan, who deceives the whole earth. He was cast down into the earth, and his angels along with him."

The rebellion of the fallen angels serves as a sobering reminder of the consequences of pride and disobedience. However, it also highlights the victory of Christ, who defeated Satan and his forces through His death and resurrection. Colossians 2:15 (TPT) declares, "Then Jesus made a public spectacle of all the powers and principalities of darkness, stripping away from them every weapon and all their spiritual authority and power to accuse us." Though the battle continues in the spiritual realm, Christ's victory is secure, and the ultimate defeat of Satan and his followers is assured.

Visual 4.2 depicts the fall of Lucifer, once an angel of light, now an angel of darkness. Jesus described his fall as being 'like lightning from heaven.'

Visual 4.2: Fall of Lucifer, cast down from heaven.
(**Source:** <u>image of fall of Lucifer and the cosmic battle - Search Images</u>)

Conclusion: Angels and the Divine Plan

Angels, as part of God's first creation, serve a crucial role in the unfolding of God's eternal purpose. They are worshipers, messengers, protectors, and warriors in the spiritual realm, carrying out God's will in ways often unseen by human eyes. Their creation reflects God's desire for order, beauty, and purpose within the heavenly realms, just as His creation of humanity reflects His desire for relationship and fellowship on earth.

While angels stand in awe of God's majesty and participate in His divine plan, humanity holds a special place in God's heart. We are not merely servants or spectators but beloved children, created to share in the divine life of the Trinity. The story of angels and their role in creation reminds us that there is more to the world than what we see with our eyes. There is a spiritual realm, filled with beings who serve God and participate in His work, and this realm intersects with our own in ways we may not always understand.

As we continue this journey through the gospel story, we will see how God's plan for humanity, though disrupted by sin, is brought to fulfilment through Christ. The angels, both faithful and fallen, play a part in this cosmic drama, but the central focus remains on God's love for humanity and His desire to bring us into His eternal family.

Chapter 5

Freedom, Love, and Choice

Central to God's creation is the principle of love, and for love to exist in its truest form, it must be freely given and received. God did not create humanity as robots programmed to obey or puppets on strings. Instead, He gave humanity the freedom to choose—freedom to love, trust, and walk with Him or to turn away. This freedom is the foundation of authentic relationship, but it also introduces the possibility of rejection and rebellion. In this chapter, we will explore how freedom, love, and choice are intertwined in God's design for humanity and how they reflect His ultimate plan for redemption and reconciliation.

Love's Nature: Rooted in Freedom

From the very beginning, love is woven into the fabric of creation. God, in His infinite love, desired to share His life with beings who could freely choose to love Him in return. This is the essence of true love—it is not coerced or forced but given freely. When God created humanity in His image, He endowed us with the capacity to choose, knowing that love without freedom is not love at all.

In Genesis 2:16-17 (TPT), God's command to Adam and Eve reveals this dynamic: "And the Lord God commanded the man, saying, 'You may freely eat the fruit of every tree in the garden—except the tree of the knowledge of good and evil. If you eat its fruit, you are sure to die.'" Here, we see both the freedom and the boundary established by God. Adam and Eve were given access to the abundance of the garden, including the Tree of Life, but they were also given the freedom to choose otherwise. The presence of the Tree of the Knowledge of Good and Evil represented the choice humanity would face—whether to trust in God's goodness or seek knowledge and autonomy apart from Him.

The inclusion of this choice demonstrates the value God places on human agency. Though God knew the potential consequences of this freedom, He chose to give it because love cannot exist without the possibility of rejection. This freedom is what distinguishes humanity from the rest of creation. While animals act on instinct and angels serve in willing obedience, humanity was uniquely designed to reflect God's relational nature through the exercise of free will.

God's desire for relationship is seen in His interaction with Adam and Eve. In the cool of the day, He walked with them in the Garden of Eden (Genesis 3:8, TPT), a beautiful picture of fellowship and intimacy. This relational dynamic—where God seeks communion with His creation—reveals that God's ultimate intention for humanity is not merely obedience but love and partnership. Yet for this partnership to be genuine, humanity had to be given the freedom to choose.

The concept of choice is central to our relationship with God, as illustrated by the two trees in Eden. The Sidebar delves deeper into this symbolism, highlighting how each tree represents a distinct path and relationship with God.

Sidebar: Freedom of Choice: The Two Trees

In the Garden of Eden, God granted humanity the freedom of choice, symbolized by two trees with vastly different outcomes: the Tree of Life and the Tree of Knowledge of Good and Evil. Each tree represents a distinct path in the human experience.

- The Tree of Life – This tree embodies the essence of life in unity with God, where all creation "consists" and exists in Him (Colossians 1:17). Choosing the Tree of Life signifies dependence on God, where we live, move, and have our being in Him (Acts 17:28). Life flows effortlessly in this connection because, in God's presence, there is no striving or separation—only a fullness of life and purpose.

- The Tree of Knowledge of Good and Evil – Choosing this tree symbolizes a life of self-reliance and independence from God's design, leading to the separation and toil that define life outside of divine connection. This choice brings about the burden of self-sufficiency, the struggle of "sweat and toil," and ultimately, spiritual death. Living apart from God is, in essence, a life without true existence, as all life is sustained by God.

In choosing between these trees, humanity faces the ongoing choice between being and doing, between a life grounded in God's presence and identity, or one rooted in striving to attain what only God can provide. While one path leads to fullness, peace, and connection, the other leads to a sense of lack and striving. True freedom lies in choosing the Tree of Life, allowing God to be the source of our existence, purpose, and sustenance.

The Risk of Freedom: The Possibility of Rejection

The gift of freedom comes with an inherent risk—the possibility that it may be misused. In granting humanity the freedom to choose, God allowed for the possibility of rebellion, and as the narrative of Genesis unfolds, we see that Adam and Eve did, indeed, make the choice to turn away from God's command.

Genesis 3 tells the story of how the serpent deceived Eve into eating from the Tree of the Knowledge of Good and Evil, and Adam followed suit. This act of disobedience was not just about breaking a rule; it was about rejecting trust in God's wisdom and attempting to define good and evil on their own terms. In Genesis 3:6 (TPT), we read, "When the woman saw that the tree produced delightful fruit and was pleasing to look at, and a tree desirable to give one insight, she took some of its fruit and ate it. She also gave some to her husband who was with her, and he ate it."

This choice to eat the forbidden fruit represented a deeper decision: to turn away from God's life-giving authority and pursue autonomy. By choosing to disobey, humanity severed the relationship of trust and love with God, and as a result, sin and death entered the world. The consequences of this choice were not only spiritual but cosmic. The harmony between humanity, God, and creation was disrupted, and the world became subject to decay and suffering.

Yet even in this moment of rebellion, we see God's love at work. Rather than immediately condemning Adam and Eve, God seeks them out, calling, "Where are you?" (Genesis 3:9, TPT). This question is not one of ignorance but of invitation. God, in His love, continues to pursue humanity even after the fall, offering the possibility of redemption and restoration.

Visual 5.1 depicts Adam and Eve faced with a choice between the Tree of Life—symbolizing a dependent relationship with God—and the Tree of Knowledge of Good and Evil, representing a life of independence from God. One path leads to life; the other, to death.

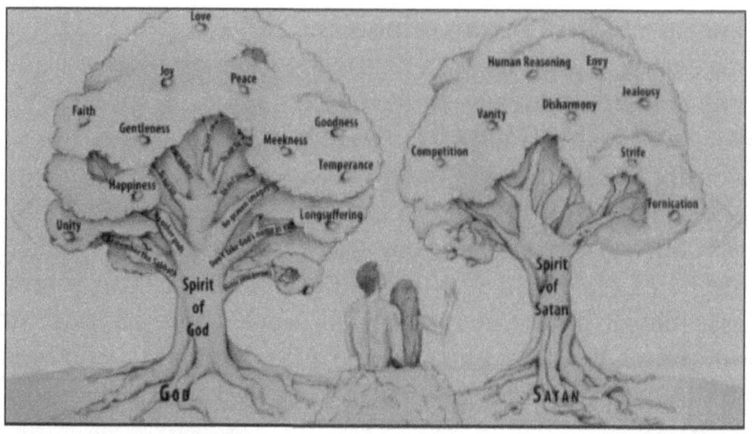

Visual 5.1: Adam and Eve had to make a choice between living in relationship with God or living independently of God. (**Source:** <u>image of Adam and Eve before the Tree of the Knowledge of Good and Evil, representing the moment of choice - Search Images</u>)

Freedom and Responsibility: The Weight of Choice

The choice that Adam and Eve made in the garden was not the last time humanity would face the tension between freedom and responsibility. Throughout Scripture, we see the recurring theme of choice—whether it's Israel choosing to follow God's covenant or the individual choices we make in our daily lives.

In Deuteronomy 30:19 (TPT), Moses presents the people of Israel with a stark choice: "I have set before you life and death, blessings and curses. Now choose life, so that you and your children may live." Here, the same dynamic seen in the Garden of Eden is repeated. God sets before His people the path of life, offering them the freedom to choose to walk in it. But with that freedom comes the responsibility to bear the consequences of those choices.

This principle applies not only to humanity's relationship with God but also to our relationships with one another and with creation. Every choice we make, whether to love or to hate, to give or to take, carries consequences. God's desire is that we use our freedom for good, to reflect His love and goodness in the world. But the misuse of freedom—choosing selfishness, hatred, or violence—leads to the unraveling of the very fabric of creation.

The freedom that God has given humanity is not something to be taken lightly. It is a sacred gift that reflects His trust in us as His image-bearers. To choose love, even in the face of difficulty, is to participate in the divine nature. To choose to trust in God's wisdom, even when we do not fully understand, is to live in harmony with the purpose for which we were created. Yet God does not force these choices upon us. He invites, He guides, but ultimately, the decision is ours to make.

Redemption Through Freedom: God's Plan for Restoration

The story of humanity's misuse of freedom does not end with the fall. From the moment of Adam and Eve's disobedience, God set in motion a plan for redemption. This plan was not to revoke humanity's freedom but to restore it, to heal the broken relationship, and to offer humanity the opportunity to choose life once again.

Throughout the Old Testament, we see God repeatedly reaching out to His people, calling them back to Himself. He sends prophets, establishes covenants, and offers guidance, all with the intention of bringing humanity back into relationship with Him. But it is in the coming of Jesus Christ that God's ultimate plan for redemption is revealed. In Christ, we see the perfect union of divine love and human freedom.

Jesus, the second [last] Adam, faced the same choice that humanity has always faced—whether to submit to God's will or to seek His own way. In the Garden of Gethsemane, on the night before His crucifixion, Jesus prayed, "Father, if you are willing, take this cup of agony away from me. But no matter what, your will must be mine" (Luke 22:42, TPT). In this moment, Jesus freely chose to submit to the Father's will, even though it led to suffering and death. His obedience was not forced but freely given, and through His choice, the possibility of redemption was opened for all humanity.

Through Jesus' death and resurrection, God offers humanity the ultimate choice—life in Him or continued separation. In John 3:16 (TPT), we are reminded, "For this is how much God loved the world—he gave his one and only, unique Son as a gift. So now everyone who believes in him will never perish but experience everlasting life." The invitation to choose life is extended to all, and through the power of the Holy Spirit, we are enabled to make that choice.

But this redemption is not just about individual salvation. It is about the restoration of all creation. The freedom that was lost in the fall is being restored, and humanity is once again invited to participate in God's divine plan. In Christ, we are given the freedom to love, to trust, and to walk in relationship with God, fulfilling the purpose for which we were created.

Conclusion: The Beauty of Freedom and the Power of Choice

The story of freedom, love, and choice is central to the gospel. God, in His infinite love, gave humanity the freedom to choose, knowing the risks but valuing the relationship that true freedom makes possible. While humanity's initial choice led to rebellion and separation, God's plan for redemption was always at work, offering the possibility of restoration.

In Christ, we see the perfect balance of freedom and obedience, love and sacrifice. And through Him, we are invited to choose life, to enter into the divine relationship for which we were created, and to reflect God's love in the world. The power of choice remains, and each day we are called to use our freedom in ways that honor God, love others, and participate in His plan for the renewal of all things.

As we move forward in the gospel narrative, we will see how this divine plan unfolds, leading to the ultimate redemption of humanity and the restoration of creation. Freedom, though risky, is a gift from God, and through it, we are called to love and live in union with Him.

PART 2

The Great Disruption

Chapter 6

Two Trees: Relationship versus Religion

At the heart of the creation story, we find a garden and two trees: the Tree of Life and the Tree of the Knowledge of Good and Evil. These trees are not just part of a historical narrative; they carry profound symbolic meaning for all of humanity. They represent two fundamental ways of relating to God—relationship or religion, trust or self-reliance, life or death. This chapter delves into the meaning of these two trees and how the choice they presented to Adam and Eve is the same choice each of us faces today: to live in intimate relationship with God or to rely on our own understanding and abilities.

The Garden of Relationship: The Tree of Life

The Tree of Life stands as a symbol of God's desire for humanity to live in eternal fellowship with Him. Placed in the center of the Garden of Eden, the Tree of Life represents a relationship built on trust, dependency, and the reception of divine life from God Himself. Genesis 2:9 (TPT) describes this tree: "The Lord God made all kinds of trees grow out of the ground—trees that were pleasing to the eye and good for food. In the middle of the garden were the tree of life and the tree of the knowledge of good and evil."

50

The Tree of Life embodies the life-giving presence of God. By partaking of this tree, Adam and Eve would continue to live in unbroken fellowship with their Creator, enjoying the fullness of life that flows from God's own being. In the book of Revelation, the Tree of Life reappears as a symbol of eternal life in the new heaven and new earth, showing that it is not merely a physical tree but a representation of the abundant, eternal life God offers to those who trust Him.

Eating from the Tree of Life symbolizes complete dependence on God for wisdom, guidance, and sustenance. It is a recognition that true life comes from Him alone, and that apart from God, there is no life. This tree points to the life Jesus speaks of when He declares, "I have come to give you everything in abundance, more than you expect—life in its fullness until you overflow!" (John 10:10, TPT). The Tree of Life is not just about physical existence but about spiritual vitality, about living in the fullness of God's presence and love.

For Adam and Eve, the Tree of Life was a daily reminder of God's goodness and their need for Him. Every time they ate from its fruit, they were affirming their trust in God's provision and acknowledging that He alone is the source of all that is good. This tree, then, stands as a metaphor for relationship with God—a relationship that is marked by trust, dependency, and the reception of divine life.

The Tree of the Knowledge of Good and Evil: The Choice for Self-Reliance

In stark contrast to the Tree of Life stands the Tree of the Knowledge of Good and Evil. While the Tree of Life represents relationship with God, the Tree of the Knowledge of Good and Evil represents the temptation to live independently from Him. Genesis 2:16-17 (TPT) contains God's command regarding this tree: "And the Lord God commanded the man, saying, 'You may freely eat the fruit of every tree in the garden—except the tree of the knowledge of good and evil. If you eat its fruit, you are sure to die.'"

What exactly does the Tree of the Knowledge of Good and Evil represent? At its core, it symbolizes the desire to determine right and wrong, good and evil, apart from God's wisdom. To eat from this tree is to assert one's autonomy and to reject God's authority. It is the pursuit of moral independence—the idea that humanity can decide for itself what is good without relying on God's wisdom.

This tree presents a stark choice: trust in God's wisdom or trust in your own understanding. Proverbs 3:5-6 (TPT) echoes this dilemma: "Trust in the Lord completely, and do not rely on your own opinions. With all your heart rely on him to guide you, and he will lead you in every decision you make. Become intimate with him in whatever you do, and he will lead you wherever you go." The Tree of the Knowledge of Good and Evil represents the opposite of this: relying on oneself, rather than trusting in God's wisdom and guidance.

When Adam and Eve chose to eat from the Tree of the Knowledge of Good and Evil, they were making a decision to step out of relationship with God and into a posture of self-reliance. Genesis 3:6 (TPT) describes their reasoning: "The woman was convinced. She saw that the tree was beautiful, and its fruit looked delicious, and she wanted the wisdom it would give her. So, she took some of the fruit and ate it. Then she gave some to her husband, who was with her, and he ate it, too."

Their desire for wisdom was not inherently wrong, but the problem lay in the way they sought it. Instead of trusting in God to provide wisdom, they chose to seize it for themselves. This is the essence of religion—humanity's attempt to reach God or attain righteousness through self-effort, rather than through relationship. Religion says, "I can do it myself," whereas relationship says, "I trust You, God, to guide and provide for me."

Visual 6.1 depicts Adam and Eve standing before the Tree of Life and the Tree of Knowledge of Good and Evil, faced with the decision to choose either the path of relationship with God or the path of independence.

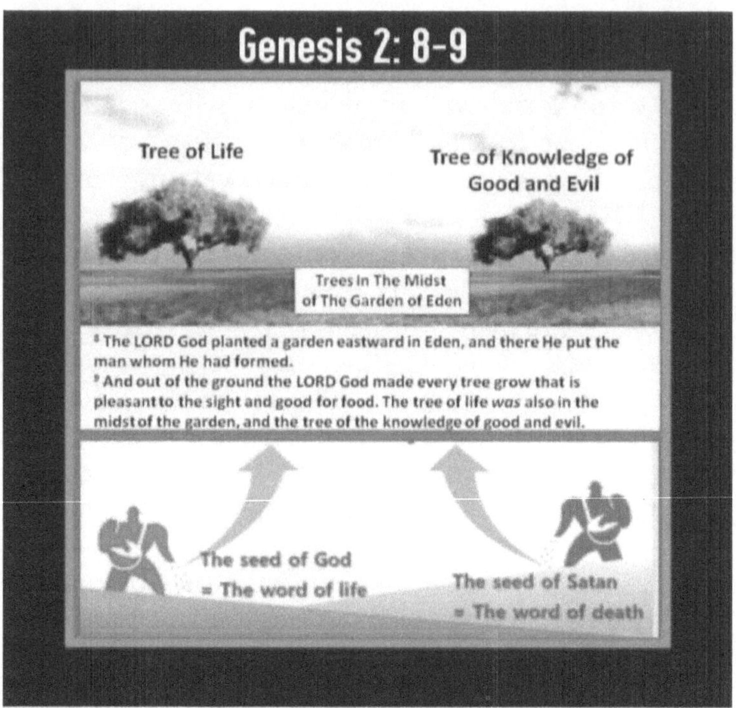

Visual 6.1: Adam and Eve standing before the Tree of Life and the Tree of the Knowledge of Good and Evil. (**Source:** image to tree of life and tree of good and evil - Search Images)

The Consequences of Choice: Relationship Lost

The moment Adam and Eve ate from the Tree of the Knowledge of Good and Evil, everything changed. Their relationship with God, which had been based on trust and intimacy, was broken. Immediately, they experienced the consequences of their choice—shame, fear, and separation from God. Genesis 3:7 (TPT) describes the aftermath: "At that moment their eyes were opened, and they suddenly felt shame at their nakedness. So they sewed fig leaves together to cover themselves."

What was once a relationship built on openness and trust was now marked by fear and hiding. Adam and Eve's choice to rely on their own understanding rather than God's wisdom led to their separation from Him. This separation is the essence of spiritual death—cut off from the source of life, humanity was now subject to decay, suffering, and mortality.

God's response to their disobedience is telling. He does not immediately destroy them or abandon them. Instead, He comes searching for them, calling out, "Where are you?" (Genesis 3:9, TPT). This question reveals God's heart. Even in their rebellion, He is still seeking relationship. But the consequences of their choice cannot be undone. As Genesis 3:22 (TPT) says, "Then the Lord God said, 'Look, the human beings have become like us, knowing both good and evil. What if they reach out, take fruit from the tree of life, and eat it? Then they will live forever!'"

In this state of brokenness, humanity could no longer partake of the Tree of Life. Their access to eternal life, to the fullness of relationship with God, was cut off. This is the tragedy of sin: it separates us from the very source of life and love. And yet, even in this moment of judgment, there is a glimmer of hope. God's plan for redemption is already at work. He clothes Adam and Eve in garments of skin, a foreshadowing of the sacrifice that will one day cover their sin and restore their relationship with Him.

Understanding the impact of Adam and Eve's choice requires us to distinguish between 'Sin' as a state of separation and 'sins' as individual actions. The Sidebar expands on this distinction, shedding light on how sin affects our perception of God and our relationship with Him.

Relationship versus Religion: A Choice We Face Today

The two trees in the Garden of Eden are not just ancient symbols; they represent a choice that each of us faces today. Will we choose to live in relationship with God, trusting in His wisdom and provision, or will we choose the path of religion, relying on our own efforts and understanding? The Tree of Life invites us into a relationship of trust, where we acknowledge our dependence on God for everything—our life, our purpose, our direction. This is the path of grace, where we receive from God and walk in the fullness of His love.

In contrast, the Tree of the Knowledge of Good and Evil represents the temptation to rely on ourselves, to seek wisdom and righteousness apart from God. This is the path of religion—where we strive to attain something that can only be received as a gift. Religion says, "If I work hard enough, if I am good enough, I can earn God's favor." But relationship says, "God has already given me His favor through Christ. I trust in Him alone."

The Apostle Paul contrasts these two approaches in his letter to the Galatians. Speaking of those who sought to be justified by the law (the way of religion), he writes, "But if you seek to be made right with God through the law, you have been severed from Christ! You have fallen from grace" (Galatians 5:4, TPT). Paul's message is clear: true life is found not in religious striving but in relationship with God through faith in Christ.

Jesus Himself offers us the invitation to return to the Tree of Life. In John 15:5 (TPT), He says, "I am the sprouting vine, and you're my branches. As you live in union with me as your source, fruitfulness will stream from within you—but when you live separated from me, you are powerless." The way of relationship is about abiding in Christ, receiving His life, and bearing fruit through His power, not our own.

Conclusion: The Invitation to Choose Life

The story of the two trees in the Garden of Eden is ultimately about choice—God's gift of freedom to humanity and our response to that gift. Will we choose the path of relationship, represented by the Tree of Life, or the path of religion, represented by the Tree of the Knowledge of Good and Evil? The choice Adam and Eve faced is the same choice we face today: to trust in God's wisdom and provision or to rely on our own efforts.

Through Christ, the way to the Tree of Life has been reopened. He is the ultimate fulfilment of God's promise to restore what was lost in the Garden. In Him, we are invited back into relationship with the Father, to partake once again of the eternal life that flows from God's presence. As we continue to explore the story of redemption, we will see how God's plan to restore humanity unfolds, leading us back to the Tree of Life and the fullness of life in Him.

Chapter 7

The Fall: Identity Lost

The fall of humanity in the Garden of Eden marks a pivotal moment in the story of creation. It is not just about disobedience to a command but about the deep fracture in humanity's understanding of its identity and purpose. In one act, Adam and Eve turned from the life God offered them and sought independence, leading to the loss of their true identity. This chapter explores how humanity's identity was lost in the fall, the consequences of this loss, and how it continues to affect us today.

A Life of Perfect Harmony: Humanity's Identity Before the Fall

Before the fall, Adam and Eve's identity was secure and rooted in their relationship with God. They were created in His image, fully alive, and lived in perfect harmony with Him and the world around them. Their purpose was clear—they were called to tend the garden, steward the earth, and reflect God's glory in all they did. Genesis 1:27-28 (TPT) tells us, "So God created man in his own image, in the image of God he created him; male and female he created them. And God blessed them and said to them, 'Be fruitful and multiply and fill the earth and subdue it, and have dominion...'"

Adam and Eve were created to live from a place of abundance, not lack. Everything they needed was provided by God. Their identity was not something they had to earn or strive for; it was a gift from their Creator. They were children of God, loved and accepted, and they lived in the joy of that relationship. In the garden, they experienced the fullness of life—no fear, no shame, no striving—just peace and trust in their Creator.

Moreover, their innocence before God was reflected in their relationship with each other. Genesis 2:25 (TPT) states, "Now the man and his wife were both naked, but they felt no shame." This lack of shame is significant because it points to their perfect understanding of themselves and each other. There was no need to hide or cover up, physically or emotionally. They were fully known and fully loved.

The Deception: Questioning God's Goodness

The fall begins not with a bite of fruit but with a question. The serpent, who embodies deceit and rebellion, approaches Eve with subtlety and craftiness. His goal is to undermine her trust in God and sow seeds of doubt in her heart. In Genesis 3:1 (TPT), the serpent asks, "Did God really say you must not eat the fruit from any of the trees in the garden?" This question is designed to confuse and distort God's words. God had not forbidden all the trees—only one—but the serpent's question introduces doubt about God's fairness and generosity.

The real turning point comes in Genesis 3:4-5 (TPT), when the serpent directly contradicts God's warning: "You won't die!" the serpent replied to the woman. "God knows that your eyes will be opened as soon as you eat it, and you will be like God, knowing both good and evil."

Here, the serpent appeals to Eve's desire for wisdom and independence. He suggests that God is withholding something good from her, that she could be more than what she already is. In doing so, the serpent shifts Eve's focus away from her identity as a beloved child of God to a desire for something more—something that, ironically, she already had.

Eve's temptation, then, was not just about physical hunger but about a deeper spiritual hunger. She was enticed by the idea of self-sufficiency, the ability to determine her own path and define good and evil for herself. The serpent's lie—that she could be "like God"—was a distortion of the truth. Adam and Eve were already created in God's image, already sharing in His life and wisdom. But the lie made them feel inadequate, as though their identity was incomplete, as though they needed to take matters into their own hands to achieve fullness.

The Fall: The Consequences of Disobedience

When Adam and Eve chose to eat from the Tree of the Knowledge of Good and Evil, they did more than break a command. They made a fundamental shift in their relationship with God. Instead of trusting Him and living in His wisdom, they chose to rely on their own understanding. Genesis 3:6 (TPT) describes the moment: "The woman was convinced. She saw that the tree was beautiful, and its fruit looked delicious, and she wanted the wisdom it would give her. So, she took some of the fruit and ate it. Then she gave some to her husband, who was with her, and he ate it, too."

In that moment, something inside them changed. They immediately became aware of their nakedness, a sign that their innocence was gone and their relationship with God had been broken. Genesis 3:7 (TPT) says, "At that moment their eyes were opened, and they suddenly felt shame at their nakedness. So, they sewed fig leaves together to cover themselves." The intimacy they once shared with God was replaced by fear, and the transparency they had with each other was replaced by shame.

The consequences of their disobedience were far-reaching. Genesis 3:16-19 (TPT) outlines the curse that fell upon humanity and the earth. Eve would now experience pain in childbirth, and Adam would toil and struggle to cultivate the ground. Creation itself was affected by their rebellion, and the harmony that once existed between humanity and nature was broken.

Most tragically, Adam and Eve were banished from the Garden of Eden and cut off from the Tree of Life. Genesis 3:23-24 (TPT) recounts, "So the Lord God banished them from the Garden of Eden, and he sent Adam out to cultivate the ground from which he had been made. After sending them out, the Lord God stationed mighty cherubim to the east of the Garden of Eden. And he placed a flaming sword that flashed back and forth to guard the way to the tree of life."

The Loss of Identity: A Deep Spiritual Wound

The fall was not just a physical separation from the garden; it was a spiritual and relational separation from God. Adam and Eve's identity as children of God was marred. No longer secure in their relationship with their Creator, they now lived in fear, guilt, and shame. Where they once lived from a place of trust and abundance, they now lived from a place of striving and insecurity.

This loss of identity has been passed down through generations. Every human being born since Adam and Eve has inherited this fractured identity. We are born into a world where our natural inclination is to seek identity and purpose apart from God. Like Adam and Eve, we often look to external things—our achievements, possessions, relationships, or knowledge—to define who we are. But these things cannot restore the identity that was lost in the fall.

Paul speaks to this condition in Romans 5:12 (TPT): "When Adam sinned, the entire world was affected. Sin entered human experience, and death was the result. And so death followed this sin, casting its shadow over all humanity, because all have sinned." The shadow of death that hangs over humanity is not just physical death but spiritual death—separation from the life and love of God.

The Fall not only separated humanity from God but also distorted our sense of self. The Sidebar explores the difference between our 'false self' formed through separation and our 'true self' restored in Christ.

Sidebar: False Self vs. True Self - Discovering Our Identity in Christ

One of the greatest journeys in our faith is discovering and living from our true identity—our true self as God designed, rather than the distorted "false self" that sin and the world shape. This true self is the person God created in His image, reconciled, forgiven, and adopted through Christ. Jesus has paid it all—past, present, and future; we are already reconciled, forgiven, accepted, justified, and adopted. Our identity in Christ is not conditional but a finished reality, freely given by grace.

Jesus speaks of two people working in the field, with "one taken and the other left" (Matthew 24:40). This passage can symbolize the distinction between our false self and our true self. Our false self, shaped by fear, insecurity, and separation, "passes away," while our true self—the person we were always meant to be in Christ—remains.

Jesus also spoke of those He never "knew" (Matthew 7:23), referring to those who acted from a distorted identity rather than from the truth of their relationship with Him. This false self is marked by striving, works, and a separation from the heart of God. But God's judgment and purifying fire are not meant to condemn or destroy. They are a refining process—a fiery furnace that purifies and restores us to our wholeness, helping us shed the false self and live from our true identity.

Knowing our true self in Christ is crucial to healing and wholeness. It transforms how we relate to ourselves, others, and God, bringing freedom from depression, fear, and self-rejection. Psychology and counseling can be deeply effective when rooted in identity-based healing, focusing on who we truly are in Christ. Without this foundation, we risk only addressing symptoms rather than the core of our being.

The parable of the two prodigal sons (Luke 15) illustrates this. Both sons misunderstood their father and themselves. The younger, "wasteful" son felt unworthy, while the older "religious" son relied on self-righteousness. Yet the father loved them both, embracing them as his true sons. Whether near or far, God waits patiently for each of us to come home to our true identity, living in His grace, peace, and purpose.

When we enter into the finished work of Christ, hearing and believing the gospel, it becomes a real, transformative experience. Our true self—the one already reconciled, forgiven, and empowered—comes alive. As we align with our identity in Christ, we live out the fullness of new life in Him.

Hope Amid the Fall: The Promise of Redemption

Yet even in the midst of the fall, God's plan for redemption was already at work. Genesis 3:15 (TPT) contains the first hint of the gospel, often referred to as the "protoevangelium" (the first gospel). God, speaking to the serpent, declares, "I will cause hostility between you and the woman, and between your offspring and her offspring. He will strike your head, and you will strike his heel." This verse foreshadows the coming of Christ, who would one day defeat the serpent and restore what was lost in the fall.

Though Adam and Eve were banished from the garden, God did not abandon them. He provided for them, covering their nakedness with garments of skin (Genesis 3:21, TPT), a foreshadowing of the ultimate covering that Christ would provide through His sacrifice. God's love and mercy were still at work, even as humanity faced the consequences of their rebellion.

The fall, then, is not the end of the story. It is the beginning of God's redemptive plan to restore humanity to its original identity and purpose. In Christ, we find the promise of new life—a life that is rooted not in our own efforts or understanding but in the grace and love of God.

Conclusion: From Identity Lost to Identity Restored

The fall represents the tragic moment when humanity lost its true identity. In seeking independence from God, Adam and Eve severed the relationship that gave them life, purpose, and meaning. The consequences of that choice have affected every human being since, leaving us with a deep spiritual wound—a loss of identity that can only be healed through a restored relationship with God.

But the story does not end with the fall. God's plan for redemption, revealed in the promise of Genesis 3:15, is fulfilled in Christ. Through His life, death, and resurrection, Christ restores what was lost, offering us the opportunity to reclaim our identity as children of God. The journey from the fall to redemption is the story of the gospel, a story that invites us to return to the life and relationship we were created for.

As we move forward, we will explore how God's plan for redemption unfolds and how, in Christ, we find our true identity once again.

Chapter 8

The DNA War: Corrupting the Human Design

The fall of humanity in the Garden of Eden not only brought spiritual death but also set the stage for a cosmic struggle over humanity's very nature. After Adam and Eve's disobedience, sin entered the world, corrupting the original design that God intended for humanity. But more than that, there began a deeper, more insidious battle—a war for the very DNA of humanity. This chapter explores the theological implications of this DNA war, how sin and evil sought to corrupt God's creation, and the ultimate plan of redemption that restores humanity to its intended design.

The Introduction of Sin: A Corruption of the Original Design

When Adam and Eve sinned, their disobedience was not just a moral failure but a corruption of the very fabric of human nature. The spiritual consequences of the fall went far beyond a simple act of rebellion; they introduced sin into the world, which affected every aspect of human existence, including our physical bodies, minds, and spirits. Genesis 3:17-19 (TPT) reveals the immediate consequences of this corruption: "Cursed is the ground because of you; through painful toil you will eat food from it all the days of your life. It will produce thorns and thistles for you, and you will eat the plants of the field. By the sweat of your brow you will eat your food until you return to the ground, since from it you were taken; for dust you are and to dust you will return."

Before the fall, humanity was created in God's image—perfect, whole, and untainted by sin. But with the entrance of sin, the image of God in humanity became marred. This corruption affected not only the spiritual life of humanity but also its physical nature. Death, decay, sickness, and disease became part of the human experience, all of which were never part of God's original design. Humanity's DNA was affected by sin, leading to the inevitable breakdown of the human body and the separation of spirit from body at death.

The Apostle Paul addresses this reality in Romans 5:12 (TPT): "When Adam sinned, the entire world was affected. Sin entered human experience, and death was the result. And so death followed this sin, casting its shadow over all humanity, because all have sinned." The sin nature, passed down from generation to generation, is a spiritual and physical inheritance that we all carry. We are born into this world with a corrupted nature, and our physical bodies bear the marks of this corruption through sickness, aging, and death.

The Serpent's Strategy: A War on Humanity's Genetic Code

The consequences of the fall go beyond the physical and spiritual realms. There is a deeper, more insidious plan at work—one that seeks to corrupt humanity's very genetic makeup. Throughout biblical history, we see that the enemy's strategy has been to attack the human seed, attempting to corrupt the line through which God would bring His Messiah.

One of the clearest examples of this strategy is found in Genesis 6, where the "sons of God" (fallen angels) took human wives and produced offspring known as the Nephilim. Genesis 6:4 (TPT) describes this: "In those days, and for some time after, giant Nephilites lived on the earth, for whenever the sons of God had intercourse with women, they gave birth to children who became the heroes and famous warriors of ancient times." This intermingling between the divine and human was not part of God's design, but a perversion meant to corrupt the human bloodline.

Why is this significant? God's promise to Adam and Eve in Genesis 3:15 (TPT) was that the seed of the woman would crush the serpent's head, foreshadowing the coming of the Messiah. The enemy's goal was to corrupt that seed, to prevent the Messiah from coming by introducing genetic corruption into the human race. The introduction of the Nephilim represented an attempt to distort God's plan for redemption by mingling human DNA with something outside of God's created order.

This battle over humanity's genetic purity continued throughout biblical history, manifesting in various forms of rebellion, idolatry, and sin that sought to distort and destroy the image of God in humanity. The flood in Noah's time was God's response to this widespread corruption. Genesis 6:5-7 (TPT) describes God's sorrow over the state of humanity: "The Lord observed the extent of human wickedness on the earth, and he saw that everything they thought or imagined was consistently and totally evil. So, the Lord was sorry he had ever made them and put them on the earth. It broke his heart."

God's judgment in the flood was not just about punishing wickedness; it was about preserving the purity of the human line through which His plan for redemption would be fulfilled. Noah, described as "righteous" in Genesis 6:9 (TPT), was chosen to preserve the untainted human line, and through him, God restarted His plan for humanity.

Visual 8.1 illustrates the Nephilim, hybrid giants who corrupted humanity's DNA and lineage, distorting the image and likeness of God in humankind.

Visual 8.1: Nephilim and the corruption of humanity's line. (**Source:** image of Nephilim and the corruption of humanity's line. - Search Images)

The Spiritual and Physical Consequences of Corruption

The corruption of human DNA is not just a metaphor; it reflects the deep spiritual reality of sin's effect on the whole person—spirit, soul, and body. This corruption manifests in many ways, including the brokenness we experience in our relationships, the diseases that plague our bodies, and the separation we feel from God. Romans 8:20-22 (TPT) explains that "against its will, the universe itself has had to endure the empty futility resulting from the consequences of human sin. But now, with eager expectation, all creation longs for freedom from its slavery to decay and to experience with us the wonderful freedom coming to God's children."

This "slavery to decay" is a direct result of the fall and the corruption of human nature. But it is not limited to humanity; the entire creation suffers under the weight of sin. From natural disasters to disease outbreaks, the world itself is groaning under the consequences of humanity's rebellion. Our bodies, once designed for eternal life, are now subject to aging, disease, and death. These physical realities are reminders of the spiritual corruption that entered the world through Adam and Eve's disobedience.

This corruption extends to our DNA—the genetic code that defines our physical makeup. Scientists have long studied the human genome, discovering the genetic mutations and errors that lead to diseases, disorders, and death. These mutations are a physical representation of the spiritual corruption that has infected humanity since the fall. We are not as we were meant to be. The image of God in us, though not completely lost, has been marred and distorted by sin.

In exploring the corruption of humanity's design, it's crucial to understand God's stance on maintaining the purity of His creation. The Sidebar offers insight into the prohibition against genetic manipulation, underscoring the importance of preserving God's intended design.

Sidebar: The Prohibition of Genetic Manipulation

In Scripture, God's law reflects a commitment to preserving the purity of His creation. Leviticus 19:19 strictly forbids the unnatural mixing of species, emphasizing the importance of maintaining God's original design without tampering. This prohibition is significant when viewed alongside the events described in Genesis 6:2-4 and the Book of Enoch, which detail the actions of certain angels known as "watchers."

According to the Book of Enoch, 200 watcher angels were sent to guide and minister to humanity, helping them prepare for their calling to rule on earth. However, these angels abandoned their God-given purpose and crossed forbidden boundaries. They left their own realm, took human women, and produced hybrid offspring known as the Nephilim—giants who did not bear the image and likeness of God. These beings could not be part of God's family, as they were outside His design for humanity. The watchers imparted forbidden knowledge to humanity, teaching them how to manipulate genes, create weapons, make potions, and other practices that went against God's purpose for His creation.

This genetic corruption brought devastation upon the earth, leading to widespread violence and moral chaos. To preserve the line through which the Messiah would come, God had to intervene to prevent this genetic corruption from overtaking His people. The flood in Noah's time was a response to this corruption, as the Nephilim and those influenced by the watchers' rebellion threatened to derail God's plan for redemption. Like Lucifer, these fallen watchers sought to thwart God's design and purpose for humanity, further illustrating the dangers of tampering with creation.

By prohibiting genetic mixing, God calls humanity to honor the integrity of His creation, reflecting His image without alteration. Humanity's unique role is to reflect God's likeness and live out His purpose. By resisting genetic corruption and tampering, we align with God's design, upholding the purity of His image within us. The fallen watchers' rebellion serves as a warning of the consequences of genetic manipulation, emphasizing God's desire for His creation to remain as He intended, bearing His image and aligning with His purpose.

The Ultimate Redemption: Restoring the Human Design

Despite the pervasive corruption of humanity's nature, God's plan for redemption has always been at work. The war over humanity's DNA, both spiritual and physical, finds its resolution in the person of Jesus Christ. As the promised seed of the woman, Jesus came to restore what was lost in the fall and to undo the corruption that had affected humanity's genetic and spiritual makeup.

Jesus' incarnation—His becoming fully human while remaining fully divine—was the first step in this restoration. In Jesus, we see the perfect human, untainted by sin, living in perfect harmony with the

Father. Hebrews 4:15 (TPT) reminds us that "He understands humanity, for as a Man, our magnificent King-Priest was tempted in every way just as we are, and conquered sin." Jesus took on human flesh, not only to atone for sin but to restore the human design to its original purpose.

Through His death and resurrection, Jesus defeated the power of sin and death, breaking the chains of corruption that had bound humanity since the fall. His resurrection body, described as glorified and incorruptible, is a foretaste of what is to come for all who believe in Him. 1 Corinthians 15:42-44 (TPT) declares, "It's the same way with the resurrection of the dead. The body is 'sown' in decay but will be raised in immortality. It is sown in humiliation but will be raised in glorification. It is sown in weakness but will be raised in power."

The ultimate redemption is not just spiritual but physical as well. With Christ's active presence in us through the Spirit, the corruption of human nature will be completely undone. Our bodies, which are now subject to decay, will be transformed into glorified bodies, free from sickness, death, and the consequences of sin. Revelation 21:4 (TPT) promises that in the new creation, "He will wipe away every tear from their eyes, and eliminate death entirely. No one will mourn or weep any longer. The pain of wounds will no longer exist, for the old order has ceased."

The DNA war—the battle to corrupt and destroy humanity's design—will end in victory for those who are in Christ. The image of God, which was marred in the fall, will be fully restored in the new creation. As children of God, we will once again live in the fullness of life for which we were created, free from the corruption of sin and death.

Conclusion: The Restoration of Humanity's True Design

The DNA war, both physical and spiritual, has been raging since the fall of humanity. Sin introduced corruption into God's perfect design, affecting every aspect of human existence. But God's plan for redemption has always been in motion, and through Jesus Christ, the corruption of humanity's nature is being undone.

In Christ, we find not only forgiveness for sin but the promise of complete restoration—spirit, soul, and body. The war over humanity's DNA will ultimately end in victory when Jesus returns, and we are raised with incorruptible bodies, free from death, disease, and decay. The promise of eternal life, foreshadowed in the Tree of Life, will be fully realized in the new creation, where we will live in perfect relationship with God, just as He intended from the beginning.

As we continue to explore the story of redemption, we will see how God's plan unfolds, leading to the ultimate restoration of all things and the fulfilment of His original design for humanity.

Chapter 9

Creation Compromised

When sin entered the world through Adam and Eve's disobedience, it didn't just affect their relationship with God or distort humanity's identity. The consequences of the fall rippled through all of creation. What was once perfect, vibrant, and teeming with life became subject to decay, corruption, and death. Creation itself became compromised, and the harmony that existed between God, humanity, and the natural world was broken. This chapter explores how sin compromised the entirety of creation, the theological implications of this brokenness, and God's ultimate plan to redeem not just humanity but the whole of creation.

The Effects of the Fall on Creation

Before the fall, the natural world operated in perfect harmony. Every aspect of creation reflected God's glory and goodness. There was no death, no suffering, and no destruction. Genesis 1:31 (TPT) describes the state of creation before sin: "Then God looked over all He had made, and He saw that it was very good!" Every element of creation was good because it was an expression of God's creative power, beauty, and love. The plants, animals, and humans lived in peaceful coexistence, with humanity tasked with stewarding the earth.

However, when Adam and Eve sinned, the consequences of their rebellion extended beyond their own lives. The very ground they were called to cultivate became cursed. In Genesis 3:17-19 (TPT), God says to Adam, "Cursed is the ground because of you; through painful toil you will eat food from it all the days of your life. It will produce thorns and thistles for you, and you will eat the plants of the field. By the sweat of your brow you will eat your food until you return to the ground, since from it you were taken; for dust you are and to dust you will return."

This curse on the ground represents the brokenness that entered the natural world as a result of sin. Instead of the earth cooperating with humanity in a fruitful partnership, it now resists human effort, producing thorns and thistles. Nature itself became subject to decay, disease, and death. What was once a flourishing, life-giving environment was now marked by struggle and suffering.

The Groaning of Creation: Longing for Redemption

The Apostle Paul vividly describes the effects of sin on creation in Romans 8:19-22 (TPT): "The entire universe is standing on tiptoe, yearning to see the unveiling of God's glorious sons and daughters! For against its will, the universe itself has had to endure the empty futility resulting from the consequences of human sin. But now, with eager expectation, all creation longs for freedom from its slavery to decay and to experience with us the wonderful freedom coming to God's children."

This passage highlights an important truth: creation is not just passively affected by sin; it actively longs for restoration. The phrase "slavery to decay" reflects the reality that the natural world is now bound by the same forces of death and corruption that affect humanity. Disease, natural disasters, environmental degradation, and the cycle of life and death all point to the brokenness of the world as a result of sin. Creation itself is groaning, waiting for the time when it will be liberated from the curse and restored to its original glory.

Paul's words also reveal that the redemption of creation is tied to the redemption of humanity. When God's children are fully restored to their rightful place, creation will share in that redemption. The brokenness of the natural world is not a permanent condition; it is temporary, awaiting the fulfilment of God's plan to make all things new.

Visual 9.1 contrasts the original beauty of creation with its current state of groaning under the weight of sin.

Visual 9.1: Creation's groaning—beauty of nature and the destruction caused by sin.
(**Source:** image of Creation's groaning—images of both the beauty of nature and the destruction caused by sin. - Search Images)

The Interconnectedness of Creation and Humanity

One of the key theological truths that emerges from the story of the fall is the interconnectedness of creation and humanity. Humanity was created to be the stewards of the earth, tasked with caring for and cultivating it in partnership with God. Genesis 2:15 (TPT) says, "The Lord God placed the man in the Garden of Eden to tend and watch over it." This stewardship was not a distant, detached responsibility; it was part of humanity's identity and purpose.

When Adam and Eve fell, they not only lost their spiritual connection with God but also compromised their ability to fulfil their role as stewards of creation. The curse that fell upon the ground was a direct result of their disobedience, and their fractured relationship with God led to a fractured relationship with the earth. Humanity's sin distorted the natural order, and the world that was once a paradise became a place of suffering and toil.

This interconnectedness is still evident today. Environmental degradation, climate change, and the exploitation of natural resources are all modern-day manifestations of humanity's broken relationship with creation. The abuse of the earth's resources for selfish gain reflects the same heart of rebellion that led Adam and Eve to disobey God in the first place. When we fail to honor our role as stewards of the earth, we perpetuate the cycle of brokenness and corruption that began in the Garden.

However, the interconnectedness between humanity and creation also means that when humanity is restored, creation will be restored as well. The promise of

Scripture is that God's redemption extends beyond individual salvation—it encompasses all of creation. Isaiah 65:17 (TPT) speaks of this future restoration: "For I am creating a new heaven and a new earth, and no one will even think about the old ones anymore." The new creation will be free from the effects of sin, and humanity will once again fulfil its role as stewards of a renewed earth.

Theological Implications of a Compromised Creation

The compromised state of creation has deep theological implications. It shows that sin is not just a personal issue between individuals and God; it is a cosmic issue that affects every part of the universe. The fall of humanity has distorted not only human nature but also the natural order, resulting in a world that is out of balance and in need of restoration.

This brokenness is evident in the ongoing tension between the beauty and majesty of creation and the destruction and suffering we see around us. Nature still reflects the glory of God, as Psalm 19:1 (TPT) says, "God's splendor is a tale that is told; His testament is written in the stars. Space itself speaks His story every day through the marvels of the heavens." Yet, at the same time, creation is marked by the scars of sin—natural disasters, extinctions, and environmental crises all remind us that the world is not as it should be.

The fact that creation suffers as a result of humanity's sin underscores the seriousness of our rebellion against God. Sin's impact is not limited to individual souls; it has far-reaching consequences that affect the physical world as well. This reality should prompt us to take seriously our responsibility as stewards of the earth and to recognize that our actions—both good and bad—have an impact on the world around us.

Theologically, the compromised state of creation also points to the need for a cosmic Savior. The redemption that Jesus offers is not just for human souls; it is for the entire cosmos. Colossians 1:19-20 (TPT) tells us, "For God is satisfied to have all His fullness dwelling in Christ, and by the blood of His cross, everything in heaven and earth is brought back to Himself—back to its original intent, restored to innocence again!" Jesus' work on the cross extends to all of creation, ensuring that the brokenness of the world will one day be healed.

Visual 9.2 depicts Jesus as the Savior not only of humanity but of all creation—healing the earth and restoring its beauty and balance. Revelation 21:5 assures us that He is going to make all things new.

Visual 9.2: Jesus as the Savior not only of humanity but of all creation—healing the earth, restoring its beauty and balance. (**Source:** image of Jesus as the Savior not only of humanity but of all creation, making all things new - Search Images)

As we consider the impact of the Fall on creation, it's important to remember that creation is awaiting restoration through God's children. The Sidebar explores how creation responds to the revealing of mature sons of God, offering hope for a renewed world.

Sidebar: Creation's Response to the Sons of God

Romans 8:19 describes creation eagerly awaiting the revealing of the mature sons of God. As believers align with God's heart, creation responds positively, reflecting the glory and purpose God intended. Jesus exemplified this maturity, commanding storms to cease, raising the dead, healing the sick, and even guiding fish into nets. In His footsteps, as sons and daughters of God, we are called to bring healing and restoration to creation, stewarding it in alignment with God's will.

This commission to govern creation was originally given to Adam and is now passed to the Church. God does not retract His gifts or callings (Romans 11:29), so this responsibility remains with us. Our role requires maturity and intimacy with God, knowing His heart so that we can act as His representatives, bringing His order and blessing into every part of creation.

However, creation can also respond negatively to human actions. When we collectively engage in pursuits that oppose God's design, creation can suffer—through natural disasters, environmental degradation, and a loss of harmony. This adverse response reflects the consequences of humanity's disconnection from God's purpose, seen in the effects of pollution, resource depletion, and the breakdown of ecosystems.

God invites us into a partnership of restoration, empowering us to shape creation for good. As we grow into our identity as His children, creation will respond in kind, reflecting God's glory, beauty, and order. This divine partnership calls us to engage responsibly with creation, bringing God's life and peace into the world and spreading His goodness everywhere.

The Hope of Restoration: God's Plan to Redeem Creation

While creation is currently compromised, the story of the gospel gives us hope that this is not the final state of the world. God's plan for redemption includes the restoration of the natural world, and the Scriptures are filled with promises of a new creation—a world where sin, death, and decay no longer reign. Revelation 21:1 (TPT) echoes this promise: "Then in a vision I saw a new heaven and a new earth. The first heaven and earth had passed away, and the sea no longer existed."

This new creation will be free from the effects of sin and will reflect God's original design. In this restored world, humanity will once again live in harmony with God, each other, and the natural world. The thorns and thistles of Genesis 3 will be replaced with fruitfulness and abundance. Isaiah 11:6-9 (TPT) paints a picture of this restored creation: "The wolf will dwell with the lamb, the leopard will lie down with the young goat... The earth will be filled with the knowledge of the Lord, as the waters cover the sea."

This vision of restoration is not just a distant hope; it is a reminder that God is actively working to bring about His plan of redemption. Every act of healing, every moment of restoration, and every step toward justice and reconciliation is a foretaste of the new creation to come. As believers, we are called to participate in this work, partnering with God in the restoration of all things.

Conclusion: From Compromise to Redemption

Creation may be compromised, but it is not beyond hope. The story of the fall reminds us of the far-reaching effects of sin, but the story of redemption assures us that God is not finished with His creation. The groaning of the natural world will one day be replaced with joy as the entire cosmos is restored to its original glory.

As we continue through the narrative of redemption, we will see how God's plan to restore creation is intertwined with His plan to redeem humanity. The restoration of all things—including the natural world—will come through Jesus Christ, the Savior of the world, who makes all things new. The compromised state of creation points us to the hope of a new creation, where God's presence will dwell with humanity once again, and the earth will be filled with His glory.

Chapter 10

God's Preparation for Redemption

As the story of humanity unfolds after the fall, the consequences of sin spread throughout the world, affecting not only individuals but all of creation. However, even in the midst of this brokenness, God's plan for redemption was already in motion. From the very beginning, God's heart was set on restoring humanity and all creation to their original design. In this chapter, we explore how God, through various stages and revelations, prepared the way for His ultimate act of redemption in Jesus Christ. This preparation reveals God's character—His patience, love, and commitment to His creation—and sets the stage for the salvation of the world.

The Promise of Redemption: A Seed of Hope

The story of redemption begins immediately after the fall. Even as God pronounces judgment on Adam and Eve, He gives them a promise that one day the serpent would be defeated and humanity would be restored. In Genesis 3:15 (TPT), God declares to the serpent, "I will cause hostility between you and the woman, and between your offspring and her offspring. He will strike your head, and you will strike his heel." This verse, often called the 'protoevangelium' or the "first gospel," contains the first hint of the coming Messiah, who would crush the serpent and undo the effects of the fall.

This promise of redemption is significant because it shows that God's plan for salvation was not an afterthought. From the moment humanity fell into sin, God had already set in motion His plan to redeem His people. The rest of the biblical narrative can be seen as the unfolding of this plan, as God works through history to prepare the way for Jesus, the ultimate Savior.

Throughout the Old Testament, we see this promise of redemption repeated and expanded. From the covenant with Noah after the flood to the promises made to Abraham, Isaac, and Jacob, God consistently reassures His people that He has not abandoned them. Each covenant, each act of deliverance, points toward the fulfilment of the promise made in Genesis 3:15—the coming of a Savior who would rescue humanity from sin and death.

The Covenant with Abraham: Establishing a People

One of the most significant steps in God's preparation for redemption was His covenant with Abraham. In Genesis 12:2-3 (TPT), God calls Abraham and promises, "I will make you into a great nation. I will bless you and make you famous, and you will be a blessing to others. I will bless those who bless you and curse those who treat you with contempt. All the families on earth will be blessed through you."

This covenant marks the beginning of God's special relationship with the people of Israel. Through Abraham and his descendants, God would establish a people set apart for Himself—a people through whom the Messiah would come. God's choice of Abraham was not based on Abraham's merit but on His own sovereign will and grace. By establishing this covenant, God set the stage for the eventual coming of Christ, the descendant of Abraham who would bring salvation to all the nations of the world.

The covenant with Abraham also emphasizes God's commitment to working through human history to accomplish His purposes. God's plan for redemption would unfold over centuries, with each generation playing a role in bringing about the fulfilment of His promises. Despite humanity's ongoing rebellion and failure, God remained faithful to His covenant, ensuring that His plan for salvation would be realized.

Visual 10.1 depicts Abraham receiving God's covenant promise, with the stars in the sky symbolizing the countless descendants he would have.

Visual 10.1: Abraham receiving God's covenant promise, showing the stars of the sky as symbols of his descendants. (**Source:** image of Abraham receiving God's covenant promise, showing the stars of the sky as symbols of his descendants. - Search)

The Law and the Prophets: Pointing to a Savior

As the nation of Israel grew, God gave them the law through Moses. The law served multiple purposes in God's plan of redemption. On one level, it provided guidelines for living in right relationship with God and with others. The Ten Commandments and other laws given at Mount Sinai established a moral and ethical framework for the people of Israel, reflecting God's holiness and justice.

However, the law also revealed humanity's inability to live up to God's perfect standards. Romans 3:20 (TPT) explains, "For by the merit of observing the law, no one earns the status of being declared righteous before God, for the law reveals the sin in us." The law, rather than being a means of salvation, showed humanity's deep need for a Savior. It exposed the sinfulness of the human heart and pointed to the fact that no amount of human effort could restore the relationship with God that had been broken by sin.

The prophets of Israel also played a crucial role in preparing the way for redemption. Throughout the Old Testament, the prophets called the people back to God, warning them of the consequences of their disobedience and reminding them of God's promise of restoration. Isaiah, in particular, spoke of a coming Messiah who would bring healing and salvation to God's people. In Isaiah 53:5 (TPT), the prophet describes the suffering servant, saying, "But he was pierced for our rebellion, crushed for our sins. He was beaten so we could be whole. He was whipped so we could be healed."

The message of the prophets was clear: humanity's hope for redemption would not come through their own efforts but through the work of a suffering Savior who would bear the sins of the world. The prophets pointed forward to the coming of Christ, preparing the people of Israel—and the world—for the day when God's promise of redemption would be fulfilled.

The Sacrificial System: A Foreshadowing of Redemption

One of the central elements of the Old Testament law was the sacrificial system. The sacrifices offered at the tabernacle and later at the temple were intended to atone for the sins of the people. Through the shedding of blood, the people were reminded of the seriousness of sin and the cost of forgiveness. Leviticus 17:11 (TPT) explains, "For the life of the body is in its blood. I have given you the blood on the altar to purify you, making you right with the Lord. It is the blood, given in exchange for a life, that makes purification possible."

However, the sacrifices of the Old Testament were never intended to provide a permanent solution to the problem of sin. Hebrews 10:4 (TPT) reminds us, "For it is not possible for the blood of bulls and goats to take away sins." Instead, the sacrificial system was a temporary measure, pointing forward to the ultimate sacrifice that would be made by Jesus Christ on the cross. Every lamb offered on the altar, every drop of blood spilled, foreshadowed the coming of the Lamb of God who would take away the sins of the world.

The sacrificial system also highlighted the need for a mediator between God and humanity. The priests, who offered sacrifices on behalf of the people, represented the need for someone to stand between sinful humanity and a holy God. In Jesus, we find the perfect High Priest who not only offers the sacrifice but becomes the sacrifice Himself. Hebrews 9:12 (TPT) declares, "With his own blood—not the blood of goats and calves—he entered the Most Holy Place once for all time and secured our redemption forever."

Visual 10.2 depicts the recurring temple sacrifices, foreshadowing the once-for-all sacrifice of Jesus.

Visual 10.2: Temple sacrifices replaced by the sacrifice of Jesus.
(**Source:** image of Temple sacrifices, with the shadow of a cross looming in the background, symbolizing the ultimate sacrifice to come. - Search Images)

The Waiting for the Messiah: Hope in the Midst of Darkness

As the centuries passed, the people of Israel experienced both moments of faithfulness and times of rebellion. They were taken into exile, faced foreign oppression, and longed for the day when God's promises of redemption would be fulfilled. Yet even in the midst of their suffering, the hope of a coming Messiah remained alive. The prophets continued to speak of a day when God would send His anointed one to save His people and establish His kingdom on earth.

The Old Testament ends with a sense of anticipation. The people are back in their land after the exile, but they are still under the control of foreign powers. The sacrificial system continues, but the ultimate redemption has not yet come. The people are waiting, longing for the fulfilment of God's promises.

Malachi 4:2 (TPT) gives one final promise of hope: "But for you who fear my name, the Sun of Righteousness will rise with healing in his wings. And you will go free, leaping with joy like calves let out to pasture." This promise points to the coming of Christ, the one who would bring healing, freedom, and joy to all who trust in Him.

As God prepared humanity for redemption, He revealed glimpses of the Messiah through prophetic promises. The Sidebar highlights some of these Old Testament prophecies, emphasizing how they pointed to Christ and His redemptive work.

Sidebar: Old Testament Prophecies of Christ

Throughout the Old Testament, God's redemptive plan is revealed in prophecies that point to Jesus, the promised "seed" who would bring restoration, conquer evil, and bless all nations. These prophecies reveal a consistent thread of hope, foreshadowing the coming Messiah who would reconcile humanity to God.

Genesis 3:15 – After the fall, God declared to the serpent, "I will put enmity between you and the woman, and between your seed and her seed; He shall bruise your head, and you shall bruise His heel." This verse is often called the "Protoevangelium," the first gospel, as it foreshadows Jesus' victory over Satan. Though the serpent would "bruise His heel" at the cross, Jesus would ultimately crush Satan's head, overcoming sin and death.

Genesis 12:3 – God's covenant with Abraham promises that through him "all families of the earth shall be blessed." This blessing reaches its fulfillment in Christ, the descendant of Abraham, who brings salvation to all nations. Later in Genesis 26:4-5, God reaffirms this promise, saying that Abraham's offspring (singular) would be a blessing to all nations, pointing to Jesus as the ultimate source of redemption.

Hosea 6:2 – This passage speaks of resurrection: "After two days He will revive us; on the third day He will raise us up, that we may live in His sight." This prophecy reflects the three days Jesus spent in the tomb and His resurrection on the third day, which brings life to all who believe in Him. The prophecy extends hope to all humanity, showing that through Christ's resurrection, all are invited to be raised to new life.

Isaiah 53 – Known as the "Suffering Servant" passage, Isaiah 53 portrays the Messiah who would be "pierced for our transgressions" and "crushed for our iniquities." His suffering brings healing and redemption, fulfilling God's plan to reconcile humanity to Himself. This prophecy points directly to the sacrificial death of Jesus, who bore our sins and made peace between God and humanity.

Psalm 22 - Written by David, this psalm prophetically describes Jesus' crucifixion, including specific details like His hands and feet being pierced and His garments divided by casting lots. Jesus referenced this psalm on the cross, underscoring its fulfillment in His suffering and sacrificial death.

Micah 5:2 - Micah foretold that the Messiah would be born in Bethlehem, a small town in Judah. "But you, Bethlehem Ephrathah, though you are small among the clans of Judah, out of you will come for me one who will be ruler over Israel, whose origins are from of old, from ancient times." This prophecy pointed to Jesus' humble birth, fulfilling God's promise through the Davidic line.

Isaiah 9:6-7 - This prophecy proclaims the coming of a child who will be called "Wonderful Counselor, Mighty God, Everlasting Father, Prince of Peace." His reign will be one of justice and righteousness, fulfilling God's promise of a perfect and everlasting kingdom.

Zechariah 12:10 - This verse foreshadows the Messiah's suffering and humanity's response: "They will look on Me whom they have pierced; they will mourn for Him as one mourns for an only child." This prophecy was fulfilled in Jesus' crucifixion, as those who witnessed His death realized He was the promised Savior.

Each of these prophecies builds a picture of God's redemptive plan, culminating in Jesus, the seed of Abraham and the Son of God, who would conquer sin and death for all humanity. In Christ, every promise is fulfilled (2 Corinthians 1:20), as He restores the relationship between God and humanity, ultimately reconciling "all things, whether on earth or in heaven" (Colossians 1:20). These prophecies reflect God's desire to bring all people into His family through Jesus, the fulfilment of the Old Testament hope and the Savior of the world.

God's Perfect Timing: The Fulfilment of Redemption in Christ

Galatians 4:4 (TPT) tells us, "But when the time was right, God sent His Son, born of a woman, subject to the law." God's preparation for redemption spanned centuries, but at the perfect moment, Jesus came into the world to fulfil all that had been promised. In Him, all of the covenants, prophecies, and sacrifices find their fulfilment. He is the promised seed of the woman, the descendant of Abraham, the suffering servant of Isaiah, and the ultimate sacrifice for sin.

God's preparation for redemption demonstrates His faithfulness, patience, and love. He did not abandon humanity after the fall but worked through history to bring about the restoration of all things. Through the covenants, the law, the prophets, and the sacrificial system, God prepared the way for Jesus, the Redeemer who would make all things new.

Conclusion: The Unfolding of God's Redemption Plan

God's preparation for redemption is a testament to His love and faithfulness. From the moment humanity fell, God set in motion a plan to restore what had been lost. He worked through history, establishing covenants, giving the law, sending prophets, and instituting the sacrificial system, all to prepare the way for the coming of Christ.

The story of redemption is not just about the salvation of individuals but the restoration of all creation. Through Jesus, God's promises are fulfilled, and the hope of the new creation becomes a reality. As we continue to explore the gospel story, we will see how the work of Christ brings to fruition the plan that God set in motion from the very beginning.

PART 3

The Vicarious Humanity of Christ

Chapter 11

The Incarnation: God Becomes Man

At the heart of the Christian faith is the profound mystery of the incarnation: the eternal Son of God, who existed before all things, took on human flesh and entered into our world. The incarnation is the ultimate expression of God's love for humanity and the climax of His plan for redemption. In Jesus Christ, God and humanity are united in a way that forever changes the course of history. This chapter explores the significance of the incarnation, how it reveals God's love and commitment to His creation, and what it means for humanity's redemption and restoration.

The Eternal Word Made Flesh

The incarnation begins with a staggering truth: the Creator of the universe became part of His creation. John 1:14 (TPT) declares, "And so the Living Expression became a man and lived among us! And we gazed upon his glory, the glory of the One and Only who came from the Father, overflowing with tender mercy and truth!" In this verse, John describes the miracle of the incarnation—the eternal Word, who was with God and who was God (John 1:1), entered into the world as a human being.

The significance of this cannot be overstated. In becoming man, God bridged the infinite gap between divinity and humanity. He did not simply visit His creation; He became one with it. This act of divine humility is unparalleled—God, who is infinite and all-powerful, took on the limitations of human flesh, subjecting Himself to the constraints of time, space, and physicality. In Jesus, the fullness of God dwelt in human form (Colossians 2:9, TPT), making Him fully God and fully man.

Why is this important? The incarnation reveals the lengths to which God would go to restore His relationship with humanity. Sin had separated humanity from God, creating a divide that could not be crossed by human effort. But in the person of Jesus, God crossed that divide, stepping into our broken world to bring healing and restoration. The incarnation shows that God's love is not distant or abstract but tangible and personal. He didn't just send a message; He came Himself.

Visual 11.1 depicts the nativity scene, where God became man in humble surroundings—a stable.

Visual 11.1: The nativity scene, emphasizing the divine mystery of God becoming man in the humble setting of a stable.

The Purpose of the Incarnation: A Plan for Redemption

The incarnation is not just about God's identification with humanity; it is part of His redemptive plan. Jesus didn't come simply to teach or to model a good life—He came to save. His very name, "Jesus," means "Yahweh saves" (Matthew 1:21, TPT), pointing to His mission from the moment of His birth. The incarnation was necessary for humanity's redemption because only God could restore what sin had broken, and only a human could represent humanity.

The Apostle Paul explains the purpose of the incarnation in Philippians 2:6-8 (TPT): "He existed in the form of God, yet he gave no thought to seizing equality with God as his supreme prize. Instead, he emptied himself of his outward glory by reducing himself to the form of a lowly servant. He became human! He humbled himself and became vulnerable, choosing to be revealed as a man and was obedient. He was a perfect example, even in his death—a criminal's death by crucifixion!"

Jesus became man to do what no other human could— live a perfect, sinless life and offer Himself as the ultimate sacrifice for sin. In His humanity, He experienced every temptation, every pain, and every struggle that we face, yet He remained without sin (Hebrews 4:15, TPT). This made Him the perfect Lamb of God, able to take away the sins of the world (John 1:29, TPT). Through His death on the cross, Jesus bore the punishment that we deserved, and through His resurrection, He conquered death and opened the way for eternal life.

The incarnation is also the key to understanding how God's justice and mercy come together in the gospel. God's justice demands that sin be punished, but His mercy desires to forgive and restore. In Jesus, both justice and mercy are perfectly fulfilled. As God, Jesus satisfies the requirements of justice, and as man, He represents humanity, offering mercy and grace to all who believe.

God with Us: The Emmanuel Promise

One of the most beautiful names given to Jesus in Scripture is "Emmanuel," which means "God with us." This name, prophesied in Isaiah 7:14 and fulfilled in Matthew 1:23 (TPT), captures the heart of the incarnation. In Jesus, God is no longer distant or removed from our experience. He is with us, fully present in our human condition.

The reality of "God with us" is transformative. It means that in every moment of human suffering, every trial, every fear, God is not far away—He is with us. Jesus experienced the full range of human emotions and trials. He knew hunger, thirst, weariness, and grief. He wept at the tomb of Lazarus (John 11:35), felt compassion for the crowds (Matthew 9:36), and endured the agony of the cross. Because He is fully human, He is able to sympathize with our weaknesses and offer comfort in our struggles.

The incarnation also means that God has forever united Himself with humanity. Jesus didn't just take on human flesh temporarily; He is eternally the God-Man. Even after His resurrection and ascension, He remains fully God and fully human. This truth is profound because it means that our humanity has been taken up into the very life of God. In Christ, humanity and divinity are united, and this union will never be undone.

Visual 11.2 shows Jesus offering comfort to people in their suffering and grief.

Visual 11.2: Image of Jesus offering comfort to people in their suffering and grief.
(**Source:** Image of Jesus Comforting - Search Images)

The Union of Divinity and Humanity: Restoring the Image of God

One of the primary purposes of the incarnation is to restore humanity to its original identity as image-bearers of God. Before the fall, Adam and Eve were created in the image of God, designed to reflect His glory and live in relationship with Him. But sin distorted that image, breaking the relationship and marring humanity's reflection of God.

In Jesus, the perfect image of God is restored. Colossians 1:15 (TPT) declares, "Christ is the visible image of the invisible God." As the perfect human, Jesus shows us what it means to live in perfect harmony with God. His life is the model of true humanity—one that is fully surrendered to God's will, fully dependent on the Father, and fully empowered by the Holy Spirit.

Through the incarnation, Jesus not only restores the image of God in humanity but also enables us to share in His divine life. 2 Peter 1:4 (TPT) speaks of the "precious and magnificent promises that... enable you to share in the divine nature." Because of Jesus' union with humanity, we are invited to partake in the life of the Trinity, to be filled with God's Spirit, and to live in intimate relationship with Him.

This restoration of the image of God is not just about moral improvement; it's about transformation. In Christ, we become new creations (2 Corinthians 5:17, TPT). Our old nature, corrupted by sin, is crucified with Christ, and we are given new life in Him. The incarnation is the means by which God brings about this transformation, making us more like Jesus and restoring us to our original purpose as His image-bearers.

The Incarnation and the New Creation: A Foreshadowing of What Is to Come

The incarnation also points forward to the new creation, where heaven and earth will be fully united, and God's presence will dwell with humanity forever. In Jesus, we see a glimpse of what is to come—the full restoration of creation and the union of God and humanity. Revelation 21:3-4 (TPT) paints this picture: "Look! God's dwelling place is now among the people, and He will dwell with them. They will be His people, and God Himself will be with them and be their God. He will wipe every tear from their eyes. There will be no more death or mourning or crying or pain, for the old order of things has passed away."

The incarnation is the first step toward this new creation. In Jesus, the Kingdom of God has broken into the world, and through His life, death, and resurrection, the power of sin and death has been defeated. The full consummation of this victory will come when Jesus returns, but even now, we experience the firstfruits of the new creation. As followers of Jesus, we are called to live as citizens of His kingdom, reflecting His love, justice, and grace in the world.

The incarnation reminds us that God's plan for redemption is not just about saving individual souls but about renewing all of creation. The union of divinity and humanity in Jesus is the beginning of the reconciliation of all things—heaven and earth, God and humanity. The story of redemption culminates in the new creation, where God's presence will fill the earth, and all things will be made new.

In becoming fully human, Jesus set a pattern for us as the Firstborn, modeling the path of growth and maturity in God's family. The Sidebar expands on how Jesus, as our elder brother, shows us the way to live in alignment with God's purposes.

Sidebar: Jesus, the Firstborn - Our Pattern for Growth and Maturity

Jesus, as the firstborn Son of God, is the pattern for our journey of spiritual growth and maturity. Though He was fully divine, He grew and matured in His humanity, learning obedience and aligning Himself with the heart of the Father (Hebrews 5:8). Jesus received the Holy Spirit at His baptism, fulfilling all righteousness on behalf of humanity. At that moment, the Father's affirmation, "This is my beloved Son, in whom I am well pleased" (Matthew 3:17), was a declaration for all believers who would follow after Him.

The same Spirit that was in Jesus now dwells in us, empowering us to walk in alignment with God's heart and purpose. Jesus' life exemplified perfect obedience, saying and doing only what He heard and saw the Father doing (John 5:19). This alignment is not restrictive but liberating, allowing us to operate in God's power and will with divine purpose. Just as Jesus performed signs and wonders in tune with God's will, so too are we called to mature in our relationship with God, becoming expressions of His love, wisdom, and authority.

In Ephesians 4, Paul speaks of "one Lord, one faith, one baptism, one God and Father of all, who is over all and through all and in all." Through the Spirit, we are united in this oneness, sharing in the life and power of Christ. As we grow in Christ, we are patterned after Jesus, the firstborn, who leads us into maturity as sons and daughters, equipped to bring God's presence into the world.

Conclusion: The Miracle and Mystery of the Incarnation

The incarnation is the cornerstone of the gospel—the miracle of God becoming man to save His creation. In Jesus, we see the fullness of God's love, humility, and commitment to restoring what was lost in the fall. The union of divinity and humanity in the person of Jesus Christ brings hope, healing, and redemption to the world.

As we reflect on the incarnation, we are reminded that God is not distant or removed from our struggles. He is with us—fully present in our humanity, offering us the life and love that only He can give. Through Jesus, we are invited into a restored relationship with God, where we can once again live as His image-bearers, sharing in His divine life.

The incarnation is not just an event in history; it is a truth that continues to shape our lives today. In Jesus, we find the fulfilment of God's promise to redeem and restore His creation, and we look forward to the day when He will return to make all things new.

Chapter 12

The Perfect Human Life

Jesus Christ did not only come into the world to die for our sins; He also lived the perfect human life, embodying what it means to be truly human in relationship with God. Every moment of His life was a reflection of God's original design for humanity. Through His actions, words, and character, Jesus demonstrated the fullness of life that God intended from the beginning—life lived in complete trust and obedience to the Father, filled with love for God and others. In this chapter, we explore the significance of Jesus' life on earth, how it perfectly fulfilled the will of God, and what it means for us to follow in His steps.

Jesus: The Second Adam

To understand the perfection of Jesus' human life, we must first recognize Him as the Second (Last) Adam. The Apostle Paul makes this comparison in Romans 5:18-19 (TPT): "In other words, just as condemnation came upon all people through one transgression, so through one righteous act of Jesus' sacrifice, the perfect righteousness that makes us right with God and leads us to a victorious life is now available to all. One man's disobedience opened the door for all humanity to become sinners, so also one man's obedience opened the door for many to be made perfectly right with God and acceptable to Him."

Where the first Adam failed by disobeying God and bringing sin and death into the world, Jesus succeeded by living a life of perfect obedience and righteousness. He came to undo the effects of Adam's sin and to restore humanity to its original purpose. From His birth to His death, Jesus lived in perfect alignment with God's will, showing us what it means to be fully human. He did what Adam and all of humanity could not do—He fulfilled God's law perfectly and lived a sinless life.

The significance of this cannot be overstated. Jesus' perfect life is not just an example for us to follow; it is the foundation of our salvation. His righteousness is credited to us through faith, making us acceptable to God. 2 Corinthians 5:21 (TPT) tells us, "For God made the only one who did not know sin to become sin for us, so that we who did not know righteousness might become the righteousness of God through our union with Him." In Christ, we are not only forgiven but also given His perfect righteousness, which restores our relationship with God.

A Life of Perfect Obedience to the Father

One of the most remarkable aspects of Jesus' life was His complete obedience to the Father. Throughout the Gospels, we see Jesus constantly seeking the Father's will and submitting Himself to it, even when it meant suffering and death. In John 5:19 (TPT), Jesus says, "I speak to you timeless truth. The Son is not able to do anything from Himself or through My own initiative. I only do the works that I see the Father doing, for the Son does the same works as His Father."

This radical dependence on the Father defines Jesus' entire life. Every decision He made, every miracle He performed, every word He spoke came from His intimate relationship with the Father. His obedience was not begrudging or forced; it was rooted in love and trust. Jesus' life shows us that true freedom comes not from asserting our own will but from surrendering to God's will.

This obedience reached its climax in the Garden of Gethsemane, where Jesus prayed before His arrest and crucifixion. Knowing the suffering that lay ahead, He cried out, "Father, if You are willing, take this cup of agony away from Me. But no matter what, Your will must be Mine" (Luke 22:42, TPT). Even in the face of unimaginable pain, Jesus chose to submit to the Father's plan. His obedience in this moment reversed the disobedience of Adam and opened the way for our redemption.

Visual 12.1 depicts Jesus praying in the Garden of Gethsemane, fully submitting to the Father's will.

Visual 12.1: Jesus praying in the Garden of Gethsemane, fully submitting to the Father's will.

(**Source:** <u>Image of Jesus praying in the Garden of Gethsemane, - Search Images</u>)

A Life Filled with Compassion and Love

Another defining characteristic of Jesus' perfect human life was His compassion and love for others. Everywhere He went, He was moved by the suffering of those around Him and responded with healing, forgiveness, and grace. Matthew 9:36 (TPT) says, "When He saw the vast crowds of people, Jesus' heart was deeply moved with compassion, because they seemed weary and helpless, like wandering sheep without a shepherd."

Jesus' compassion was not limited to those who followed Him or believed in Him. He reached out to the marginalized, the outcasts, and even those who opposed Him. He healed lepers, restored sight to the blind, and forgave sinners. In doing so, He demonstrated the heart of God, who desires all people to come to Him and experience His love.

One of the most profound examples of Jesus' love is found in His interaction with the woman caught in adultery. In John 8, the religious leaders brought the woman before Jesus, hoping to trap Him into condemning her. Instead, Jesus responded with mercy, saying, "Let the one who has never sinned throw the first stone!" (John 8:7, TPT). After her accusers left, Jesus said to the woman, "Dear woman, where are your accusers? Is there no one here to condemn you?" When she replied that no one remained, Jesus said, "Then I certainly don't condemn you either. Go, and from now on, be free from a life of sin" (John 8:10-11, TPT).

In this encounter, we see the perfect balance of grace and truth. Jesus does not condone sin, but neither does He condemn the sinner. Instead, He offers forgiveness and the power to live a transformed life. This same love is extended to all of us—Jesus meets us in our brokenness and offers us the grace to be made whole.

Jesus as the Model of True Humanity

In addition to being our Savior, Jesus is also the model of true humanity. His life shows us what it means to live as image-bearers of God. He lived in perfect harmony with the Father, fully surrendered to His will, and filled with the Holy Spirit. He embodied love, justice, mercy, and humility. In every situation, Jesus responded in a way that reflected the heart of God.

Ephesians 5:1-2 (TPT) calls us to follow His example: "Be imitators of God in everything you do, for then you will represent your Father as His beloved sons and daughters. And continue to walk surrendered to the extravagant love of Christ, for He surrendered His life as a sacrifice for us." Following Jesus means more than simply obeying rules or trying to be a good person—it means living a life of surrender to God, filled with His love and empowered by His Spirit.

Jesus' perfect human life also shows us what it means to live in community. He gathered around Him a group of disciples, teaching them, encouraging them, and loving them. He shared meals with them, prayed with them, and invited them into His mission. Jesus modeled a life of relational love, showing us that true humanity is lived in fellowship with others, not in isolation.

The ultimate goal of following Jesus is not just to imitate His actions but to be transformed into His likeness. Romans 8:29 (TPT) tells us that God's plan is for us to "become like His Son, so that His Son would be the firstborn among many brothers and sisters." As we walk with Jesus, the Holy Spirit works within us to shape us into the image of Christ, restoring us to the true humanity that God intended from the beginning.

Visual 12.2 depicts Jesus' walking with His disciples, symbolizing relational love and the essence of shared community.

Visual 12.2: Jesus walking with His disciples, symbolizing relational love and shared community.
(**Source:** Image of Jesus walking with His disciples, symbolizing relational love - Search Images)

The Significance of Jesus' Sinlessness

One of the unique aspects of Jesus' humanity is His sinlessness. While every other human being has fallen short of God's glory, Jesus lived a life without sin. Hebrews 4:15 (TPT) emphasizes this truth: "He understands humanity, for as a Man, our magnificent

King-Priest was tempted in every way just as we are, and conquered sin."

Jesus' sinlessness is crucial to our salvation. Because He was without sin, He could offer Himself as the perfect sacrifice for our sins. If He had sinned, He would have needed a Savior Himself. But because He remained sinless, He could stand in our place and bear the punishment that we deserved. His perfect life and His sacrificial death are two sides of the same coin—both are essential for our redemption.

Moreover, Jesus' sinlessness gives us hope for our own transformation. While we will never be sinless in this life, we are being conformed to the image of Christ. As we grow in our relationship with Him, we experience the power of the Holy Spirit working within us, enabling us to overcome sin and live in greater holiness. Jesus' life shows us that it is possible to live a life that pleases God, not by our own strength but by the power of the Spirit.

Jesus' life of perfect obedience accomplished everything needed for our salvation, leaving nothing unfinished. The Sidebar explains how we are invited to enter into the fullness of His completed work, experiencing the life He offers.

Sidebar: The Finished Work of Christ - Entering into Fullness

The "finished work of Christ" on the cross encompasses the entirety of His life, death, resurrection, and ascension. Jesus did not accomplish part of the work and leave the rest for us to complete. Rather, He finished it fully (John

19:30), providing complete reconciliation, forgiveness, acceptance, and justification for all humanity. Through His work, we are invited to enter into this finished reality, not by our own efforts, but by simply receiving His gift of grace.

This finished work means that salvation is by grace alone. We don't "add to" Christ's work or strive to complete it ourselves. Instead, we receive and live out what He has already done, stepping into the new life He has given. As we embrace this truth, we begin to experience the fullness of life in Christ, knowing that we are already forgiven, accepted, and justified—not by our works, but by His grace.

In Christ, we are invited to rest in His finished work, rather than striving to earn what He has already provided. This truth frees us from the pressure of "finishing the race" ourselves. It is God's grace that empowers us, and His Spirit that enables us to live in alignment with His purpose. Our journey is not about achieving salvation, but about living out the reality of the gift we have received.

Conclusion: The Life We Were Meant to Live

Jesus lived the perfect human life, fully obedient to the Father, filled with love and compassion, and free from sin. His life is not only the foundation of our salvation but also the model for how we are called to live. In Him, we see the true image of God, restored and perfected. He shows us what it means to live in relationship with God, to love others selflessly, and to walk in holiness.

As followers of Jesus, we are invited to participate in His life. Through His death and resurrection, we have been given new life in Him—a life that is no longer defined by sin and death but by the power of the Spirit. We are called to walk as He walked, to love as He loved, and to surrender to the Father as He did. The life of Jesus is the life we were meant to live, and through Him, it is now possible for us to live in the fullness of God's purpose for us.

The perfect human life of Jesus sets the stage for His ultimate act of love—the cross. In the next chapter, we will explore how Jesus' life culminated in His sacrificial death, where He took upon Himself the sins of the world and opened the way for our reconciliation with God.

Chapter 13

The Cross: Including All Humanity

The cross stands at the center of the Christian faith, representing the ultimate act of love and sacrifice. It is through the cross that Jesus fulfilled His mission to redeem humanity and reconcile us to God. Yet, the significance of the cross goes far beyond individual forgiveness. In His death, Jesus included all of humanity in His redemptive work, opening the way for every person to experience new life in Him. This chapter explores the profound meaning of the cross, the scope of its impact, and how it encompasses all humanity in God's plan for salvation.

The Necessity of the Cross: A Response to Sin

To understand the cross, we must first recognize the gravity of sin and its effects on humanity. Sin is more than just breaking God's laws; it is a rupture in the relationship between humanity and God. Since the fall, sin has infected every aspect of human life, leading to spiritual death and separation from God. Romans 3:23 (TPT) reminds us, "For we all have sinned and are in need of the glory of God."

The justice of God requires that sin be dealt with. God's holiness cannot tolerate sin, and His justice demands that the penalty for sin—death—be paid. But God's love desires to save humanity, not condemn it. This tension between God's justice and His mercy finds its resolution in the cross. Jesus, the sinless Son of God, became the sacrifice for sin, taking upon Himself the punishment that we deserved. In doing so, He satisfied the demands of justice while extending mercy to all.

Romans 6:23 (TPT) explains, "For sin's meager wages is death, but God's lavish gift is life eternal, found in your union with our Lord Jesus, the Anointed One." The cross, then, is God's response to the problem of sin. It is the means by which humanity's broken relationship with God is healed. Jesus' death on the cross was not an accident or a tragic end to His life; it was the fulfilment of God's eternal plan to restore humanity.

Visual 13.1 illustrates the cross on Calvary, symbolizing the intersection of God's love, justice, and mercy.

Visual 13.1: The cross on Calvary, symbolizing the intersection of God's justice and mercy.
(**Source:** Image of The cross on Calvary, - Search Images)

The Inclusive Nature of the Cross: A Sacrifice for All

The cross was not an act of redemption for a select few. From the very beginning, God's plan for salvation has been inclusive, extending to all people regardless of their background, ethnicity, or social status. 1 Timothy 2:4-6 (TPT) declares, "He longs for everyone to embrace His life and return to the full knowledge of the truth. For God is one, and there is one Mediator between God and the sons of men—the true man, Jesus, the Anointed One. He gave Himself as a ransom payment for everyone."

Jesus' death on the cross was for all of humanity. Every person, no matter who they are or what they have done, is included in the offer of salvation. John 3:16 (TPT) reminds us, "For this is how much God loved the world— He gave His one and only, unique Son as a gift. So now everyone who believes in Him will never perish but experience everlasting life." This message of inclusion is at the heart of the gospel.

Throughout His ministry, Jesus demonstrated that His mission was for all people. He welcomed the outcasts, healed the sick, and forgave sinners. He broke down social and cultural barriers, showing that the kingdom of God was open to all. The cross is the culmination of this mission. In His death, Jesus reconciled humanity to God, making it possible for anyone who believes in Him to receive forgiveness and new life.

The Apostle Paul emphasizes this inclusivity in Galatians 3:28 (TPT): "And we no longer see each other in our former state—Jew or non-Jew, rich or poor, male or female—because we're all one through our union with Jesus Christ." The cross erases the divisions that separate people from one another and from God. In Christ, we are united as one family, reconciled to God and to each other.

Jesus as the Lamb of God: The Final Sacrifice

The cross is the ultimate fulfilment of the Old Testament sacrificial system. For centuries, the people of Israel offered sacrifices to atone for their sins, but these sacrifices were temporary and could never fully remove sin. Hebrews 10:4 (TPT) states, "For it is not possible for the blood of bulls and goats to take away sins."

Jesus, however, is the perfect and final sacrifice. John the Baptist identified Him as the "Lamb of God who takes away the sin of the world" (John 1:29, TPT). As the spotless Lamb, Jesus took upon Himself the sins of the world, offering His life in exchange for ours. His sacrifice was once for all—sufficient to atone for the sins of every person who has ever lived or will ever live.

Hebrews 10:12 (TPT) explains, "But when this Priest had offered the one supreme sacrifice for sin for all time, He sat down on a throne at the right hand of God." The cross marked the end of the need for further sacrifices. In Jesus' death, the price for sin was paid in full, and through His resurrection, the power of sin and death was defeated. His sacrifice opened the way for humanity to be reconciled to God once and for all.

Visual 13.2 depicts a sacrificial lamb, symbolizing Jesus as the ultimate and final sacrifice.

Visual 13.2: The sacrificial lamb, symbolizing Jesus as the ultimate and final sacrifice.
(**Source:** Image of The sacrificial lamb, symbolizing Jesus as the ultimate and final sacrifice. - Search Images)

The Power of the Cross: Breaking the Curse of Sin and Death

The cross is not only the place where Jesus paid the penalty for sin; it is also the place where He broke the power of sin and death. Sin's hold over humanity was broken through Jesus' victory on the cross. Colossians 2:14-15 (TPT) describes this triumph: "He canceled out every legal violation we had on our record and the old arrest warrant that stood to indict us. He erased it all—our sins, our stained soul—He deleted it all and they cannot be retrieved! Everything we once were in Adam has been placed onto His cross and nailed permanently there as a public display of cancellation."

Jesus' death and resurrection broke the curse of death that had entered the world through Adam's sin. Death no longer has the final word over those who are in Christ. Romans 6:9-10 (TPT) proclaims, "We know that since the Anointed One has been raised from the dead to die no more, His resurrection life has vanquished death and its power over Him is finished. For by His sacrifice, He died to sin's power once and for all, but He now lives continuously for the Father's pleasure."

The power of the cross extends beyond the forgiveness of sins—it transforms lives. Through the cross, we are set free from the bondage of sin, given a new identity in Christ, and empowered to live in victory. The cross is the ultimate declaration of God's love and power, and it invites all people to experience the life-changing freedom that comes through Jesus.

The Universal Invitation: "It Is Finished"

As Jesus hung on the cross, His final words were, "It is finished" (John 19:30, TPT). These words signify the completion of His work of salvation. The debt of sin had been paid, and the way to eternal life was opened. The cross is God's universal invitation to all people—an invitation to come, believe, and receive the gift of salvation.

The cross stands as a beacon of hope for the world. No one is excluded from the love of God. No sin is too great, no past too dark, no failure too deep to be forgiven through the blood of Jesus. The cross is the great equalizer—it reminds us that all have sinned and fallen short of God's glory, but it also assures us that all can be saved through faith in Jesus Christ.

Jesus' words, "It is finished," echo through history, calling every person to receive the gift of redemption. Revelation 22:17 (TPT) extends this invitation: "Come," says the Holy Spirit and the bride in divine duet. Let everyone who hears this duet join them in saying, "Come." Let everyone gripped with spiritual thirst say, "Come." And let everyone who craves the gift of living water come and drink it freely. "It is My gift to you! Come."

Through the Cross, Jesus opened the way for eternal life, defeating death and offering us the hope of resurrection. The Sidebar explores the promise of immortality we receive in Christ's victory over the grave.

Sidebar: Immortality through Resurrection

Through Jesus' death, resurrection, and ascension, believers receive the incredible promise of immortality and transformation. Jesus didn't merely die for us; He died as us, taking on the full consequence of sin. In Him, we were co-crucified (Galatians 2:20), and through this profound union, we also share in His resurrection and ascension, becoming a new creation (2 Corinthians 5:17). This transformation is as radical as the metamorphosis of a caterpillar into a butterfly—where what was once bound by limitations becomes something entirely new and glorious.

- 1 Corinthians 15:53-54 assures us that mortality is exchanged for immortality, where "death is swallowed up in victory." Jesus overcame sin and death, transferring to us His victory, righteousness, and eternal life. In His resurrection, we too have the assurance of a glorified existence, where the hidden glory of Christ in us will one day be fully revealed (Colossians 1:27).

- Romans 6:5 states, "If we have been united with Him in a death like His, we will certainly also be united with Him in a resurrection like His." Jesus' resurrection marks the defeat of death, not as an escape to heaven but as the beginning of a new, eternal quality of life in God's presence. The death of a saint is described as "costly" in Psalm 116:15, not because it is precious in a sentimental sense, but because each life carries immense value and purpose in God's kingdom.

- Jesus' ascension to the Father also becomes ours: "I am ascending to My Father and your Father, to My God and your God" (John 20:17). Through this, we inherit His relationship with the Father, living in union with God as members of His family. Whether part of the cloud of witnesses (Hebrews 12:1) or living on earth, we are united with God, participating in the fullness of His life.

In Colossians 2:15, Paul explains that Jesus "disarmed the powers and authorities" and paraded them in victory, symbolizing the defeat of all enemies. We share in this triumph, as Jesus' victory over death, sin, and every opposing force becomes ours. This promise of immortality and transformation fuels our hope, knowing that our present struggles are temporary, and we await the day when we will fully experience our glorified state.

Just as Jesus' glory was momentarily veiled in His humanity, our true glory is hidden until the day of full transformation. Through Jesus, we are being conformed to His glorious image, destined to live eternally with God in a transformed, victorious state. Death is not an end but a transition, a stepping into the reality of our true, eternal life with Him.

Conclusion: The Cross and the Inclusion of All Humanity

The cross of Christ is the central moment in the story of redemption. It is the place where God's justice and mercy meet, where the sinless Savior takes upon Himself the sins of the world, and where the power of sin and death is broken forever. Through the cross, Jesus included all humanity in His redemptive work, offering forgiveness, freedom, and new life to every person.

As we reflect on the significance of the cross, we are reminded that it is not only a symbol of individual salvation but a declaration of God's love for all people. Jesus' sacrifice was for the whole world, and His invitation to experience new life extends to everyone. The cross calls us to embrace the grace of God, to surrender our lives to Him, and to walk in the freedom that He has secured for us.

The story of the cross does not end in death but in resurrection. In the next chapter, we will explore the significance of Jesus' resurrection and how it marks the beginning of the new creation, where death is defeated, and new life is offered to all who believe.

125

Chapter 14

Resurrection: The New Creation Begins

The resurrection of Jesus Christ is the turning point in history, the moment when death itself was defeated, and the promise of new creation was inaugurated. Through His resurrection, Jesus not only conquered death but opened the way for humanity to experience eternal life and the renewal of all creation. The resurrection is the foundation of the Christian faith and the proof that Jesus is who He claimed to be—the Son of God and the Savior of the world. In this chapter, we explore the significance of the resurrection, its implications for humanity and the world, and how it marks the beginning of the new creation.

The Triumph Over Death

The resurrection is the central event of the Christian gospel, the ultimate victory over sin, death, and the powers of darkness. When Jesus rose from the dead, He demonstrated that death no longer had dominion over Him or over those who belong to Him. The resurrection was not just a spiritual event but a physical one—Jesus' body was raised to new life, transformed and glorified. In doing so, He fulfilled God's promise to defeat death and restore life.

In 1 Corinthians 15:20-22 (TPT), Paul writes, "But the truth is, Christ is risen from the dead, as the firstfruit of a great resurrection harvest of those who have died. For since death came through a man, it's fitting that the resurrection of the dead has also come through a man. Even as all who are in Adam die, so also all who are in Christ will be made alive." Paul emphasizes that Jesus' resurrection is not just about His victory but also about the promise that all who are in Him will share in that victory.

The resurrection marks the undoing of the curse of death that entered the world through Adam's sin. Jesus is the "firstfruits" of a new humanity—a humanity that will one day experience resurrection life in the same way He did. The resurrection is the beginning of a new era in which death no longer has the final word. In Jesus, death has been defeated once and for all.

The Resurrection marks our passage from death to life, symbolized by crossing into new territory just as Israel crossed the Jordan. The Sidebar highlights this powerful imagery, connecting it with our transition into the new creation through Christ.

life cannot flourish, symbolizing the ultimate destination of a life separated from God.

Crossing the Jordan marked a decisive break from the wilderness wanderings and entry into a new life in God's promises. For the Israelites, this journey was not only a geographical transition but a spiritual progression—moving from a life marked by the old identity, tied to Adam and the effects of sin, to a new life in covenant with God, where they could flourish in the fullness of His promises.

In a broader sense, the Jordan represents the transition from death to life, illustrating the journey of leaving behind an old self and stepping into the resurrection life promised in Christ. Just as the Israelites left behind the wilderness, crossing the Jordan symbolizes moving beyond the limitations, struggles, and spiritual "deadness" tied to sin and entering a new identity in God.

The path from Adam to life parallels the spiritual transformation that takes place in every believer. Through faith in Christ, we, too, cross our own Jordan, leaving behind the past, marked by the limitations of the flesh, and moving into a life shaped by the Spirit. This crossing is not just an escape from sin but a stepping into the fullness of God's promise and identity as His children, possessing the inheritance He has given us.

This journey also reflects resurrection power, as we die to the old self and rise to a new life, following Christ. Jesus, who called Himself the "resurrection and the life" (John 11:25), leads us through our personal "Jordan" into a life of purpose, freedom, and union with God. Crossing the Jordan is thus a symbol of faith and resurrection, where the barriers of sin and death are rolled back, and we step into the abundant life God has prepared for us.

The Physical Reality of the Resurrection

One of the most important aspects of the resurrection is its physical reality. Jesus' body was not merely resuscitated but transformed into a new, glorified body. After His resurrection, Jesus appeared to His disciples, ate with them, and invited them to touch His wounds, proving that He was not a ghost or a mere spirit but physically alive (Luke 24:39-43, TPT). This physical resurrection is crucial because it affirms the goodness of God's creation and His plan to redeem and restore the entire created order.

The physicality of Jesus' resurrection points to the future hope of bodily resurrection for all believers. As Paul writes in Philippians 3:21 (TPT), "He will transform our humble bodies and transfigure us into the identical likeness of His glorified body. And using His matchless power, He continually subdues everything to Himself." Our future resurrection bodies will be like Jesus'— glorified, imperishable, and free from the effects of sin and death.

This promise of bodily resurrection is central to the Christian hope. It reminds us that salvation is not just about escaping this world and going to heaven; it is about the renewal and restoration of all things, including our physical bodies. The resurrection shows us that God's plan is to bring wholeness and redemption to every part of creation.

Visual 14.1 shows the empty tomb, symbolizing Jesus' triumph of life over death.

Visual 14.1: An empty tomb, symbolizing Jesus' triumph of life over death.
(Source: <u>Image of An empty tomb - Search Images</u>)

The Inauguration of the New Creation

The resurrection of Jesus is not only the defeat of death but also the beginning of the new creation. In His resurrection, Jesus becomes the firstborn of a new humanity and the first glimpse of what the renewed creation will be like. Colossians 1:18 (TPT) says, "He is the head of His body, which is the church. And since He is the beginning and the firstborn heir in resurrection, He is the most exalted one, holding first place in everything."

Jesus' resurrection signals the beginning of God's plan to renew and restore the entire universe. The curse of sin, which affected not only humanity but all of creation, is being undone through the resurrection of Jesus. Romans 8:19-21 (TPT) explains, "The entire universe is standing on tiptoe, yearning to see the unveiling of God's glorious sons and daughters! For against its will, the universe itself has had to endure the empty futility resulting from the consequences of human sin. But now, with eager expectation, all creation longs for freedom from its slavery to decay and to experience with us the wonderful freedom coming to God's children."

The resurrection is the beginning of this cosmic restoration. Through Jesus, the new creation has already been inaugurated, and as His followers, we are invited to participate in this work of renewal. We are not simply waiting for the future restoration of all things; we are called to live as new creations in the present. 2 Corinthians 5:17 (TPT) proclaims, "Now, if anyone is enfolded into Christ, he has become an entirely new creation. All that is related to the old order has vanished. Behold, everything is fresh and new."

As new creations in Christ, we are called to reflect the reality of the resurrection in our lives. This means living in the power of the Holy Spirit, embodying the values of God's kingdom, and working toward the restoration of justice, peace, and reconciliation in the world. The resurrection is not just a future hope; it is a present reality that transforms the way we live here and now.

Victory Over the Powers of Darkness

The resurrection also signifies Jesus' victory over the powers of darkness. Throughout His ministry, Jesus confronted the forces of evil—casting out demons, healing the sick, and proclaiming the arrival of God's kingdom. But it was in His death and resurrection that Jesus delivered the final blow to the powers of sin, Satan, and death.

In Colossians 2:15 (TPT), Paul describes this victory: "Then Jesus made a public spectacle of all the powers and principalities of darkness, stripping away from them every weapon and all their spiritual authority and power to accuse us. And by the power of the cross, Jesus led them around as prisoners in a procession of triumph. He was not their prisoner; they were His!" The resurrection is the ultimate demonstration of Jesus' authority over the forces of evil. Through His resurrection, He disarmed the powers of darkness and secured victory for all who belong to Him.

This victory is not just theoretical; it has real implications for our lives today. Because of Jesus' resurrection, we are no longer slaves to sin or under the dominion of darkness. We have been set free to live in the light of God's kingdom. Romans 6:4 (TPT) affirms this truth: "We have been co-resurrected with Him so that we could be empowered to walk in the freshness of new life."

The resurrection empowers us to live in victory over sin and to resist the temptations and lies of the enemy. It assures us that no matter what struggles or battles we face in this life, the ultimate victory has already been won through Jesus' death and resurrection.

Visual 14.2 symbolizes Jesus' victory over the forces of darkness and the triumph of good over evil.

Visual 14.2: Jesus' victory over the forces of darkness, symbolizing the triumph of good over evil.
(**Source:** Image of Jesus' victory over the forces of darkness, symbolizing the triumph of good over evil. - Search Images)

The Promise of Eternal Life

The resurrection is also the guarantee of eternal life for all who believe in Jesus. Because Jesus has risen from the dead, we can have confidence that death is not the end. John 11:25-26 (TPT) records Jesus' words: "I am the resurrection and I am life eternal. Anyone who clings to Me in faith, even though he dies, will live forever. And the one who lives by believing in Me will never die."

Jesus' resurrection assures us that those who are in Christ will be raised to new life with Him. This eternal life is not just about living forever; it is about living in the fullness of God's presence, free from the power of sin and death. Revelation 21:4 (TPT) gives us a glimpse of this eternal reality: "He will wipe away every tear from their eyes, and eliminate death entirely. No one will mourn or weep any longer. The pain of wounds will no longer exist, for the old order has ceased."

The promise of eternal life through the resurrection gives us hope in the midst of suffering and loss. We know that death does not have the final word and that we will one day be raised with Christ to live in the new creation. This hope empowers us to live with courage and purpose, knowing that our lives are part of God's eternal plan.

The Commission of the Resurrected Jesus: Empowering His Disciples

After His resurrection, Jesus appeared to His disciples and gave them a mission: to go into the world and proclaim the good news of His victory over death. In Matthew 28:18-20 (TPT), Jesus says, "All the authority of the universe has been given to Me. Now, wherever you go, make disciples of all nations, baptizing them in the name of the Father, the Son, and the Holy Spirit. And teach them to faithfully follow all that I have commanded you. And never forget that I am with you every day, even to the completion of this age."

The resurrection is not only a personal victory for Jesus but the commissioning of His followers to continue His mission. The same power that raised Jesus from the dead is now at work in us, empowering us to be His witnesses and ambassadors in the world. We are called to proclaim the good news of the resurrection, to invite others into the new creation, and to participate in God's work of renewal in the world.

Conclusion: The Beginning of the New Creation

The resurrection of Jesus marks the beginning of the new creation. It is the moment when death was defeated, and the power of sin was broken. Through His resurrection, Jesus inaugurated a new era in which all things are being made new, and He invites all of humanity to participate in this renewal.

The resurrection is not just a future hope but a present reality that transforms the way we live today. As followers of the risen Christ, we are called to live as new creations, reflecting the reality of the resurrection in our lives and in the world around us. We are empowered by the Holy Spirit to proclaim the good news, resist the powers of darkness, and participate in the renewal of all things.

As we look forward to the full consummation of the new creation when Jesus returns, we live in the confidence that the resurrection has already secured the victory. In Christ, we are part of a new humanity, and we look forward to the day when death will be no more, and God's kingdom will be fully realized.

In the next chapter, we will explore the significance of Jesus' ascension and what it means for humanity to enter into glory with Him.

Chapter 15

Ascension: Humanity Enters Glory

The ascension of Jesus Christ is often less discussed than His resurrection, yet it is a profound and essential part of God's redemptive plan. The ascension is not merely Jesus' return to heaven; it marks the exaltation of His humanity into divine glory, a reality that forever changes the destiny of humanity. Jesus, fully God and fully man, entered into the highest realm of glory and now reigns at the right hand of the Father. In this chapter, we will explore the significance of Jesus' ascension, how it affects our understanding of human destiny, and the promises it holds for those who are in Christ.

The Ascension: The Exaltation of Jesus' Humanity

After His resurrection, Jesus spent forty days with His disciples, teaching them about the kingdom of God and preparing them for the mission He was about to give them. Then, in an awe-inspiring moment, Jesus ascended into heaven. Luke 24:51 (TPT) describes the event: "While He was blessing them, He floated off the ground into the sky, ascending into heaven before their eyes." In this act, Jesus was taken from the physical realm into the heavenly realm, returning to the Father and entering His glory.

However, the ascension was not simply a return to where Jesus had come from before His incarnation.

Something profound had changed—Jesus was now fully human as well as fully divine. The humanity that He had taken on in the incarnation was now forever exalted in the presence of God. Hebrews 1:3 (TPT) says, "The Son is the dazzling radiance of God's splendor, the exact expression of God's true nature—His mirror image! He holds the universe together and expands it by the mighty power of His spoken word. He accomplished for us the complete cleansing of sins, and then took His seat on the highest throne at the right hand of the majestic One."

The ascension of Jesus reveals that humanity, in the person of Jesus, has been lifted into the divine presence. Jesus is seated at the right hand of God, the position of highest honor and authority. This means that humanity, which had fallen so far from God in the Garden of Eden, is now exalted in Christ, seated in heavenly places (Ephesians 2:6). Jesus is not only our Savior; He is the pioneer of our destiny, leading the way for humanity to enter into glory with Him.

Visual 15.1 illustrates Jesus ascending into the clouds, symbolizing His ascension and return to the Father.

Visual 15.1: Jesus' ascending into the clouds symbolizing His exaltation and return to the Father.
(**Source:** Image of Jesus ascending into the clouds - Search Images)

The Significance of the Ascension for Humanity

The ascension is more than a dramatic exit; it carries deep theological meaning. Through His ascension, Jesus brings humanity into the very presence of God. He does not leave His humanity behind; He takes it with Him. This truth has profound implications for every believer.

First, the ascension reveals that Jesus' work on earth was complete. When He ascended, He took His place at the Father's right hand, a position of rest and authority. Hebrews 10:12 (TPT) says, "But when this Priest had offered the one supreme sacrifice for sin for all time, He sat down on a throne at the right hand of God." Jesus' ascension signifies that the work of redemption is finished. The sacrifice has been made, the victory over sin and death has been won, and Jesus now reigns as King.

Second, the ascension means that we, as believers, are united with Christ in His exaltation. Colossians 3:1 (TPT) tells us, "Christ's resurrection is your resurrection too. This is why we are to yearn for all that is above, for that's where Christ sits enthroned at the place of all power, honor, and authority!" Because we are united with Christ through faith, we are seated with Him in heavenly places. Our citizenship is no longer of this world; it is in heaven (Philippians 3:20). The ascension assures us that our ultimate destiny is to share in Christ's glory.

Third, the ascension is a promise that Jesus will return. As the disciples watched Jesus ascend into heaven, two angels appeared and said, "Men of Galilee, why are you standing here staring into heaven? Jesus has been taken from you into heaven, but someday He will return from heaven in the same way you saw Him go!" (Acts 1:11, TPT). The ascension points forward to the day when Jesus will come again to fully establish His kingdom on earth.

Jesus as Our High Priest and Mediator

One of the most profound aspects of the ascension is that Jesus, in His humanity, now serves as our High Priest and Mediator before God. Hebrews 4:14-16 (TPT) says, "So then, we must cling in faith to all we know to be true. For we have a magnificent King-Priest, Jesus Christ, the Son of God, who rose into the heavenly realm for us, and now sympathizes with us in our frailty. He understands humanity, for as a Man, our magnificent King-Priest was tempted in every way just as we are, and conquered sin."

Jesus' role as High Priest means that He is continually interceding for us before the Father. He is our advocate, representing us in the presence of God. Romans 8:34 (TPT) assures us, "Who then is left to condemn us? Certainly not Jesus, the Anointed One! For He gave His life for us, and even more than that, He has conquered death and is now risen, exalted, and enthroned by God at His right hand. So how could He possibly condemn us since He is continually praying for our triumph?"

Jesus, fully God and fully man, is forever the bridge between humanity and God. His ascension guarantees that we have an advocate in heaven, someone who understands our struggles, prays for us, and ensures that we are always welcome in the presence of God. This is the ultimate assurance of God's love and acceptance.

Visual 15.2 depicts Jesus as the High Priest, mediating and interceding between the Father and humanity.

Visual 15.2: Jesus as the High Priest, standing before the Father, interceding on behalf of humanity.
(**Source:** <u>Image of Jesus as the High Priest - Search Images</u>)

The Sending of the Holy Spirit: Empowerment for the Church

One of the greatest gifts that came through Jesus' ascension is the sending of the Holy Spirit. Before His ascension, Jesus told His disciples, "But I promise you this—the Holy Spirit will come upon you and you will be seized with power. You will be My messengers to Jerusalem, throughout Judea, the distant provinces—even to the remotest places on earth!" (Acts 1:8, TPT).

Jesus' ascension made way for the Holy Spirit to come and dwell within every believer. The Spirit is the presence of Christ in us, empowering us to live out the mission of the kingdom of God. Through the Holy Spirit, we are equipped to be witnesses of Jesus' resurrection and to carry forward His work on earth.

The Holy Spirit also serves as the guarantee of our future inheritance. Ephesians 1:13-14 (TPT) explains, "The Holy Spirit is given to us like an engagement ring, as the first instalment of what's coming! He is our hope-promise of a future inheritance, which seals us until we have all of redemption's promises and experience complete freedom—all for the supreme glory and honor of God!"

The Spirit's presence in our lives is a foretaste of the glory that awaits us in the new creation. The ascension assures us that, while Jesus reigns in heaven, He has not left us alone. We have the Spirit of God within us, guiding, teaching, and empowering us as we await His return.

The Hope of Glorification: Sharing in Christ's Glory

The ascension of Jesus is not only about His glory; it is also about our future glorification. As believers, we are destined to share in Christ's glory. Romans 8:17 (TPT) tells us, "And since we are His true children, we qualify to share all His treasures, for indeed, we are heirs of God Himself. And since we are joined to Christ, we also inherit all that He is and all that He has. We will experience being co-glorified with Him provided that we accept His sufferings as our own."

Jesus' ascension points us to our future hope—just as He was raised and glorified, so too will we be raised and glorified with Him. Philippians 3:20-21 (TPT) reminds us that "we are a colony of heaven on earth as we cling tightly to our life-giver, the Lord Jesus Christ, who will transform our humble bodies and transfigure us into the identical likeness of His glorified body."

This promise of glorification gives us hope and purpose as we navigate the challenges and trials of life. We know that our current suffering is not the end of the story. Just as Jesus entered into glory, so will we. The ascension is a reminder that our ultimate destiny is not rooted in this world but in the kingdom of God.

Visual 15.3 shows Jesus in His glorified state, promising believers a share in His glory and symbolizing our future hope.

Visual 15.3: Jesus in glorified state, promising believers a sharing in His glory and symbolizing our future hope. (**Source:** Image of Jesus in glory - Search Images)

The Ascension elevated humanity to a place of glory, making us God's permanent dwelling place on earth. The Sidebar further explores how we, as the living temple, carry His presence and reflect His glory wherever we go.

Sidebar: The Living Temple - God's Permanent Dwelling Place

Throughout Scripture, the concept of God's dwelling place evolved, revealing His deep desire to be present with His people. In the wilderness, Moses' mobile tabernacle was a temporary structure made of materials like skin, hair, and cloth. This tabernacle housed God's presence intermittently, appearing on sacred occasions such as the Day of Atonement. Later, Solomon built a stone temple, providing a more enduring but still conditional dwelling place for God's glory, which filled the temple only at certain times.

During Jesus' earthly ministry, He taught and ministered in the temple, but as His ministry reached its climax, He drove out the money changers who had turned it into a marketplace. This act symbolized a pivotal moment—the departure of God's presence from the physical temple. Jesus then foretold a new kind of temple, saying, "Destroy this temple, and I will raise it again in three days" (John 2:19), referring to His own body as the new, eternal dwelling of God's Spirit.

Despite this, the Jewish people continued their worship in the physical temple, unaware that Jesus had prophesied its imminent destruction. "Not one stone here will be left on another," He warned (Matthew 24:2). This prophecy was fulfilled in AD 70, when the Romans destroyed the temple, bringing an end to the era of worship centered on physical buildings.

Under the new covenant, we are now God's living temples—His permanent, mobile dwelling place on earth. As believers, God's Spirit dwells in us constantly; we are His address on earth, carrying

His presence wherever we go. This reality also emphasizes the importance of the redemption of our bodies as part of God's complete work of restoration. Even those who have gone before us, the cloud of witnesses (Hebrews 12:1), await this redemption (Hebrews 11:39-40), where body, soul, and spirit are wholly transformed in His presence.

We are, therefore, not just symbolic temples but living, sacred vessels of His Spirit, designed to reflect His love and embody His purposes on earth. Unlike the temporary tabernacle or stone temple, God's presence resides within us permanently, making each believer a dwelling place of the Most High. This union with God is our true and eternal identity, revealing His glory and purpose to the world.

Conclusion: Humanity in Glory with Christ

The ascension of Jesus is the final act of His earthly ministry, but it opens the door to a new era of redemption. Through His ascension, Jesus takes His place as King and High Priest, interceding for humanity and preparing the way for our future glorification. He has brought humanity into the presence of God, and through Him, we have the hope of eternal life and glory.

The ascension is not the end of the story but the beginning of a new chapter in God's redemptive plan. Jesus reigns

in glory, and we are united with Him in that glory. We are seated with Him in heavenly places, empowered by the Holy Spirit to carry out His mission on earth.

As we reflect on the ascension, we are reminded that our destiny is bound up with Christ's. We are called to live as citizens of heaven, with our eyes fixed on the future glory that awaits us. Jesus' ascension assures us that He has gone ahead to prepare a place for us, and one day, we will be with Him in the fullness of His kingdom, sharing in His glory forever.

The story of redemption continues as we move forward, anticipating the ultimate restoration of all things in the new creation.

PART 4

The New Creation Reality

Chapter 16

Christ's Life Becoming Our Life

The Christian life is not about merely following the teachings of Jesus from a distance. It is about entering into a union with Christ in such a way that His life becomes our life. The mystery of the gospel is that through faith, we are not only forgiven of our sins but also invited to participate in the very life of Christ. His death, resurrection, and ascension are not just historical events but realities that transform our existence. In this chapter, we explore what it means for Christ's life to become our life, how we share in His death and resurrection, and how this profound union changes everything about how we live.

The Mystery of Union with Christ

At the heart of the Christian faith is the concept of union with Christ. This union is a mystery beyond human comprehension, yet it is one of the most foundational truths of the gospel. Through faith, we are united with Christ in such a way that His experiences—His death, resurrection, and ascension—become our experiences. Colossians 3:3-4 (TPT) captures this reality: "Your crucifixion with Christ has severed the tie to this life, and now your true life is hidden away in God in Christ. And as Christ Himself is seen for who He really is, who you really are will also be revealed, for you are now one with Him in His glory!"

This union means that when Christ died, we died with Him; when He rose, we rose with Him; and when He ascended, we ascended with Him. Our identity is no longer rooted in our old nature or our old way of life but in Christ Himself. The Apostle Paul frequently speaks of believers being "in Christ," a phrase that signifies this intimate and transformative connection.

In Galatians 2:20 (TPT), Paul writes, "My old identity has been co-crucified with Messiah and no longer lives, for the nails of His cross crucified me with Him. And now the essence of this new life is no longer mine, for the Anointed One lives His life through me—we live in union as one! My new life is empowered by the faith of the Son of God who loves me so much that He gave Himself for me, dispensing His life into mine!" This powerful statement reveals that the Christian life is not lived by our own strength or effort but through the life of Christ flowing through us.

Visual 16.1 shows a believer standing in light, symbolizing union with Christ and the transformation that occurs as His life becomes ours.

Visual 16.1: Believer standing in light, symbolizing the union with Christ and the transformation that comes from His life becoming ours.
(**Source:** <u>image of Believer standing in light, symbolizing the union with Christ and the transformation that comes from His life becoming ours - Search</u>)

Sharing in Christ's Death and Resurrection

The first aspect of this union is that we share in Christ's death and resurrection. Through baptism, we symbolically and spiritually participate in the death and burial of Jesus, as well as His resurrection to new life. Romans 6:4 (TPT) explains, "Sharing in His death by our baptism means that we were co-buried and entombed with Him, so that when the Father's glory raised Christ from the dead, we were also raised with Him. We have been co-resurrected with Him so that we could be empowered to walk in the freshness of new life."

To share in Christ's death means that our old, sinful nature has been put to death. The power of sin, which once held us in bondage, has been broken through the cross. Our old self—our identity in Adam—has been crucified, and we are no longer slaves to sin. This death is not something we must strive to achieve; it is something that has already happened in Christ. Our task is to live out the reality of what has already been accomplished.

But the Christian life is not just about dying to sin; it is also about being raised to new life. In Christ's resurrection, we are given new life—a life that is no longer dominated by sin but empowered by the Holy Spirit. This resurrection life is the source of our hope and our power to live as followers of Jesus. Ephesians

2:4-6 (TPT) reminds us, "But God still loved us with such great love. He is so rich in compassion and mercy. Even when we were dead and doomed in our many sins, He united us into the very life of Christ and saved us by His wonderful grace! He raised us up with Christ the Exalted One, and we ascended with Him into the glorious perfection and authority of the heavenly realm."

Our new life in Christ is not merely an improved version of our old life; it is an entirely new existence. We are no longer defined by the brokenness of our past or the limitations of our human nature. Instead, we live in the reality of Christ's resurrection, empowered by His Spirit to walk in victory and holiness.

Living in the Power of Christ's Life

The mystery of Christ's life becoming our life is not only about what has been done for us but also about how we live in the present. As believers, we are called to live out the reality of our union with Christ on a daily basis. This means living in the power of His resurrection and walking in the newness of life He has given us.

In practical terms, living in the power of Christ's life means that we are no longer bound by the limitations of our human nature. We are empowered by the Holy Spirit to live in ways that reflect the character and love of Jesus. Galatians 5:22-23 (TPT) describes the fruit of this life: "But the fruit produced by the Holy Spirit within you is divine love in all its varied expressions: joy that overflows, peace that subdues, patience that endures, kindness in action, a life full of virtue, faith that prevails, gentleness of heart, and strength of spirit. Never set the law above these qualities, for they are meant to be limitless."

This new life in Christ is not lived by our own efforts or by trying harder to be good. It is lived by surrendering to the life of Christ within us and allowing His Spirit to produce His character in us. The Christian life is about abiding in Christ and allowing His life to flow through us, as Jesus Himself explained in John 15:5 (TPT): "I am the sprouting vine and you're My branches. As you live in union with Me as your source, fruitfulness will stream from within you—but when you live separated from Me you are powerless."

This abiding life means that we are continually connected to Christ, drawing our strength, wisdom, and guidance from Him. It is not a life of striving but a life of resting in His finished work and trusting in His presence. As we abide in Him, His life transforms us from the inside out, enabling us to bear fruit that reflects His love and grace to the world.

Visual 16.2 shows a vine with branches, symbolizing the life of Christ flowing through believers and producing fruit that reflects His character.

Visual 16.2: An image of a vine with branches, symbolizing the life of Christ flowing through believers, producing fruit that reflects His character.

(**Source:** image of An image of a vine with branches, symbolizing the life of Christ flowing through believers, producing fruit that reflects His character - Search Images)

Through Christ, our identity as God's image-bearers is fully restored, allowing His life to shine through us. The Sidebar delves deeper into what it means to reflect the restored image of God.

Sidebar: The Restored Image of God

God's redemptive plan restores humanity to His image—a likeness that was distorted by the fall but now fully restored in Christ, who is the perfect image of God (Colossians 1:15). When we accept Jesus, we enter into an exchanged life where His righteousness, holiness, and perfection are imparted to us. The risen Jesus is now our life (Colossians 3:4), and it is His presence in us that the Father sees, which is why we are holy, blameless, perfect, and righteous in His sight. We cannot be otherwise, for we are seen through the lens of Christ's finished work.

Jesus lived a vicarious humanity—a life lived not only for us but as us. Through His death and resurrection, we are included in every stage of His redemptive journey:

- We were co-crucified with Him, symbolizing the end of our old self.
- We were co-buried with Him, signifying that our past life is completely laid to rest.
- We were co-resurrected and co-ascended with Him, and we are now co-seated in the heavenly places, face-to-face with God in the spirit.

Our union with Christ means that we are in Him, and thus, everything He is, we are; everything He has, we possess. This reality establishes our identity as coheirs with Christ (Romans 8:17), where we share in His inheritance and authority. As sons and daughters, we carry His divine nature, fully restored to the image of God, equipped to live out His character, love, and purpose on earth.

In this exchanged life, we are not merely forgiven but transformed. Christ's life within us enables us to reflect God's character and love, preparing us for eternal fellowship with Him. Our restored identity is grounded in the reality of being "in Christ," where we are empowered to live in alignment with God's original design—holy, complete, and beloved. As Paul affirms, "As He is, so are we in this world" (1 John 4:17). Through Christ's finished work, we are renewed as the image-bearers we were always intended to be.

Christ's Life as the Source of Our Identity

One of the most profound implications of Christ's life becoming our life is that it redefines our identity. No longer are we defined by our past mistakes, failures, or even our achievements. Our identity is now rooted in Christ. 2 Corinthians 5:17 (TPT) declares, "Now, if anyone is enfolded into Christ, he has become an entirely new creation. All that is related to the old order has vanished. Behold, everything is fresh and new."

This new identity means that we are no longer defined by the labels that the world places on us—whether by our successes or our shortcomings. We are children of God, beloved and accepted because of what Christ has done, not because of anything we have done. Our identity is no longer shaped by our performance but by the finished work of Jesus.

Living in this new identity frees us from the pressures and anxieties of trying to earn God's approval or the approval of others. We are free to live confidently in the knowledge that we are accepted and loved by God because of Christ's life in us. This freedom allows us to live with purpose and boldness, knowing that our identity is secure in Him.

Conclusion: The Transforming Power of Christ's Life in Us

The reality of Christ's life becoming our life is at the heart of the Christian experience. It is a mystery and a miracle that changes everything about how we live.

Through our union with Christ, we have died to our old life of sin and have been raised to new life in Him. His life is now the source of our strength, our identity, and our purpose.

As we live in the power of Christ's resurrection, we are transformed from the inside out. The Christian life is not about trying harder to be good or moral; it is about allowing the life of Christ to flow through us, transforming us into His image. It is a life of abiding in Him, trusting in His presence, and living out the reality of our union with Him.

As we move forward, we will continue to explore the practical implications of this union with Christ, how it shapes our spirit, soul, and body, and how we are called to live in the fullness of His life.

Chapter 17

Spirit, Soul, and Body Design

One of the most profound revelations of the gospel is that humanity was created as a tripartite being—spirit, soul, and body—designed to live in harmony with God. This design reflects the complexity and beauty of God's creation, as well as the way in which God relates to us on different levels. However, the fall disrupted the balance between spirit, soul, and body, leading to spiritual death and confusion within humanity. Through Christ's redemptive work, the original design is restored, and believers are invited to live in alignment with their true identity as beings made in the image of God. In this chapter, we explore the biblical understanding of spirit, soul, and body, how each aspect of our being relates to God, and how the gospel restores the proper order within us.

The Biblical Understanding of Spirit, Soul, and Body

The Bible teaches that humans are created in three parts: spirit, soul, and body. Each of these aspects plays a distinct role in how we relate to God, ourselves, and the world around us. The Apostle Paul emphasizes this tripartite nature in 1 Thessalonians 5:23 (TPT): "Now, may the God of peace and harmony set you apart, making you completely holy. And may your entire being—spirit, soul, and body—be kept completely flawless in the appearing of our Lord Jesus, the Anointed One."

Spirit: The spirit is the part of us that is designed to connect with God. It is the deepest aspect of our being and reflects the image of God in a unique way. When Adam and Eve sinned, they experienced spiritual death—a separation from the life of God. However, through the work of Christ, our spirits are made alive again, and we are able to have a restored relationship with God. Ephesians 2:5 (TPT) reminds us, "Even when we were dead and doomed in our many sins, He united us into the very life of Christ and saved us by His wonderful grace!"

Soul: The soul encompasses our mind, will, and emotions. It is the seat of our personality and decision-making. Our soul is where we process thoughts, feel emotions, and make choices. While the spirit is the part of us that is in direct communion with God, the soul interprets and responds to the experiences of life. However, the fall disrupted the harmony between the soul and the spirit, causing our minds and emotions to be easily influenced by the flesh (our fallen, sinful nature). Romans 12:2 (TPT) encourages believers to "be inwardly transformed by the Holy Spirit through a total reformation of how you think."

Body: The body is our physical form and the means through which we interact with the physical world. While the body itself is not inherently sinful, it is subject to decay and death as a result of the fall. Through the resurrection of Jesus, believers are promised new, glorified bodies, free from the effects of sin and death. Romans 8:23 (TPT) speaks of the hope of redemption for our physical bodies: "And it's not just creation. We who have already experienced the firstfruits of the Spirit also inwardly groan as we passionately long to experience our full status as God's sons and daughters—including our physical bodies being transformed."

Visual 17.1 illustrates humanity as a tri-partite being, comprised of spirit, soul, and body, highlighting the distinct yet interconnected aspects of human existence.

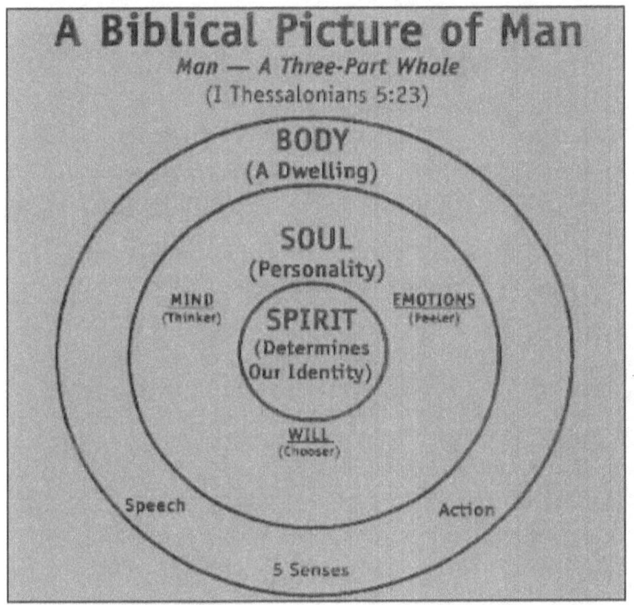

Visual 17.1: Illustrates man is a tri-partitie being with spirit, soul, and body.
(**Source:** image of Illustrates man is tri-partitie with spirit, soul, and body - Search Images)

Our design as spirit, soul, and body connects us deeply to God's nature, sharing in His divine essence. The Sidebar expands on this idea, explaining how we are born of the same 'species' as God through spiritual birth.

Sidebar: Born of the Same Species: Humanity and Divinity

Scripture reveals a profound truth about our identity: through spiritual birth, we are born of God—we are no longer just human beings, but sons and daughters of God. This rebirth places us in a unique relationship with God, not as distant creations but as His very children, sharing in His divine nature.

- John 3:6-7 – Jesus taught that "that which is born of the Spirit is spirit," emphasizing that we must be "born again" to enter God's kingdom. This spiritual birth marks our transformation from a purely earthly existence to a life sourced in God Himself, aligning us with our true identity as His children, born from above and empowered by the Spirit.

- 1 John 3:1-3 – The apostle John declares, "See what great love the Father has lavished on us, that we should be called children of God! And that is what we are." This passage confirms that our new identity is rooted in God's love and calls us to live with the expectation of becoming like Him in glory. This family likeness means that we are not merely saved or forgiven, but truly part of God's divine family, reflecting His nature.

- Revelation 21:7 – "Those who are victorious will inherit all this, and I will be their God and they will be my children." As sons and daughters of God, we inherit His promises, reflecting His nature and bearing His image. This spiritual lineage grants us access to His divine inheritance, not only in eternity but also as His representatives on earth.

In John 14 and 17, Jesus emphasizes this unbreakable family connection: "My Father is in Me, and I am in you, and you are in Me." Through Jesus, we enter a relationship with the Father as true sons and daughters, with a shared nature that allows us to express His love, wisdom, and power in the world.

As sons and daughters born from above, we carry a divine identity—we are not just humans but a new creation, imbued with God's Spirit. This reality enables us to walk in authority, to live with divine purpose, and to co-rule with Christ. As God's offspring, we are born to reflect His nature and participate in His mission, embodying the Kingdom and manifesting His love on earth.

The Disruption of the Fall: Spirit, Soul, and Body in Disharmony

Before the fall, humanity's spirit, soul, and body existed in perfect harmony. Adam and Eve lived in full communion with God, their spirits leading their souls and bodies in alignment with God's will. They experienced no separation between the spiritual and physical realms; both were fully integrated into their daily lives.

However, when Adam and Eve sinned, spiritual death entered the picture. The direct connection between their spirits and God was broken, and their souls—no longer guided by the spirit—became influenced by the desires of the flesh. This is the essence of the human condition after the fall: the soul and body, designed to follow the spirit's lead, now operate out of alignment with God. As a result, humanity became enslaved to sin, driven by the desires of the flesh (Galatians 5:17, TPT).

The disorder introduced by the fall is evident in the way people often live today. Many people live their lives dominated by their bodily appetites and emotional desires, rather than in submission to the spirit. The soul, meant to mediate between the spirit and body, becomes the battlefield where internal conflict arises. Paul describes this inner struggle in Romans 7:23 (TPT): "But I discern another power operating in my humanity, waging a war against the moral principles of my conscience and bringing me into captivity as a prisoner to the law of sin—this unwelcome intruder in my humanity."

This disconnection between spirit, soul, and body leads to confusion, brokenness, and alienation from God. The natural inclination of the fallen human condition is to prioritize the desires of the flesh over the leading of the spirit, which leads to destructive behaviors, selfish decisions, and a deep sense of dissatisfaction.

Restoring the Divine Order through Christ

The good news of the gospel is that Jesus came to restore the harmony between spirit, soul, and body that was lost in the fall. Through His death, resurrection, and ascension, Jesus has made it possible for us to be reconciled to God and to experience the fullness of life for which we were created. This includes the realignment of our spirit, soul, and body in the proper order.

Restoring the Spirit: Through faith in Christ, our spirits are made alive again, enabling us to have direct communion with God. Ephesians 2:4-5 (TPT) says, "But God still loved us with such great love. He is so rich in compassion and mercy. Even when we were dead and doomed in our many sins, He united us into the very life of Christ." Our spirits are no longer dead in sin but alive to God, allowing us to live in intimate relationship with Him.

Renewing the Soul: The process of sanctification—the gradual transformation of the believer into the image of Christ—primarily takes place in the soul. As we renew our minds through the Word of God, our thoughts, emotions, and will come into alignment with the spirit. Romans 12:2 (TPT) speaks to this transformation: "Stop imitating the ideals and opinions of the culture around you, but be inwardly transformed by the Holy Spirit through a total reformation of how you think." As we submit our soul to the leading of the spirit, we begin to experience healing, clarity, and freedom in our inner life.

Redeeming the Body: While our physical bodies still experience the effects of the fall—sickness, aging, and eventually death—there is a future hope of resurrection. Just as Jesus was raised with a glorified body, so too will believers be raised with glorified bodies that are free from decay and corruption. This is the ultimate redemption of the body, which will be fully realized in the new creation. Philippians 3:21 (TPT) promises that Christ "will transform our humble bodies and transfigure us into the identical likeness of His glorified body."

Visual 17.2 depicts the transformation of spirit, soul, and body through the redemptive work of Christ, illustrating the holistic renewal that believers experience in Him.

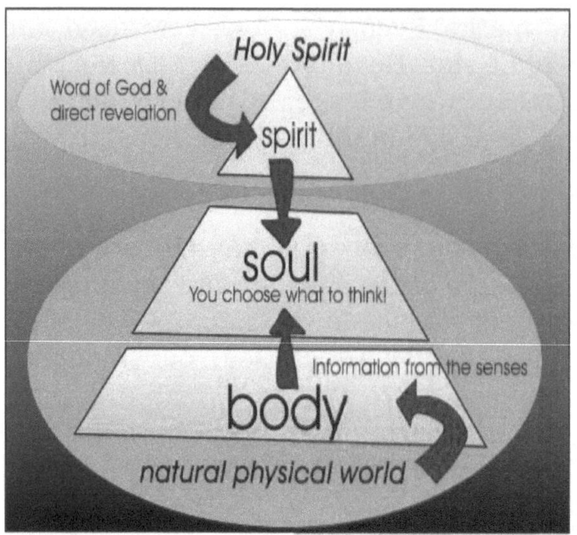

Visual 17.2: Transformation of spirit, soul, and body through Christ's redemptive work.
(**Source:** image of Depiction of the transformation of spirit, soul, and body through Christ's redemptive work. - Search Images)

Living in Alignment: Walking by the Spirit

As believers, we are called to live in alignment with our new identity in Christ, where the spirit leads the soul and the body follows. Paul encourages believers to "walk by the Spirit" and not to be driven by the desires of the flesh (Galatians 5:16, TPT). This means that we are to live from the inside out, allowing the Holy Spirit to direct our lives through our regenerated spirit.

Walking by the Spirit is not about denying the needs of the body or suppressing the emotions of the soul but about living in proper balance. When our spirit is in communion with God, it naturally leads our soul and body in ways that are life-giving and aligned with God's will. The desires of the flesh are put in their proper place, and the soul finds peace and wholeness as it submits to the Spirit's leading.

The more we align ourselves with the Spirit, the more we will experience the abundant life that Jesus promised (John 10:10, TPT). This is the life of freedom, peace, and joy that comes from living in harmony with God and within ourselves.

Conclusion: Embracing the Fullness of Our Design

The design of spirit, soul, and body reflects the beauty and complexity of God's creation. While the fall introduced disorder and separation, Christ's redemptive work restores the original harmony and invites us into a life of wholeness and alignment. As we walk by the Spirit, we experience the fullness of life that God intended, living as integrated beings in relationship with Him.

As we continue to explore the implications of this restored design, we will see how the Holy Spirit works in our lives to make Christ's life real in us, bringing about the transformation that leads to a life of victory and peace.

Chapter 18

The Holy Spirit: Making Christ Real

The role of the Holy Spirit in the life of a believer is both profound and essential. Without the Holy Spirit, the truths of the gospel would remain abstract and distant, but through Him, Christ becomes real and present in our lives. The Holy Spirit is not only the Spirit of God but also the Spirit of Christ, sent to dwell in us and to bring the reality of Christ's life, death, resurrection, and ascension into our daily experience. In this chapter, we will explore the transformative work of the Holy Spirit, how He makes Christ real in our lives, and how He empowers us to live in alignment with God's purpose.

The Promise of the Holy Spirit: God's Gift to Believers

Before His ascension, Jesus made a promise to His disciples that He would not leave them as orphans but would send the Holy Spirit to be with them and in them. This promise was fulfilled on the day of Pentecost when the Holy Spirit descended upon the disciples, empowering them to carry forward the mission of Christ. Acts 1:8 (TPT) records Jesus' words: "But I promise you this—the Holy Spirit will come upon you and you will be seized with power. You will be My messengers to Jerusalem, throughout Judea, the distant provinces—even to the remotest places on earth!"

The sending of the Holy Spirit is one of the greatest gifts of the gospel. Through the Holy Spirit, we are not only connected to Christ but also empowered to live the Christian life. The Spirit makes the presence of Christ a living reality in us. Jesus assured His disciples that it was for their benefit that He would go to the Father, because through His departure, the Spirit would come (John 16:7, TPT). The Holy Spirit continues the ministry of Jesus in the world by working in and through His followers.

The indwelling of the Holy Spirit is a defining characteristic of the new covenant. In the Old Testament, the Holy Spirit would come upon certain individuals for specific tasks, but under the new covenant, the Spirit permanently dwells within all who believe in Christ. This indwelling presence is the guarantee of our salvation and the ongoing work of transformation in our lives.

The Holy Spirit's Role in Making Christ Real

The Holy Spirit's primary role is to make Christ real in the life of the believer. He does this in several ways:

Revealing Christ: The Holy Spirit opens our spiritual eyes to see and know Christ more deeply. Without the Spirit, we cannot fully comprehend the truth of the gospel or the person of Jesus. 1 Corinthians 2:10 (TPT) explains, "But God now unveils these profound realities to us by the Spirit. Yes, He has revealed to us His inmost heart and deepest mysteries through the Holy Spirit, who constantly explores all things." The Spirit illuminates the Scriptures, enabling us to see Christ in every part of the Bible and to experience the truth of His promises personally.

Transforming Us into the Image of Christ: The Holy Spirit is the agent of sanctification, working within us to transform us into the image of Christ. 2 Corinthians 3:18 (TPT) says, "We can all draw close to Him with the veil removed from our faces. And with no veil we all become like mirrors who brightly reflect the glory of the Lord Jesus. We are being transfigured into His very image as we move from one brighter level of glory to another. And this glorious transfiguration comes from the Lord, who is the Spirit." Through the Spirit's work, we are being changed from the inside out, reflecting more and more of Christ's character in our daily lives.

Empowering Us to Live the Christian Life: The Holy Spirit not only reveals Christ to us but also empowers us to live in accordance with God's will. The Christian life is impossible to live in our own strength, but through the power of the Holy Spirit, we are enabled to walk in obedience and victory. Galatians 5:16 (TPT) urges us to "let the Holy Spirit guide your life. Then you won't be doing what your sinful nature craves." The Spirit produces the fruit of righteousness in us, helping us to overcome the desires of the flesh and live in freedom.

Making Christ's Presence Tangible: One of the most profound ways the Holy Spirit makes Christ real is by manifesting the presence of Jesus in our everyday lives. The Spirit brings the peace, joy, and love of Christ into our hearts, enabling us to experience God's presence in a personal and intimate way. Romans 5:5 (TPT) declares, "And this hope is not a disappointing fantasy, because we can now experience the endless love of God cascading into our hearts through the Holy Spirit who lives in us!" The Holy Spirit fills our hearts with the reality of God's love, making the presence of Christ tangible and transformative.

Visual 18.1 illustrates the Holy Spirit descending like a dove, symbolizing His presence and work within believers.

Visual 18.1: Image of the Holy Spirit descending like a dove, symbolizing His presence and work in believers.
(**Source:** image of Image of the Holy Spirit descending on man like a dove - Search Images)

Living in the Power of the Holy Spirit

Living by the power of the Holy Spirit is the key to experiencing the fullness of life in Christ. The Holy Spirit empowers us not only to understand the truth of the gospel but to live it out in practical ways. This power is not just for moments of spiritual highs but for everyday life—empowering us to love others, resist sin, and bear witness to Christ.

The Apostle Paul often contrasted living by the flesh (our fallen, sinful nature) with living by the Spirit. Galatians 5:25 (TPT) calls us to align ourselves with the Spirit: "If the Spirit is the source of our life, we must also allow the Spirit to direct every aspect of our lives." This means that we must actively choose to surrender to the leading of the Holy Spirit, allowing Him to guide our thoughts, actions, and decisions.

Walking in Step with the Spirit: To walk in the Spirit is to live in continual dependence on His power and guidance. It involves daily surrender to God's will and a sensitivity to the promptings of the Spirit. As we cultivate a life of prayer, worship, and time in God's Word, we become more attuned to the Spirit's leading. This leads to a life of peace and fruitfulness, as described in Galatians 5:22-23 (TPT): "But the fruit produced by the Holy Spirit within you is divine love in all its varied expressions: joy that overflows, peace that subdues, patience that endures, kindness in action, a life full of virtue, faith that prevails, gentleness of heart, and strength of spirit."

Overcoming the Flesh through the Spirit: One of the primary ways the Holy Spirit works in us is by empowering us to overcome the desires of the flesh. The flesh represents the fallen, sinful nature that still tries to exert influence over us, but the Spirit gives us the strength to resist these temptations. Romans 8:13 (TPT) encourages us, "For when you live controlled by the flesh, you are about to die. But if the life of the Spirit puts to death the corrupt ways of the flesh, we then taste His abundant life." The Spirit empowers us to live in victory over sin and to walk in the freedom that Christ has won for us.

Bearing Witness to Christ through the Spirit: The Holy Spirit empowers us not only for personal transformation but also for the mission of proclaiming the gospel. Jesus promised that His disciples would receive power when the Holy Spirit came upon them, enabling them to be His witnesses to the ends of the earth (Acts 1:8, TPT). This same power is available to every believer today. The Spirit equips us with boldness, wisdom, and spiritual gifts to share the good news of Jesus with others and to live as ambassadors of His kingdom.

Visual 18.2 shows believers being filled with the Holy Spirit, symbolizing empowerment, guidance, and the transformative presence of God within them.

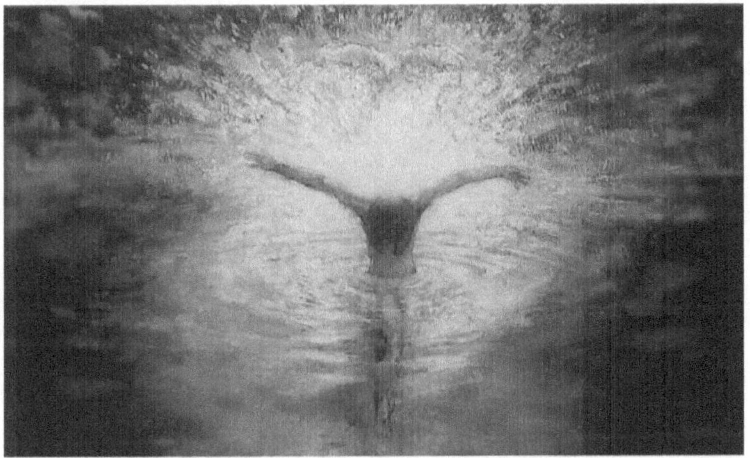

Visual 18.2: Believers being filled with the Holy Spirit (**Source:** image of Believers being filled with the Holy Spirit - Search Images)

The Holy Spirit initiates a transformative journey in us, often represented by baptisms in water, Spirit, and fire. The Sidebar explores these stages, highlighting how each baptism shapes our spiritual life.

Sidebar: Baptisms: Water, Spirit, and Fire

In the believer's journey, three baptisms—water, Spirit, and fire—represent a progression into deeper intimacy and transformation in God's presence. These baptisms parallel not only Israel's journey but also reflect the 30, 60, and 100-fold harvest described in the parable of the sower, illustrating the heart's openness to God's goodness and our response to His calling.

Water Baptism – Water baptism symbolizes repentance, turning away from the old self, and stepping into new life with Christ. This baptism marks the 30-fold harvest, representing the heart condition that trusts God with forgiveness and eternal life. Here, we believe God has settled our sin, but the relationship may still feel limited—where we look to God primarily for deliverance from sin and assurance of salvation. The heart at this stage knows God as loving but may yet be growing in the fullness of His goodness.

Spirit Baptism – Baptism of the Holy Spirit signifies empowerment and the beginning of a life led by the Spirit. Just as the Holy Spirit empowered the early Church at Pentecost, so this baptism invites believers into a 60-fold harvest—where God's goodness is recognized not just in salvation, but in His willingness to heal, deliver, and answer prayer. The heart is more open to God's active presence, calling upon Him for miracles, healing, and guidance. While we may still approach Him as a supplier of blessings, this stage reflects a growing trust in His power and faithfulness.

Fire Baptism – The baptism by fire brings purification and transformation, preparing believers to carry God's authority and to align fully with His will. Representing the 100-fold harvest, this level of maturity is reached when the heart truly grasps the fullness of God's goodness—seeing Him not just as a distant provider but as the source of life, purpose, and identity. God is understood not merely as someone who blesses from afar, but as One who shares His very life with us, living and working within us. Here, believers know God as a super-abundant, all-sufficient Father who invites them to partner with Him, restoring His creation and manifesting His kingdom on earth.

This journey of 30, 60, and 100-fold response reflects the heart's condition, deepening as it comes to understand God's nature and intentions. We move from seeing God as "okay," to "good," to "super good"—a Father who not only blesses but brings us into union with His divine life. Each baptism and harvest represent a deeper intimacy with God, leading believers to embody the fullness of their identity as His sons and daughters on earth.

The Spirit of Adoption: Our Identity as Children of God

Another powerful aspect of the Holy Spirit's work is that He confirms our identity as children of God. The Spirit not only makes Christ real to us but also assures us of our relationship with the Father. Romans 8:15-16 (TPT) says, "And you did not receive the 'spirit of religious duty,' leading you back into the fear of never being good enough. But you have received the 'Spirit of full acceptance,' enfolding you into the family of God. And you will never feel orphaned, for as He rises up within us, our spirits join Him in saying the words of tender affection, 'Beloved Father!' For the Holy Spirit makes God's fatherhood real to us as He whispers into our innermost being, 'You are God's beloved child!'"

This work of the Holy Spirit is foundational to our sense of belonging and security in God. Through the Spirit, we are able to call God "Abba, Father," and to experience the love and acceptance of being His children. The Spirit's presence in our lives is the guarantee that we are heirs with Christ and that we will share in His glory.

Conclusion: The Holy Spirit's Ongoing Work in Us

The Holy Spirit is the one who makes Christ real in our lives. Through His presence, we experience the reality of Christ's love, power, and grace. He transforms us into the image of Christ, empowers us to live in victory, and equips us to carry out the mission of the gospel.

As we walk in step with the Spirit, we experience the fullness of life that God intends for us. The Spirit is not just a distant force or an occasional influence; He is our constant companion, guiding us, empowering us, and making Christ's life a living reality within us. The more we yield to His leading, the more we will reflect the character of Christ and fulfil God's purpose for our lives.

As we continue this journey, we will explore what it means to live from our perfect union with Christ and how the grace of God empowers us to live in His fullness.

Chapter 19

Living from Perfect Union

The central truth of the Christian life is that, through Christ, we are brought into perfect union with God. This union is not a distant or abstract concept but a living reality that transforms every aspect of our existence. When we come to faith in Christ, we are united with Him in a deep and intimate way, and this union forms the foundation for how we live, think, and relate to God. Living from this perfect union means recognizing and embracing the fullness of what Christ has accomplished for us and allowing His life to flow through us daily. In this chapter, we explore the meaning of living from our union with Christ, the profound implications it has for our spiritual lives, and how it empowers us to walk in the freedom and grace of God.

The Nature of Our Union with Christ

At the heart of the gospel is the mystery that believers are "in Christ." This phrase, repeated throughout the New Testament, signifies the profound reality that our lives are now bound up with Christ's life. In Galatians 2:20 (TPT), Paul captures this truth: "My old identity has been co-crucified with Messiah and no longer lives, for the nails of His cross crucified me with Him. And now the essence of this new life is no longer mine, for the Anointed One lives His life through me—we live in union as one!"

Our union with Christ means that we share in everything He accomplished through His life, death, resurrection, and ascension. This is not just a symbolic or metaphorical connection but a real, spiritual union in which Christ's life becomes our life. In Romans 6:5 (TPT), Paul writes, "For since we are permanently grafted into Him to experience a death like His, then we are permanently grafted into Him to experience a resurrection like His and the new life that it imparts."

This union is both a mystery and a miracle. While we continue to live in our physical bodies, our true life is hidden with Christ in God (Colossians 3:3, TPT). We are no longer separated from God by sin or death; we are now intimately connected to Him, sharing in His victory over the powers of darkness and in the new creation that has begun in Christ.

Visual 19.1 illustrates the vine and its branches, symbolizing the believer's connection to Christ as described in John 15:5, with the life of Christ flowing through the believer.

Visual 19.1: Vine and its branches, symbolizing the believer's connection to Christ, showing the life of Christ flowing through the believer.
(**Source:** image of Vine and its branches, symbolizing the believer's connection to Christ - Search Images)

Living from Union: Abiding in Christ

One of the most profound images of our union with Christ is found in Jesus' teaching about the vine and the branches. In John 15:5 (TPT), Jesus says, "I am the sprouting vine and you're My branches. As you live in union with Me as your source, fruitfulness will stream from within you—but when you live separated from Me you are powerless."

This picture of the vine and branches reveals the essence of living from union with Christ: abiding. To abide means to remain, to dwell, to stay connected. Just as a branch draws its life from the vine, so we draw our life from Christ. The Christian life is not about striving or performing for God's approval; it is about resting in our union with Christ and allowing His life to flow through us.

Abiding in Christ involves living in a posture of dependence, trust, and surrender. It means recognizing that apart from Him, we can do nothing of eternal significance. But as we abide in Him, His life flows through us, producing the fruit of the Spirit—love, joy, peace, patience, kindness, goodness, faithfulness, gentleness, and self-control (Galatians 5:22-23, TPT). This fruit is not something we can manufacture on our own; it is the natural result of Christ's life within us.

Living in perfect union with God reveals that separation from Him is an illusion. The Sidebar explains the depth of our oneness with God, showing that we are fully embraced in His presence.

Sidebar: No Separation - The Union of God and Humanity

The idea of separation between God and humanity is a misunderstanding. While sin has caused alienation in humanity's mind (Colossians 1:21, Isaiah 59:2), God has never turned away from us. From the very beginning, when Adam sinned, it was God who sought him out, demonstrating His desire to remain close. This separation exists only in our perception, not in reality.

In John 14 and 17, Jesus describes a profound union, saying, "I am in the Father, and you are in Me, and I am in you." This divine relationship is not one of distance, but of oneness and inclusion. Acts 17:28 affirms this, declaring that "in Him we live, move, and have our being." God is not a distant deity, but One who is fully present within us, sustaining and filling all things.

The apostle Paul expresses this reality in Galatians 1:16, when he says that God "revealed His Son in me," emphasizing the inner presence of Christ. As believers, we are the temple of God; His Spirit dwells in us continually. God is not in some far-off place, waiting for us to reach Him. He is closer than we can imagine, residing in our hearts, fully engaged with our lives here and now.

This intimate union means that God is not a distant future hope, but a present reality. Any belief that God is "not here, not now, not me" is a misconception. God's nearness, as both Creator and Redeemer, assures us that He is always with us, dwelling in us as a source of love, strength, and purpose. The truth of our union with Him means we are never separated, but fully embraced in His presence.

The Freedom of Living from Union

One of the most liberating aspects of living from our union with Christ is the freedom it brings. Many Christians struggle with feelings of inadequacy, guilt, or the pressure to perform in order to earn God's favor. But when we understand that we are already fully united with Christ, we are set free from these burdens.

Because of our union with Christ, we are fully accepted by God. We are no longer defined by our past mistakes or by our performance; we are defined by Christ's righteousness. 2 Corinthians 5:21 (TPT) tells us, "For God made the only one who did not know sin to become sin for us, so that we who did not know righteousness might become the righteousness of God through our union with Him." This means that when God looks at us, He sees us clothed in the perfect righteousness of Christ. We are completely forgiven, completely loved, and completely accepted—not because of anything we have done, but because of what Christ has done.

Living from union also means living in the freedom from striving. The Christian life is not about trying harder to be holy or righteous; it is about surrendering to the life of Christ within us. In Matthew 11:28-30 (TPT), Jesus invites us to rest in Him: "Are you weary, carrying a heavy burden? Then come to Me. I will refresh your life, for I am your oasis. Simply join your life with Mine. Learn My ways and you'll discover that I'm gentle, humble, easy to please. You will find refreshment and rest in Me. For all that I require of you will be pleasant and easy to bear."

This invitation to rest in Christ is central to living from our union with Him. We are not called to strive, but to abide. We are not called to perform, but to rest. We are not called to do things for God in our own strength, but to allow Him to live His life through us.

Visual 19.2 depicts a believer at peace, resting in the presence of Christ, symbolizing the rest and freedom that come from abiding in Him.

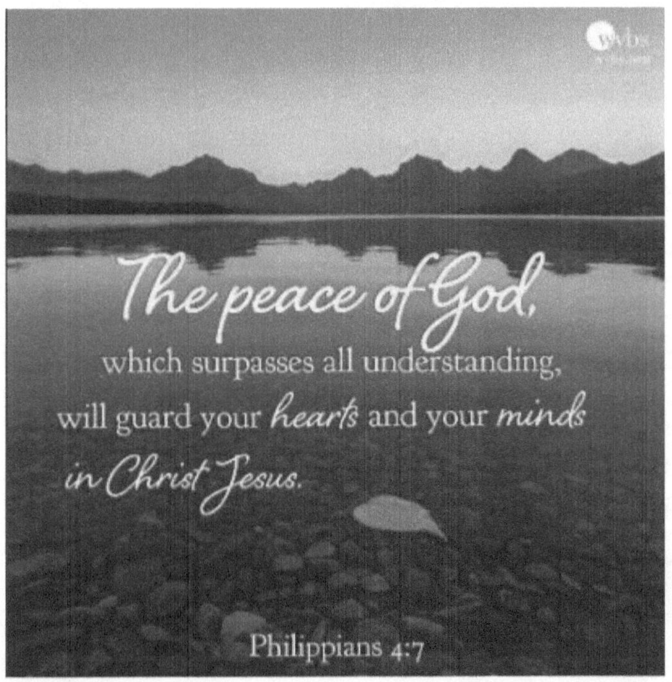

Visual 19.2: Believer at peace, resting in the presence of Christ.
(**Source:** <u>image of Believer at peace, resting in the presence of Christ - Search Images</u>)

The Power of Living from Union

While living from union brings freedom, it also brings power. The same power that raised Jesus from the dead is now at work in us because of our union with Him. Ephesians 1:19-20 (TPT) speaks of "the unlimited magnitude of His power made available to you through faith. Then your lives will be an advertisement of this immense power as it works through you! This is the mighty power that was released when God raised Christ from the dead and exalted Him to the place of highest honor and supreme authority in the heavenly realm!"

This power is not just for miraculous signs and wonders, though it includes those things. It is the power to live a life of victory over sin, the power to love others sacrificially, the power to endure suffering with joy, and the power to walk in the fullness of the Spirit. Living from our union with Christ means that we are no longer trying to live the Christian life in our own strength. Instead, we are relying on the supernatural power of Christ within us.

Paul understood this reality when he wrote in Philippians 4:13 (TPT), "I find that the strength of Christ's explosive power infuses me to conquer every difficulty." This is the essence of living from union: it is Christ's strength, not ours, that enables us to live the life God has called us to live.

Living in Grace: The Flow of Divine Empowerment

Living from union with Christ also means living in the flow of grace. Grace is not just God's unmerited favor; it is His divine empowerment at work in our lives. In 2 Corinthians 12:9 (TPT), Paul shares Jesus' words: "My grace is always more than enough for you, and My power finds its full expression through your weakness." This grace empowers us to live beyond our human limitations and to walk in the fullness of the life Christ has given us.

Grace is not an excuse for passivity or laziness; it is the fuel that enables us to fulfill God's purposes in our lives. As we live from our union with Christ, we experience the flow of His grace in every area of our lives. This grace strengthens us, equips us, and enables us to walk in the works that God has prepared for us to do (Ephesians 2:10, TPT).

Visual 19.3 illustrates a waterfall flowing into a river, symbolizing the flow of grace from Christ into the believer's life.

Visual 19.3: A waterfall flowing into a river, symbolizing the flow of grace from Christ into the life of the believer.
(**Source:** image of A waterfall flowing into a river, symbolizing the flow of grace from Christ into the life of the believer. - Search Images)

The Joy of Living in Union with Christ

Finally, living from union with Christ brings deep and lasting joy. Jesus promised His disciples that as they abide in Him, they would experience His joy: "I have told you these things so that My joy may be in you and your joy may be full" (John 15:11, TPT). This joy is not dependent on circumstances but is rooted in the unshakable reality of our union with Christ.

When we live from our union with Christ, we experience the joy of His presence, the joy of His love, and the joy of being fully known and fully loved by God. This joy sustains us through trials and difficulties, giving us strength and hope even in the darkest moments.

Conclusion: The Life of Union with Christ

Living from perfect union with Christ is the foundation of the Christian life. It is the reality that we are no longer separated from God but are intimately connected to Him through Christ. As we abide in Him, we experience His life flowing through us, bringing freedom, power, grace, and joy.

This union is not something we earn or achieve; it is a gift of grace, given to us through the finished work of Christ. Our role is to rest in this union, to live from it, and to allow Christ's life to flow through us in every aspect of our lives. As we do, we will experience the fullness of the abundant life that Jesus promised and walk in the power and freedom that come from being one with Him.

Chapter 20

Grace: Divine Empowerment

Grace is one of the most powerful and transformative concepts in the Christian faith. It is much more than the forgiveness of sins; it is the very power and presence of God working in and through us. Grace is the fuel of the Christian life—it is what enables us to live in the fullness of God's purpose, to overcome sin, to walk in victory, and to grow in our relationship with God. In this chapter, we explore the nature of grace, its role in our lives, and how it serves as divine empowerment for living the life God calls us to live.

The Nature of Grace: God's Gift to Humanity

At its core, grace is God's unmerited favor toward humanity. It is the expression of His love, kindness, and generosity, freely given to us even though we do not deserve it. Ephesians 2:8 (TPT) captures the essence of grace: "For by grace you have been saved by faith. Nothing you did could ever earn this salvation, for it was the love-gift from God that brought us to Christ!"

Grace is the reason we are saved—it is entirely God's initiative, not something we earn through our own efforts. But grace is not just limited to salvation; it encompasses every aspect of the Christian life. It is the ongoing source of our strength and the key to our growth in Christ. Grace transforms us from the inside out, enabling us to live lives that reflect the character of Jesus.

Grace is also deeply relational. It is not a transactional or mechanical gift but the expression of God's personal love and commitment to His people. In Jesus Christ, we see the ultimate demonstration of God's grace, as He gave His life for us, not because we were worthy, but because He loved us. Grace, then, is inseparable from the person of Jesus—it is through our relationship with Him that we receive and experience grace in its fullness.

Visual 20.1 illustrates open hands receiving light from above, symbolizing the gift of grace freely given by God and received with an open heart.

Visual 20.1: Open hands receiving light from above, symbolizing the gift of grace being freely given by God. (**Source:** image of Open hands receiving light from above, symbolizing the gift of grace - Search Images)

Grace as Divine Empowerment

While grace is often understood as God's forgiveness of sins, it is also His divine empowerment working within us. Grace is not only what saves us but also what sustains and strengthens us. In 2 Corinthians 12:9 (TPT), Jesus says to Paul, "My grace is always more than enough for you, and My power finds its full expression through your weakness." This verse highlights the truth that grace is not just about removing sin but about empowering us to live beyond our human limitations.

Grace enables us to overcome the challenges and weaknesses of our flesh. It is the strength that comes from God to do what we could never do in our own strength. The Christian life is not about trying harder to live according to God's commands; it is about relying on His grace to enable us to live in alignment with His will. Philippians 2:13 (TPT) explains, "God will continually revitalize you, implanting within you the passion to do what pleases Him."

This divine empowerment extends to every area of our lives. Grace is what helps us resist temptation, grow in holiness, and walk in the fruits of the Spirit. It is the fuel that powers our spiritual growth and allows us to serve God and others with joy and effectiveness. Grace is the antidote to both legalism (relying on our own efforts) and passivity (failing to engage in the Christian life). It calls us to active participation in God's work, but it does so by providing the strength and resources we need to fulfill His purposes.

Grace invites us into the fullness of Christ's completed work, empowering us to live out what He has already achieved. The Sidebar delves into this concept, showing how we enter into His fullness through grace.

about living out the reality of the gift we have received.

Grace and Transformation: Growing in Christlikeness

One of the most powerful ways grace works in our lives is through the process of transformation. The moment we place our faith in Christ, we are justified—made right with God through the grace of Jesus' sacrifice. But grace doesn't stop at justification; it continues to work in us, transforming us into the image of Christ. This process is often referred to as sanctification, and it is fueled by God's grace.

Titus 2:11-12 (TPT) explains, "God's marvelous grace has manifested in person, bringing salvation for everyone. This same grace teaches us how to live each day as we turn our backs on ungodliness and indulgent lifestyles, and it equips us to live self-controlled, upright, godly lives in this present age." Grace not only forgives us; it teaches us, shapes us, and empowers us to live in a way that honors God.

This transformation is an ongoing work of the Holy Spirit, who applies the grace of God to every part of our lives. As we yield to the Spirit's work, grace begins to reshape our character, desires, and actions. We begin to grow in love, patience, kindness, and humility, reflecting the character of Jesus more and more. This transformation is not something we achieve through sheer willpower; it is the result of God's grace continually working in us.

Grace also enables us to move forward despite our failures. When we fall short, God's grace picks us up, forgives us, and empowers us to keep going. Romans 5:20 (TPT) reminds us that "wherever sin increased, there was more than enough of God's grace to triumph all the more!" Grace is never exhausted, and no matter how many times we stumble, God's grace is always there to restore and renew us.

Visual 20.2 depicts a heart being transformed by rays of light, symbolizing the sanctifying work of grace in the life of a believer.

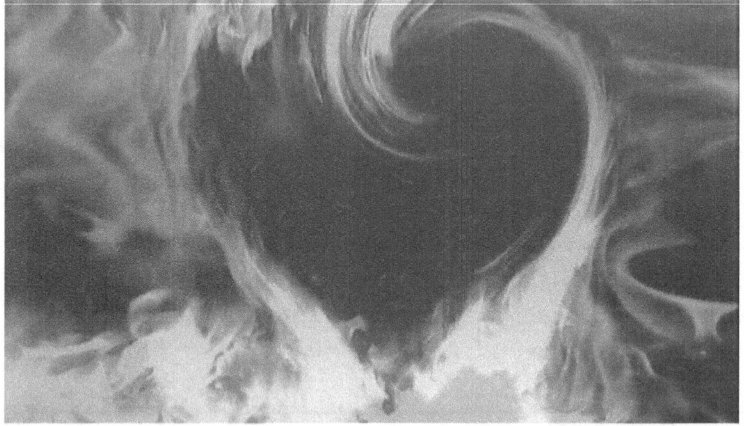

Visual 20.2: A heart being transformed by rays of light, symbolizing the sanctifying work of grace in a believer's life. (**Source:** image of A heart being transformed by rays of light, symbolizing the sanctifying work of grace in a believer's life. - Search Images

Grace and Freedom: Breaking the Power of Sin

One of the most transformative aspects of grace is the freedom it brings from the power of sin. Before we come to faith in Christ, we are enslaved to sin, unable to break free from its grip. But when we experience the grace of God, we are set free—not only from the penalty of sin but also from its dominion over our lives.

Romans 6:14 (TPT) declares, "Remember this: sin will not conquer you, for God already has! You are not governed by law but governed by the reign of the grace of God." Grace is not an excuse to continue in sin; it is the power that enables us to overcome sin. When we live under grace, we are no longer bound by the law's demands or by the guilt and shame of our failures. Instead, we live in the freedom that comes from knowing we are fully accepted and empowered by God.

This freedom does not mean that we will never struggle with sin again, but it does mean that sin no longer has the final word in our lives. Grace empowers us to resist temptation and to walk in victory over the sinful desires that once controlled us. It is by grace that we can say no to ungodliness and yes to living a life that reflects the holiness of God.

Grace and Community: Living in Grace with Others

Just as grace transforms our relationship with God, it also transforms our relationships with others. Grace teaches us to live in humility, recognizing that we are all recipients of God's unmerited favor. This humility enables us to extend grace to others, forgiving as we have been forgiven, and showing mercy as we have received mercy.

Colossians 3:13 (TPT) encourages us, "Tolerate the weaknesses of those in the family of faith, forgiving one another in the same way you have been graciously forgiven by Jesus Christ. If you find fault with someone, release this same gift of forgiveness to them." When we understand the magnitude of the grace we have received from God, we are empowered to offer that same grace to others. This grace-filled living fosters unity, love, and peace within the body of Christ.

Grace also teaches us to serve others with the gifts and abilities God has given us. 1 Peter 4:10 (TPT) says, "Every believer has received grace gifts, so use them to serve one another as faithful stewards of the many-colored tapestry of God's grace." Whether we are called to teach, encourage, lead, or help, our service to others flows from the grace that God has poured into our lives.

Visual 20.3 illustrates believers serving one another, reflecting the grace they have received and are now sharing with others.

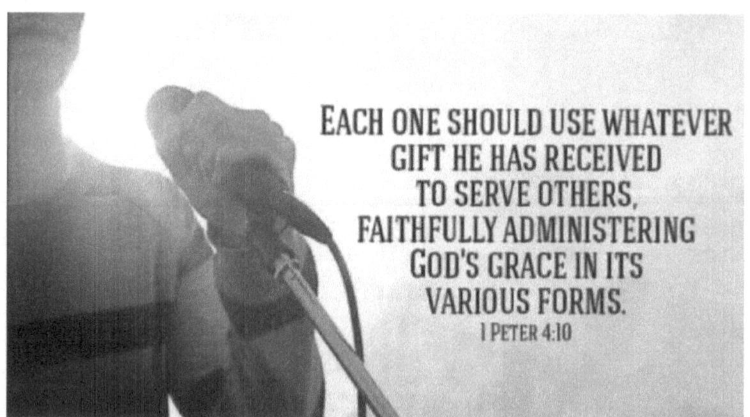

Visual 20.3: Believers serving one another, reflecting the grace they have received and shared with others.
(**Source:** image of ABelievers serving one another, reflecting the grace they have received and shared with others. - Search Images)

Conclusion: Living in the Flow of Grace

Grace is not a one-time event; it is an ongoing reality in the life of every believer. It is the divine empowerment that enables us to live in alignment with God's will, to grow in holiness, to overcome sin, and to serve others. As we embrace the fullness of God's grace, we experience a life of freedom, joy, and transformation.

Living in grace means that we are no longer striving to earn God's favor or approval; we are resting in the finished work of Christ and allowing His grace to shape every part of our lives. Grace empowers us to walk in victory, to love others, and to fulfill God's purpose for our lives. It is the foundation of our salvation, the fuel of our spiritual growth, and the power behind our daily walk with God.

As we move forward, we will explore the ways in which grace leads us to reveal our true identity as sons and daughters of God and how it equips us to live in the fullness of the inheritance that is ours in Christ.

PART 5

Sons Revealed

Chapter 21

The Journey to Mature Sonship

The Christian life is not only about salvation; it is about growing into maturity as sons and daughters of God. While we are adopted into God's family the moment we place our faith in Christ, we are called to a lifelong journey of transformation, learning to live out our identity as God's children in fullness and maturity. This journey, often referred to as "sonship," is about becoming who we were always meant to be—reflecting the image of God, walking in His authority, and fulfilling His purposes. In this chapter, we explore the process of maturing as sons and daughters of God, the challenges and opportunities we encounter along the way, and how the Holy Spirit leads us into the fullness of sonship.

The Foundation of Sonship: Our Identity in Christ

The journey to mature sonship begins with understanding our identity in Christ. When we come to faith, we are no longer orphans or slaves; we are adopted as children of God. Galatians 4:6-7 (TPT) declares, "And so that we would know for sure that we are His true children, God released the Spirit of Sonship into our hearts—moving us to cry out intimately, 'My Father, my true Father!' Now we're no longer living like slaves under the law, but we enjoy being God's very own sons and daughters! And because we're His, we can access everything our Father has—for we are heirs of God through Jesus, the Messiah!"

This passage reveals the profound truth that our identity is no longer based on our past, our performance, or our position in the world. We are children of God, loved unconditionally and given a place in His family. This identity is foundational to our growth in sonship. Understanding that we are sons and daughters—not slaves or servants—frees us to live in the security of God's love and the confidence of His grace.

However, while our position as God's children is secure, the process of growing into mature sons and daughters is ongoing. Just as a child grows and matures over time, so we, as children of God, are invited to grow into the fullness of our identity. This journey of sonship involves learning to live in the reality of God's love, authority, and purpose.

Visual 21.1 depicts a parent and child walking hand in hand, symbolizing the journey of growth and maturity in the path of sonship.

Visual 21.1: A parent and child walking hand in hand, symbolizing the journey of growth and maturity in sonship.

The Process of Maturing: From Spiritual Infancy to Fullness

The New Testament often speaks of believers progressing from spiritual infancy to maturity. In 1 Corinthians 3:1-2 (TPT), Paul addresses the church, saying, "Brothers and sisters, when I was with you, I found it impossible to speak to you as those who are spiritually mature people, for you are still dominated by the mindset of the flesh. And because you are immature infants in Christ, I had to nurse you and feed you with 'milk,' not with the solid food of more advanced teachings, because you weren't ready for it."

Spiritual infancy is characterized by a lack of understanding and experience in the ways of God. While we are fully children of God from the moment we believe, we may still be influenced by our old ways of thinking, reacting to situations in fear, insecurity, or self-reliance. Maturing in sonship means that we move beyond spiritual infancy and begin to embrace the deeper truths of God's Word and Spirit.

As we grow in our relationship with God, we move from being driven by our flesh—our old nature—and instead, we learn to be led by the Holy Spirit. Romans 8:14 (TPT) emphasizes, "The mature children of God are those who are moved by the impulses of the Holy Spirit." Maturity is marked by a life that is led by the Spirit, not by our emotions, desires, or external circumstances.

One of the key markers of maturing sonship is learning to trust in God's fatherhood. Just as a child must learn to trust their parents, we, too, must learn to trust our heavenly Father's love, wisdom, and provision. This trust grows as we experience God's faithfulness in our lives, as we face trials and difficulties that deepen our dependence on Him.

As we grow into mature sons and daughters, we look to Jesus, the Firstborn, as our example. The Sidebar explores how Jesus' life provides a pattern for growth and maturity in God's family.

Sidebar: Jesus, the Firstborn - Our Pattern for Growth and Maturity

Jesus, as the firstborn Son of God, is the pattern for our journey of spiritual growth and maturity. Though He was fully divine, He grew and matured in His humanity, learning obedience and aligning Himself with the heart of the Father (Hebrews 5:8). Jesus received the Holy Spirit at His baptism, fulfilling all righteousness on behalf of humanity. At that moment, the Father's affirmation, "This is my beloved Son, in whom I am well pleased" (Matthew 3:17), was a declaration for all believers who would follow after Him.

The same Spirit that was in Jesus now dwells in us, empowering us to walk in alignment with God's heart and purpose. Jesus' life exemplified perfect obedience, saying and doing only what He heard and saw the Father doing (John 5:19). This alignment is not restrictive but liberating, allowing us to operate in God's power and will with divine purpose. Just as

Jesus performed signs and wonders in tune with God's will, so too are we called to mature in our relationship with God, becoming expressions of His love, wisdom, and authority.

In Ephesians 4, Paul speaks of "one Lord, one faith, one baptism, one God and Father of all, who is over all and through all and in all." Through the Spirit, we are united in this oneness, sharing in the life and power of Christ. As we grow in Christ, we are patterned after Jesus, the firstborn, who leads us into maturity as sons and daughters, equipped to bring God's presence into the world.

Challenges in the Journey: Overcoming Orphan Thinking

One of the greatest obstacles to maturing in sonship is what some have called "orphan thinking." Even though we are adopted as sons and daughters of God, many of us continue to live as though we are spiritual orphans, feeling insecure, unworthy, or abandoned. This orphan mentality leads to striving, performance, fear, and self-reliance—attitudes that are rooted in the false belief that we must earn God's love or prove our worth.

Orphan thinking manifests in several ways:

Fear and Insecurity: Orphans live in fear of rejection and abandonment, always wondering if they are truly loved or accepted. This fear drives them to seek approval from others or to live in constant anxiety about their relationship with God.

Striving and Performance: Spiritual orphans feel the need to prove themselves. They are constantly working to earn God's favor or to impress others, driven by the belief that they are not enough as they are.

Self-reliance: Rather than trusting in God's provision and guidance, orphans rely on their own strength and wisdom. They have a difficult time surrendering control to God because they fear that He will not come through for them.

The journey to mature sonship involves confronting and overcoming these patterns of thinking. The Holy Spirit works within us to heal the wounds of our past, to replace lies with truth, and to lead us into the freedom of living as God's beloved children. Romans 8:15 (TPT) reminds us, "You did not receive the 'spirit of religious duty,' leading you back into the fear of never being good enough. But you have received the 'Spirit of full acceptance,' enfolding you into the family of God. And you will never feel orphaned."

The more we embrace our identity as sons and daughters, the more we are freed from the bondage of orphan thinking. We begin to live in the security of God's love, trusting that He is a good Father who provides, protects, and leads us. This security allows us to rest in His grace, knowing that we do not need to earn His love—it is freely given.

Visual 21.2 illustrates a heart transforming from chains, symbolizing orphan thinking, to wings, representing the freedom of sonship.

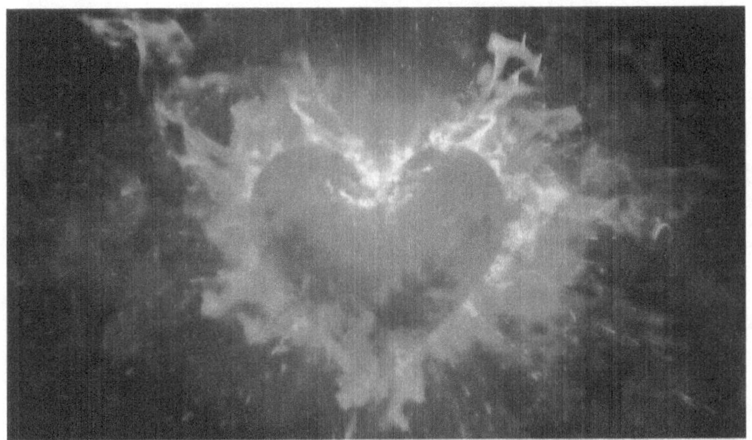

Visual 21.2: A heart being transformed from chains (representing orphan thinking) to wings (representing the freedom of sonship).
(**Source:** image of A heart being transformed from chains (representing orphan thinking) to wings (representing the freedom of sonship). - Search Images)

The Role of the Holy Spirit in Sonship

The Holy Spirit plays a crucial role in our journey to mature sonship. He is the one who continually testifies to our hearts that we are children of God, bringing us into deeper understanding and experience of our identity in Christ. Romans 8:16 (TPT) says, "For the Holy Spirit makes God's fatherhood real to us as He whispers into our innermost being, 'You are God's beloved child!'"

The Spirit leads us into the deeper truths of our inheritance as sons and daughters. As we yield to His guidance, we begin to walk in the authority, power, and purpose that come from our identity in Christ. The Spirit teaches us to live in alignment with God's will, to embrace the character of Christ, and to operate in the gifts and callings God has placed in our lives.

Moreover, the Holy Spirit empowers us to live out our sonship in practical ways. As we grow in maturity, we are called to take on greater responsibility in God's kingdom—whether in leadership, service, or in fulfilling specific callings. Just as earthly parents entrust greater responsibility to their children as they grow, so God entrusts more to us as we mature in faith. The Spirit equips us with the power and wisdom to walk in these responsibilities.

Living in Fullness: Sons and Daughters Walking in Authority

Maturing in sonship also means stepping into the authority that comes with being a child of God. Jesus, as the perfect Son of God, walked in divine authority throughout His ministry, healing the sick, casting out demons, and proclaiming the kingdom of God. As we grow in maturity, we are called to walk in that same authority, representing God's kingdom on earth.

In Luke 10:19 (TPT), Jesus tells His disciples, "Now you understand that I have imparted to you all My authority to trample over his kingdom. You will trample upon every demon before you and overcome every power Satan possesses. Absolutely nothing will harm you as you walk in this authority." This authority is not something we earn; it is part of our inheritance as sons and daughters. However, walking in this authority requires maturity and a deep understanding of our identity in Christ.

As we grow in sonship, we are called to live as ambassadors of God's kingdom, exercising the authority

He has given us to bring healing, deliverance, and hope to the world. We are not powerless in the face of darkness; we are children of the King, empowered by His Spirit to advance His kingdom.

Visual 21.3 depicts a crown being placed on a believer's head, symbolizing the authority and responsibility that come with sonship.

Visual 21.3: A crown being placed on a believer's head, symbolizing the authority and responsibility of sonship.
(**Source:** image of A crown being placed on a believer's head, symbolizing the authority and responsibility of sonship. - Search Images)

Conclusion: The Ongoing Journey of Sonship

The journey to mature sonship is a lifelong process of growth, transformation, and discovery. As we walk with God, we are continually invited to go deeper in our understanding of His love, to trust more fully in His provision, and to step more boldly into the authority He has given us. This journey is not without its challenges, but it is one filled with the promise of intimacy with God and the joy of living in the fullness of our identity as His children.

As we continue to explore the themes of sonship, we will see how this identity leads us to function as priests and kings in God's kingdom, exercising divine authority and fulfilling His purposes on earth.

Chapter 22

Sons, Priests, and Kings

As believers, our identity in Christ goes beyond being sons and daughters of God—we are also called to function as priests and kings in His kingdom. These roles are not merely symbolic titles but carry profound spiritual authority and responsibility. The priesthood speaks to our role in worship, intercession, and spiritual service, while the kingship speaks to our authority to rule and reign with Christ. Understanding our dual identity as priests and kings is essential for living in the fullness of our calling as God's people. In this chapter, we explore what it means to function as sons, priests, and kings in the kingdom of God, and how these roles are interwoven in our lives as believers.

The Priesthood of All Believers: Serving in Worship and Intercession

The concept of priesthood is central to the Christian faith. In the Old Testament, priests were the mediators between God and His people, offering sacrifices and prayers on behalf of the nation. They were set apart for the sacred task of ministering to God and leading the people in worship. However, in the New Testament, the priesthood is no longer restricted to a select few. Through Christ, all believers are called to be priests, serving God in worship and intercession.

1 Peter 2:9 (TPT) declares, "But you are God's chosen treasure—priests who are kings, a spiritual 'nation' set apart as God's devoted ones. He called you out of darkness to experience His marvelous light, and now He claims you as His very own. He did this so that you would broadcast His glorious wonders throughout the world." This passage emphasizes the priesthood of all believers. We are no longer dependent on earthly priests to mediate between us and God; we now have direct access to the Father through Jesus Christ, our High Priest (Hebrews 4:14-16, TPT).

As priests, we are called to offer spiritual sacrifices to God. These sacrifices include our worship, our prayers, and our lives lived in devotion to Him. Romans 12:1 (TPT) encourages us to "present your bodies as a living sacrifice, holy and acceptable to God, which is your spiritual worship." This means that every aspect of our lives—our work, relationships, and daily activities—can be an act of worship when done in submission to God.

The priestly role also involves intercession. Just as the priests of the Old Testament interceded for the people, we are called to stand in the gap, praying for others and bringing their needs before God. 1 Timothy 2:1 (TPT) urges us, "Most of all, I'm writing to encourage you to pray with gratitude to God. Pray for all men with all forms of prayers and requests as you intercede with intense passion." As priests, we have the privilege of partnering with God in prayer, interceding for the lost, the broken, and the world around us.

Visual 22.1 depicts a believer kneeling in prayer, with light shining down, symbolizing their priestly role in worship and intercession.

Visual 22.1: Believer kneeling in prayer, with light shining down, symbolizing their priestly role in worship and intercession.
(**Source:** image of believer kneeling in prayer, with light shining down, symbolizing their priestly role in worship and intercession - Search Images)

Kingship: Walking in Divine Authority

In addition to being priests, believers are also called to function as kings. The Bible teaches that, through Christ, we share in His authority and are called to rule and reign with Him. This kingship is not about earthly power or domination but about exercising spiritual authority in alignment with God's purposes.

Revelation 1:6 (TPT) speaks of Jesus making us "priests and kings" unto God. This dual role emphasizes that, as sons and daughters of God, we are given the authority to carry out His will on earth. Ephesians 2:6 (TPT) declares that God "raised us up with Christ the Exalted One, and we ascended with Him into the glorious perfection and authority of the heavenly realm." Our kingship is rooted in our union with Christ, who is the King of kings. We are seated with Him in heavenly places, meaning that we share in His victory over sin, death, and the powers of darkness.

Our role as kings involves exercising spiritual authority over the forces of darkness and advancing God's kingdom in the world. This authority is not something we earn; it is part of our inheritance as sons and daughters of God. Jesus Himself declared in Luke 10:19 (TPT), "Now you understand that I have imparted to you all My authority to trample over his [Satan's] kingdom. You will trample upon every demon before you and overcome every power Satan possesses. Absolutely nothing will harm you as you walk in this authority."

As kings, we are also called to bring order, justice, and righteousness into the areas where God has given us influence. Whether in our families, workplaces, communities, or ministries, we are called to reign with Christ, bringing His wisdom and authority into every situation. This means that we do not merely react to circumstances; we actively seek to align our lives with God's kingdom purposes and bring His rule to bear in our spheres of influence.

Visual 22.2 depicts a crown and scepter, symbolizing the believer's kingship and authority in Christ.

Visual 22.2: A crown and scepter, symbolizing the believer's kingship and authority in Christ.
(**Source:** image of A crown and scepter, symbolizing the believer's kingship and authority in Christ. - Search Images)

Sidebar: The Bride of Christ: A New Covenant Image

Scripture often uses the image of marriage to illustrate the deep, covenantal relationship between Christ and His Church. Just as a husband and wife become "one flesh," so Christ and His Church are united in an eternal bond of love and shared purpose.

- Revelation 19:7-9 – This passage depicts the Church as the bride of Christ, fully prepared for the marriage of the Lamb. "Let us rejoice and be glad and give him glory! For the wedding of the Lamb has come, and his bride has made herself ready." Here, the Church is seen as holy and radiant, prepared to enter into an everlasting union with Christ.

- Revelation 21:2, 9-11 – In the vision of the new Jerusalem, the city is described as "a bride beautifully dressed for her husband." This imagery reflects the eternal covenant God shares with His people, fully realized in the new creation where God dwells with His bride forever.

- Song of Solomon 2:16 – This book, a poetic portrayal of love, reflects Christ's passionate commitment to His Church. "My beloved is mine, and I am his," speaks of the intimate, mutual devotion between Christ and His people, a relationship marked by love, respect, and unwavering commitment.

- Ephesians 5:25-27 – Paul compares Christ's relationship with the Church to that of a husband and wife, saying, "Husbands, love your wives, just as Christ loved the church and gave Himself up for her." Christ cherishes His bride, the Church, giving Himself fully to sanctify and present her without blemish. In this covenant of grace, we are cleansed, made holy, and perfected by His love.

Just as Eve was drawn from Adam's side, the Church is drawn from the side of Christ. Jesus' sacrifice on the cross and His resurrection gave birth to a new humanity, bringing His people into a life-giving relationship as His bride. This union signifies that we are coheirs with Him, sharing in His life, authority, and mission on earth.

As the body of Christ, we are collectively His hands, feet, and voice in the world. United with Him, we are called to embody His love, mercy, and truth, becoming His representatives and co-laborers in God's kingdom. This profound relationship means that, just as Christ cherishes and nourishes us, we live and move in Him, expressing His presence and fulfilling His purposes on earth. He is our life, and we, His bride, are called to reflect His glory and share in His eternal inheritance.

In our role as sons, priests, and kings, we are also invited into a unique relationship with Christ as His Bride. The Sidebar explores this New Covenant image, reflecting our intimate union and co-reigning with Him.

The Interconnected Roles of Priest and King

While priesthood and kingship are distinct roles, they are deeply interconnected. As priests, we draw near to God in worship and intercession, aligning our hearts with His will. As kings, we take the authority and power we receive in God's presence and apply it to the world around us. The priestly role fuels the kingly role, and the kingly role carries out the purposes discovered in the priestly role.

1 Peter 2:9 (TPT) beautifully unites these roles by calling us "priests who are kings." This dual identity highlights the balance between intimacy with God and authority in the world. We are called to be people of prayer, deeply connected to the heart of God, but also people of action, advancing His kingdom and exercising His authority on the earth.

One of the greatest challenges in living out this dual identity is maintaining the balance between the two. It is easy to focus on one role at the expense of the other. Some may prioritize their priestly role, spending time in worship and prayer, but neglect to walk in the authority God has given them to impact the world. Others may focus on exercising their authority, but neglect the need for intimacy with God that fuels their effectiveness as kings.

The key to fulfilling both roles is to remain grounded in our identity as sons and daughters of God. Our priestly and kingly roles flow from our relationship with the Father. As we grow in our understanding of who we are in Christ, we are empowered to live out both our priesthood and our kingship with grace and balance.

Living as Priests and Kings in Everyday Life

The calling to live as priests and kings is not reserved for a select few or for specific moments of spiritual significance. It is a calling for every believer and applies to every aspect of our daily lives. Whether we are at home, at work, in church, or in the community, we are invited to live out our identity as priests and kings, bringing God's presence and authority into every situation.

Priestly Living: In our daily lives, we can live out our priestly role by cultivating a lifestyle of worship and prayer. This means setting aside time to meet with God, offering Him our praise and devotion, and interceding for others. It also means living in a posture of surrender, allowing every part of our lives to be an offering to God. As we go about our daily tasks, we can maintain an attitude of prayer, continually seeking God's guidance and interceding for those around us.

Kingly Living: In our day-to-day interactions, we can live out our kingly role by exercising spiritual authority and bringing God's kingdom to bear on the situations we face. This could involve praying for healing for someone in need, speaking truth and justice in a difficult situation, or standing firm against spiritual attacks. It also means living with intentionality, recognizing that God has placed us in specific situations and relationships to bring His rule and reign.

In practical terms, this might look like praying for your workplace, asking God for wisdom and insight to make decisions that align with His will. It might involve standing in faith for your family, declaring God's promises over your loved ones, and taking spiritual authority over any areas where the enemy is at work. As priests and kings, we are called to bring God's kingdom into every area of our lives, partnering with Him to see His will done on earth as it is in heaven (Matthew 6:10, TPT).

Visual 22.3 illustrates a believer walking in both prayer and authority, symbolizing the harmony of priesthood and kingship in everyday life.

Visual 22.3: A believer walking in both prayer and authority, symbolizing the balance of priesthood and kingship in everyday life.
(**Source:** image of A believer walking in both prayer and authority, symbolizing the balance of priesthood and kingship in everyday life - Search Images)

Conclusion: Stepping into Our Full Identity

Living as sons, priests, and kings is not an abstract spiritual concept; it is the essence of our identity in Christ. We are called to draw near to God in worship and prayer as His priests, and we are called to walk in the authority of His kingdom as His kings. These roles are not mutually exclusive but deeply connected, each empowering the other.

As we grow in our understanding of our identity in Christ, we will find that the priestly and kingly roles naturally flow from our relationship with God. The more we spend time in His presence, the more we are equipped to exercise His authority in the world. The more we walk in His authority, the more we are drawn back to His presence, knowing that all power and wisdom come from Him.

The journey to mature sonship is one of growing in these roles, learning to live in the fullness of our calling as priests and kings. As we embrace this dual identity, we will see God's kingdom advance in our lives and in the world around us, fulfilling His purposes and bringing His glory to the earth.

Chapter 23

Operating in Divine Authority

As believers in Christ, we are called not only to live in the fullness of our identity as sons and daughters of God but also to operate in the divine authority that comes with our identity. This authority is not rooted in human strength or power but flows directly from our union with Christ and the victory He accomplished through His death, resurrection, and ascension. Divine authority is the ability to exercise God's power, declare His will, and bring His kingdom into every aspect of life. In this chapter, we explore what it means to operate in divine authority, the source of that authority, and how we can walk in it in our daily lives to fulfil God's purposes on earth.

The Source of Divine Authority: Union with Christ

The authority we have as believers comes directly from our union with Christ. When we are born again, we are not only forgiven of our sins but also united with Christ in His victory over sin, death, and the powers of darkness. Ephesians 2:6 (TPT) tells us that God "raised us up with Christ the Exalted One, and we ascended with Him into the glorious perfection and authority of the heavenly realm, for we are now co-seated as one with Christ!"

Our position with Christ in the heavenly realm means that we share in His authority. This is not something we earn or achieve through our own efforts; it is part of our inheritance as children of God. Jesus Himself declared in Matthew 28:18 (TPT), "All authority of the universe has been given to Me." As those who are united with Christ, we share in that authority, empowered by His Spirit to carry out His will on earth.

Divine authority is not based on our own strength, knowledge, or resources. It is entirely dependent on our relationship with Jesus and our submission to His lordship. The closer we walk with Christ, the more we are able to operate in the authority He has given us. John 15:5 (TPT) illustrates this truth: "I am the sprouting vine and you're My branches. As you live in union with Me as your source, fruitfulness will stream from within you—but when you live separated from Me you are powerless."

Visual 23.1 illustrates Jesus extending His hand to a believer, symbolizing the transfer of authority from Christ to His followers.

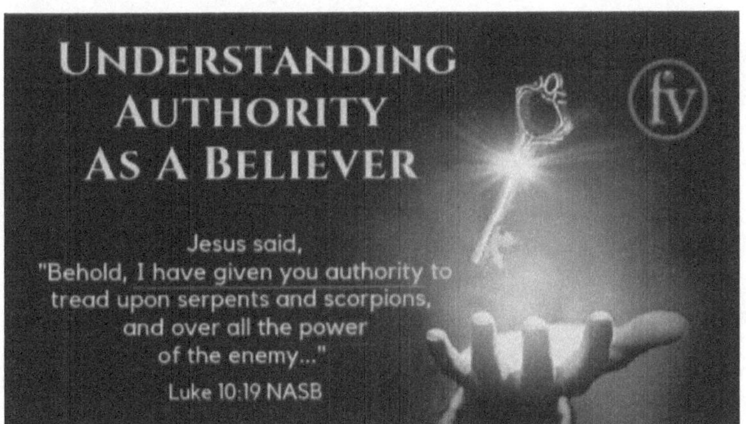

Visual 23.1: Jesus extending His hand to a believer, symbolizing the transfer of authority from Christ to His followers.

Understanding Our Authority: Exercising Dominion in Christ

Operating in divine authority means exercising the dominion that God originally intended for humanity. In Genesis 1:26-28, God gave Adam and Eve the mandate to rule over creation and to bring His order to the earth. However, this dominion was lost through sin. Jesus, as the second Adam, came to restore what was lost and to bring humanity back into its rightful place of authority under God's rule.

As believers, we are called to exercise this restored dominion in every area of life. This means that we are not passive bystanders in the spiritual realm; we are active participants in God's plan to bring His kingdom on earth as it is in heaven. Luke 10:19 (TPT) records Jesus' words to His disciples: "Now you understand that I have imparted to you all My authority to trample over his [Satan's] kingdom. You will trample upon every demon before you and overcome every power Satan possesses. Absolutely nothing will harm you as you walk in this authority."

Operating in divine authority involves several key areas:

Authority Over Sin: As believers, we are no longer slaves to sin. Romans 6:14 (TPT) assures us, "Remember this: sin will not conquer you, for God already has! You are not governed by law but governed by the reign of the grace of God." Through the authority of Christ, we have the power to resist temptation and overcome sin in our lives. This authority empowers us to walk in freedom and holiness.

Authority Over Darkness: Jesus came to destroy the works of the devil (1 John 3:8, TPT), and He has given us authority to do the same. As we walk in the authority of Christ, we are able to confront and overcome the powers of darkness, whether through prayer, deliverance, or spiritual warfare. Ephesians 6:10-12 (TPT) reminds us that we are engaged in a spiritual battle but have been equipped with divine power to overcome.

Authority in Prayer: Operating in divine authority means praying with boldness and confidence, knowing that our prayers have the power to change circumstances and bring God's will to pass. James 5:16 (TPT) tells us, "The prayer of a righteous person is powerful and effective." When we pray in the name of Jesus, we are praying with His authority, and our prayers have the potential to shift spiritual realities and bring breakthrough.

Authority to Heal and Restore: Jesus sent His disciples out to heal the sick, raise the dead, and cast out demons, saying, "Freely you have received; freely give" (Matthew 10:8, TPT). This same authority has been entrusted to us as His followers. We are called to be agents of healing and restoration, bringing the power of Christ to those who are suffering physically, emotionally, and spiritually.

Visual 23.2 illustrates a believer standing in prayer, with radiant light emanating from their hands, symbolizing the authority in prayer and healing.

Visual 23.2: A believer standing in prayer, with a radiant light emanating from their hands, symbolizing the authority of prayer and healing.
(**Source:** image of person laying hand and praying and healing - Search Images)

Operating in divine authority includes overcoming inner battles, especially in the realm of our thoughts. The Sidebar delves into spiritual warfare as a battle of the mind, emphasizing the power of aligning our beliefs with God's truth.

Sidebar: Spiritual Warfare - The Battle of the Mind

Spiritual warfare is often understood as an ongoing struggle against demonic forces, but true spiritual warfare is not about fearing or focusing on dark powers. For those who follow Christ, we can be assured that "the one who is in us is greater than the one who is in the world" (1 John 4:4), and that Jesus has already overcome all powers and authorities, living victoriously within us.

Today, much of the battle lies in the mind, where strongholds of wrong beliefs can keep us from fully experiencing the life Christ offers. 2 Corinthians 10:4-5 speaks of pulling down these strongholds, which often take the form of beliefs about ourselves, God, or others that don't align with His truth. These strongholds may include ideas that God is harsh or demanding, that we are unworthy of His love, or that we must "earn" His favor through religious actions.

The concept of "repentance" as repeated penance is a religious misunderstanding. The Greek word metanoia means a "change of mind," specifically a transformation in how we see God, ourselves, and others. Metanoia is key to spiritual renewal, as we align our thinking with God's view and purpose. Through this transformed mindset, we begin to see as God sees. 2 Corinthians 5:16-17 teaches us not to view anyone "according to the flesh" but through the lens of Christ's reconciling work. By recognizing that all people are reconciled to God's original design, we are called to see Christ in everyone, including ourselves.

As we embrace our identity in Christ and renew our minds to align with God's perspective, we break down these mental strongholds and experience true freedom. In spiritual warfare, then, the battle isn't about fighting darkness; it's about focusing on God's truth. As we accept and live in His perspective, we experience His peace, power, and victory. Aligning with the mind of Christ enables us to walk in His love, extending it to ourselves and others as we live out our true purpose.

The Relationship Between Faith and Authority

Faith is a key component of operating in divine authority. Authority without faith is ineffective, but when we combine our authority in Christ with faith in His promises, we are able to see mountains moved and obstacles overcome. Jesus said in Matthew 17:20 (TPT), "I promise you, if you have faith inside of you no bigger than the size of a small mustard seed, you can say to this mountain, 'Move away from here and go over there,' and you will see it move! There is nothing you couldn't do!"

Faith is the confidence that God's word is true and that He will act on our behalf when we step out in His authority. When we operate in divine authority, we do so not in our own power but in full reliance on God's promises and faithfulness. Hebrews 11:1 (TPT) describes faith as "the assurance of things hoped for, the evidence of realities not seen." It is this faith that activates the authority God has given us and enables us to see His kingdom come in our lives and in the world.

Operating in divine authority also requires boldness. The enemy will often try to intimidate or deceive us into believing that we have no authority. However, we must stand firm in the truth of God's word, knowing that we are seated with Christ in heavenly places and that His authority is ours to exercise. Hebrews 10:35 (TPT) encourages us, "So don't lose your bold, courageous faith, for you are destined for a great reward!"

Walking in Authority: Practical Steps for Everyday Life

Operating in divine authority is not limited to moments of spiritual warfare or miraculous signs. It is something we are called to walk in daily, in every aspect of our lives. Here are some practical ways to walk in divine authority:

Declare God's Promises: One of the simplest and most powerful ways to exercise authority is by speaking and declaring God's word over your life and circumstances. When we declare God's promises, we align ourselves with His will and release His power into our situation. Isaiah 55:11 (TPT) reminds us that God's word "will not return to Me void, but it will accomplish what I desire and achieve the purpose for which I sent it."

Take Authority Over Your Mind: The enemy often attacks our minds with fear, doubt, and discouragement. As believers, we have the authority to take every thought captive and make it obedient to Christ (2 Corinthians 10:5, TPT). This means actively resisting lies and replacing them with the truth of God's word.

Pray with Boldness: When you pray, do so with the confidence that God hears you and that your prayers carry authority. Don't pray from a place of fear or doubt; pray from your position of victory in Christ, believing that God is at work to bring about His will.

Speak Life and Blessing: Your words carry power. Proverbs 18:21 (TPT) says, "Your words are so powerful that they will kill or give life, and the talkative person will reap the consequences." Use your words to speak life, blessing, and truth over yourself, your family, and your circumstances. Speak God's promises, even when the natural reality seems contrary to them.

Stand in Faith and Don't Back Down: When exercising authority, persistence is key. There may be times when the enemy resists, and it feels as though nothing is changing. In those moments, stand firm in your authority, continuing to declare God's word and trust in His promises. Ephesians 6:13 (TPT) encourages us to "put on the full armor of God, so that when the day of evil comes, you may be able to stand your ground, and after you have done everything, to stand."

Conclusion: Walking in the Power of Divine Authority

Operating in divine authority is not reserved for the spiritually elite; it is the birthright of every believer in Christ. As sons and daughters of God, we have been given the authority to carry out His will on earth, to overcome the powers of darkness, and to bring His kingdom into every area of life. This authority flows from our union with Christ, and it is activated by faith, boldness, and reliance on God's word.

As we grow in our understanding of who we are in Christ and the authority we have been given, we will see His power at work in us and through us. Whether in prayer, spiritual warfare, or daily interactions, we are called to walk in divine authority, bringing God's rule and reign into every situation we encounter.

The journey of maturing as sons, priests, and kings continues as we embrace the authority that has been entrusted to us and seek to fulfil God's purposes on earth. As we do, we will witness the advance of His kingdom and the manifestation of His glory in our lives and the world around us.

Chapter 24

Living in Multiple Dimensions

One of the most profound truths revealed in the Scriptures is that as believers, we are not confined to the limitations of the natural world. Through our union with Christ, we are called to live in multiple dimensions—both in the physical and spiritual realms—simultaneously. This reality impacts how we perceive the world, how we engage with the supernatural, and how we fulfil our calling in God's kingdom. Living in multiple dimensions is about recognizing the interconnectedness of the seen and unseen realms and learning to operate in the authority and wisdom of God's higher realities.

In this chapter, we explore the biblical foundations for living in multiple dimensions, how we are seated in heavenly places while living on earth, and how this multidimensional life transforms our perspective, actions, and influence in the world.

Seated in Heavenly Places: A Dual Reality

The New Testament teaches that believers occupy two realms at the same time: the physical realm (earth) and the spiritual realm (heaven). This dual reality is a cornerstone of our identity in Christ and a vital part of how we are called to live and operate as His representatives on earth.

Ephesians 2:6 (TPT) reveals this dual position: "He raised us up with Christ the Exalted One, and we ascended with Him into the glorious perfection and authority of the heavenly realm, for we are now co-seated as one with Christ!" This verse shows that while we are physically present on earth, we are also spiritually seated with Christ in heavenly places. This is not a future promise but a present reality—our spiritual position in Christ gives us access to the resources, wisdom, and authority of heaven.

To live in multiple dimensions means to recognize and operate from our heavenly position while engaging with the world around us. It is a life of walking in the Spirit, aware that the unseen realm is just as real—if not more real—than the visible world. In 2 Corinthians 4:18 (TPT), Paul writes, "We don't focus our attention on what is seen but on what is unseen. For what is seen is temporary, but the unseen realm is eternal."

This dual reality impacts how we perceive life's challenges, opportunities, and decisions. When we understand that we are seated with Christ, we begin to view circumstances from a higher perspective. Rather than being overwhelmed by what is happening in the natural, we can draw on the wisdom and authority available to us from our heavenly position.

Visual 24.1 illustrates a believer's connection to multiple realms, symbolizing their access to both the spiritual and physical dimensions through Christ.

Visual 24.1: A believer standing on earth, with light extending from heaven, symbolizing their connection to both realms. (**Source:** <u>image of A believer standing on earth, with light extending from heaven, symbolizing their connection to both realms. - Search Images</u>

Walking in the Spirit: Living from the Unseen Realm

The key to living in multiple dimensions is learning to walk in the Spirit. Walking in the Spirit means being led by the Holy Spirit, who guides us into the realities of God's kingdom and helps us navigate the spiritual realm while engaging with the physical world.

Romans 8:14 (TPT) reminds us, "The mature children of God are those who are moved by the impulses of the Holy Spirit." As we grow in our relationship with God, we become more sensitive to the leading of the Spirit and more attuned to the realities of the unseen realm. This sensitivity allows us to operate in supernatural wisdom, power, and discernment, accessing the resources of heaven for the situations we encounter on earth.

Galatians 5:25 (TPT) instructs us to "live in the Holy Spirit and follow after Him." This means that our decisions, actions, and responses are informed by the Spirit's guidance, rather than by our natural instincts or external circumstances. Living in the Spirit empowers us to see beyond the immediate, to discern spiritual dynamics at play, and to respond with heaven's solutions.

Walking in the Spirit also enables us to engage in spiritual warfare. Ephesians 6:12 (TPT) reminds us, "Your hand-to-hand combat is not with human beings, but with the highest principalities and authorities operating in rebellion under the heavenly realms." Our battle is not against flesh and blood but against spiritual forces, and as we walk in the Spirit, we are equipped to confront and overcome these forces with divine authority.

As we explore the concept of living in multiple dimensions, it's essential to understand the biblical perspective on the three heavens. The Sidebar provides insight into these realms and how they connect with our spiritual journey.

Sidebar: Three Heavens: A Biblical Perspective

The Bible speaks of three distinct realms of heaven that correspond to levels of spiritual authority, maturity, and intimacy with God. These realms reflect our relationship with God and our calling as sons and daughters to bring heaven's reality to earth.

The First Heaven – This is the physical realm, the visible world of earth, sky, and cosmos, where we see God's creation. It represents the outer court of God's tabernacle, where all people, even those without a relationship with God, experience His general revelation through nature.

The Second Heaven – This is the spiritual realm, where angels, including fallen angels, reside. It represents the holy place within the tabernacle and is a place of spiritual activity where believers engage in spiritual warfare. Fallen angels still operate here, opposing God's work on earth, yet Jesus has already defeated these principalities and powers. As believers grow, they are equipped to overcome spiritual opposition, realizing their divine authority in Christ. Mature sons of God will one day judge these fallen beings (1 Corinthians 6:3), demonstrating God's justice through our alignment with His authority.

The Third Heaven – This is the realm of God's uncreated presence, where His throne is established. Represented by the Holy of Holies, this realm is accessible only through deep, intimate relationship with God. Here, believers are "seated in the heavenly places" (Ephesians 2:6), operating as ambassadors of heaven on earth, bringing God's kingdom into every area of life. Sons and daughters operate in this realm, fulfilling the call to bring heaven to earth (Matthew 6:10) and participating in God's plan to restore all creation (Romans 8:19-21).

Progression of Maturity: 30, 60, 100-Fold Harvest
Believers grow through stages of understanding and authority in the Spirit:

30-Fold – New believers in Christ know that their sins are forgiven, and they look forward to eternal life. They have entered the first heaven, the outer court, living in the assurance of salvation.

60-Fold – Believers at this stage realize God's power to heal, deliver, and answer prayers. They actively seek God's intervention and believe He can change situations. This represents the second heaven, a place of growth in faith and authority, yet with dependence on God's intervention.

100-Fold – Mature sons and daughters walk in the fullness of their identity, declaring and decreeing in alignment with God's will, bringing His kingdom to earth. Just as Jesus and the apostles spoke and healed with divine authority, mature sons and daughters co-rule with Christ, always motivated by His love and character. As He is, so are we in this world (1 John 4:17).

God's design is for us to function as heirs and coheirs with Christ, equipped with His authority to restore creation, overcome opposition, and spread His glory across the earth. By aligning with God's heart, we operate from the third heaven, embodying the reality of heaven on earth with the help of angels working alongside us. In this way, we live out the calling to bring 100-fold fruitfulness as sons and daughters fully restored to God's purpose.

Operating with Heaven's Perspective

Living in multiple dimensions means that we must learn to operate with heaven's perspective. The natural world often limits our view, focusing on immediate problems, obstacles, and limitations. However, when we embrace our position in Christ and walk in the Spirit, we begin to see things from God's perspective—a perspective that is not bound by time, space, or human limitations.

Colossians 3:1-2 (TPT) encourages us, "Christ's resurrection is your resurrection too. This is why we are to yearn for all that is above, for that's where Christ sits enthroned at the place of all power, honor, and authority! Yes, feast on all the treasures of the heavenly realm and fill your thoughts with heavenly realities, and not with the distractions of the natural realm." This passage invites us to focus our hearts and minds on the realities of heaven and to operate from a place of spiritual authority.

Operating with heaven's perspective allows us to:

See Beyond the Immediate: Instead of being overwhelmed by current circumstances, we can view life through the lens of God's eternal purpose. We understand that even in difficult seasons, God is working for our good (Romans 8:28, TPT), and His plans are far greater than what we can see in the moment.

Align with God's Will: When we operate from heaven's perspective, we seek to align our lives, decisions, and actions with God's will. Jesus taught us to pray, "Your kingdom come, Your will be done, on earth as it is in heaven" (Matthew 6:10, TPT). Our goal is to bring the realities of heaven into the earth, allowing God's kingdom to be manifested in and through us.

Access Supernatural Resources: From our position in Christ, we have access to the resources of heaven—divine wisdom, spiritual gifts, healing, and provision. James 1:5 (TPT) promises, "If anyone longs to be wise, ask God for wisdom and He will give it! He won't see your lack of wisdom as an opportunity to scold you over your failures but He will overwhelm your failures with His generous grace."

Visual 24.2 shows a man standing at a crossroads with two paths—one leading to the natural world and the other to a heavenly realm, symbolizing the choice of a divine perspective.

Visual 24.2: A man navigating dual realms.
(**Source:** image of man in dual realms. - Search Images)

Engaging with the Supernatural: Living in the Power of the Spirit

Living in multiple dimensions also means embracing the supernatural reality of God's kingdom. Throughout the Gospels, we see Jesus operating in both the natural and supernatural realms. He healed the sick, cast out demons, and performed miracles—all while walking among ordinary people. As followers of Jesus, we are called to do the same.

John 14:12 (TPT) records Jesus' words: "I tell you this timeless truth: The person who follows Me in faith, believing in Me, will do the same mighty miracles that I do—even greater miracles than these because I go to be with My Father!" Jesus made it clear that His followers are called to continue His work on earth, operating in the power of the Holy Spirit to bring healing, deliverance, and restoration.

Engaging with the supernatural requires faith and sensitivity to the Holy Spirit. It involves stepping out of our comfort zones and believing that God's power is available to us in every situation. Whether it's praying for healing, casting out fear, or trusting God for supernatural provision, living in multiple dimensions means expecting the impossible and believing that God is actively at work in the unseen realm.

Visual 24.3 illustrates Jesus healing the sick, with His followers in the background, symbolizing the continuation of His supernatural ministry through believers."

Visual 24.3: Jesus healing the sick, with His followers in the background, symbolizing the continuation of His supernatural ministry through believers.
(**Source:** <u>image of Jesus healing the sick, with His followers in the background, - Search Images</u>)

Balancing the Natural and Spiritual Realms

While we are called to live in multiple dimensions, we are also called to live with balance. We are not called to abandon our responsibilities in the natural world or to disengage from practical matters. Rather, we are called to integrate the natural and spiritual realms, bringing heaven's influence into the physical world.

This balance is seen in Jesus' life. While He operated in supernatural power, He also cared for practical needs, fed the hungry, and spent time in relationships. Living in multiple dimensions means that we bring the power and wisdom of the Spirit into our everyday lives—our work, our families, our communities—so that God's kingdom can be manifested in every area.

Living in balance requires discernment. There are times when we must engage in the practical aspects of life, but we must do so with an awareness of the spiritual realm. For example, when facing a challenge at work, we can seek God's wisdom and direction, trusting that He is at work behind the scenes. When ministering to someone in need, we can rely on the Holy Spirit to guide us in how to respond with both compassion and supernatural power.

Conclusion: Embracing the Multidimensional Life

Living in multiple dimensions is the reality of every believer in Christ. We are called to live with one foot in the natural world and one foot in the spiritual realm, engaging with both while operating from our heavenly position in Christ. As we learn to walk in the Spirit, see with heaven's perspective, and engage with the supernatural, we become more effective in advancing God's kingdom on earth.

This multidimensional life is not about escaping the challenges of the natural world but about bringing the resources, wisdom, and power of heaven into those challenges. As we embrace this reality, we will see God's kingdom manifest in our lives and in the world around us, fulfilling His purposes and revealing His glory.

As we move forward, we will explore how this multidimensional life empowers us to manifest heaven on earth and operate in divine authority to bring about God's plans for creation.

Chapter 25

Manifesting Heaven on Earth

The ultimate calling of every believer is to manifest heaven on earth. This means living in such a way that the realities of God's kingdom—His love, peace, justice, and power—are made visible in the world around us. Jesus taught us to pray, "Your kingdom come, Your will be done, on earth as it is in heaven" (Matthew 6:10, TPT), revealing that God's intention is for His heavenly kingdom to be realized in the physical world. As sons and daughters of God, we are called to be conduits through which heaven flows into every sphere of life, transforming lives, communities, and nations. In this chapter, we explore what it means to manifest heaven on earth and how we, as believers, can participate in bringing God's kingdom to the here and now.

The Mission of Manifesting Heaven: Jesus as Our Model

Jesus is the perfect example of what it means to manifest heaven on earth. Throughout His earthly ministry, Jesus demonstrated the nature and power of God's kingdom. He healed the sick, cast out demons, forgave sins, and brought hope to the marginalized. Everything He did was a reflection of the reality of heaven. In John 14:9 (TPT), Jesus said, "Whoever has seen Me has seen the Father." His life was the embodiment of God's will, showing what heaven looks like in human form.

Jesus' ministry wasn't just about performing miracles; it was about revealing the character of God and restoring what had been broken by sin. He confronted injustice, embraced the outcast, and taught the values of God's kingdom—love, mercy, righteousness, and humility. Jesus didn't just talk about heaven; He brought it into every encounter and situation, demonstrating that the kingdom of God is not just a distant reality but something that is available and accessible here and now.

As followers of Jesus, we are called to carry on His mission. In John 14:12 (TPT), Jesus tells His disciples, "I tell you this timeless truth: The person who follows Me in faith, believing in Me, will do the same mighty miracles that I do—even greater miracles than these because I go to be with My Father!" This means that we are empowered to continue the work of Jesus, manifesting the same love, power, and presence of God in the world today.

Visual 25.1 illustrates Jesus healing the sick, with His disciples and followers extending hands of compassion and power, symbolizing the continuation of His mission to bring heaven to earth.

Visual 25.1: Jesus healing the sick, with His disciples extending hands of compassion and power, symbolizing the continuation of His mission to manifest heaven on earth. (**Source:** image of Jesus healing the sick, symbolizing His mission to manifest heaven on earth. - Search Images)

The Role of the Holy Spirit: Empowerment for Manifesting Heaven

The key to manifesting heaven on earth lies in the power of the Holy Spirit. When Jesus ascended to heaven, He promised that His followers would receive the Holy Spirit, who would empower them to continue His work (Acts 1:8, TPT). The Holy Spirit is the active presence of God in our lives, enabling us to carry out the mission of bringing heaven to earth. Without the Holy Spirit, we are limited by our human abilities, but with Him, we are empowered to operate in the supernatural and accomplish things far beyond our natural capacity.

Romans 8:11 (TPT) tells us, "Yes, God raised Jesus to life! And since God's Spirit of Resurrection lives in you, He will also raise your dying body to life by the same Spirit that breathes life into you!" This resurrection power is at work in every believer, empowering us to bring healing, freedom, and restoration to a broken world. The Holy Spirit gives us access to the resources of heaven, equipping us with spiritual gifts such as wisdom, discernment, healing, prophecy, and miracles (1 Corinthians 12:7-11, TPT), which enable us to minister to others with the love and power of God.

Moreover, the Holy Spirit transforms us from the inside out, shaping our character to reflect the values of God's kingdom. The fruit of the Spirit—love, joy, peace, patience, kindness, goodness, faithfulness, gentleness, and self-control (Galatians 5:22-23, TPT)—are the attributes of heaven. As we grow in the Spirit, we not only demonstrate the power of God but also the heart of God, revealing His love and grace in every area of life.

As we live out our role in manifesting heaven on earth, creation responds to the revealing of God's children. The Sidebar highlights how creation eagerly awaits and interacts with the maturity of the sons and daughters of God.

daughters of God, we are called to bring healing and restoration to creation, stewarding it in alignment with God's will.

This commission to govern creation was originally given to Adam and is now passed to the Church. God does not retract His gifts or callings (Romans 11:29), so this responsibility remains with us. Our role requires maturity and intimacy with God, knowing His heart so that we can act as His representatives, bringing His order and blessing into every part of creation.

However, creation can also respond negatively to human actions. When we collectively engage in pursuits that oppose God's design, creation can suffer—through natural disasters, environmental degradation, and a loss of harmony. This adverse response reflects the consequences of humanity's disconnection from God's purpose, seen in the effects of pollution, resource depletion, and the breakdown of ecosystems.

God invites us into a partnership of restoration, empowering us to shape creation for good. As we grow into our identity as His children, creation will respond in kind, reflecting God's glory, beauty, and order. This divine partnership calls us to engage responsibly with creation, bringing God's life and peace into the world and spreading His goodness everywhere.

Heaven in Every Sphere: Transforming the World Around Us

Manifesting heaven on earth means bringing God's kingdom into every sphere of life—our families, workplaces, communities, and nations. It's about aligning every aspect of our lives with the values, principles, and power of God's kingdom. This calling is not limited to pastors, missionaries, or those in ministry; it applies to every believer, no matter their occupation or context. Whether you are a teacher, a businessperson, a parent, or a student, you are called to be an agent of heaven's influence wherever you go.

In Our Relationships: Manifesting heaven begins in our closest relationships. This means loving others with the same unconditional love that God has shown us. It means practicing forgiveness, humility, and kindness, and being a peacemaker in our families, friendships, and communities. When we live out the values of heaven in our relationships, we create an environment where God's love and peace can reign, transforming hearts and restoring brokenness.

In Our Workplaces: God's kingdom is not confined to the church. It extends into the marketplace, where we can bring heaven's influence into our jobs, businesses, and professional interactions. Colossians 3:23 (TPT) reminds us, "Put your heart and soul into every activity you do, as though you are doing it for the Lord Himself and not merely for others." By working with integrity, excellence, and a heart of service, we reflect the character of God and influence our workplaces with His values. Additionally, we can pray for our colleagues, seek God's wisdom in our decisions, and be a light in our professional environments.

In Our Communities: Manifesting heaven on earth also involves engaging with the needs of our communities.

Jesus demonstrated a deep compassion for the poor, the marginalized, and the oppressed, and we are called to do the same. This might involve serving the homeless, advocating for justice, supporting education, or simply being present for those in need. When we bring the love of Christ into our communities, we create opportunities for transformation and healing.

In Our Nations: Finally, manifesting heaven on earth means seeking the transformation of entire nations. This can be done through prayer, advocacy, and working for systemic change that aligns with God's kingdom principles of justice, peace, and righteousness. While we may feel powerless to influence global issues, we are called to be intercessors and advocates for change, trusting that God can move through our prayers and actions to bring about His will.

Visual 25.2 depicts believers in various settings—families, workplaces, and community service—demonstrating the kingdom of God through love, service, and integrity.

Visual 25.2: Believers in various contexts—families, workplaces, community service—demonstrating the kingdom of God through love, service, and integrity.
(**Source:** image of believers in various contexts—families, workplaces, community service—demonstrating the kingdom of God through love, service, and integrity. - Search Images)

The Power of Prayer: Bringing Heaven to Earth

Prayer is one of the most powerful tools we have for manifesting heaven on earth. Through prayer, we partner with God to bring His will and purposes into reality. Jesus taught His disciples to pray, "Your kingdom come, Your will be done, on earth as it is in heaven" (Matthew 6:10, TPT), showing us that prayer is the means by which we invite heaven's influence into the earth.

Prayer is not just a passive exercise; it is an active declaration of faith and alignment with God's purposes. James 5:16 (TPT) reminds us, "The prayer of a righteous person is powerful and effective." When we pray in faith, we release the power of heaven into situations that seem impossible, and we invite God to move in supernatural ways.

Through prayer, we can:

Intercede for Others: Prayer allows us to stand in the gap for those who are hurting, lost, or in need of healing. We can intercede for our families, communities, and nations, asking God to bring His kingdom into their lives.

Pray for Healing: Jesus often healed the sick through prayer, and we are called to do the same. By praying for physical, emotional, and spiritual healing, we invite the resurrection power of Jesus to bring restoration to those who are suffering.

Declare God's Promises: Prayer is a way of declaring God's promises and aligning our hearts with His will. When we pray God's Word, we are releasing His truth into our circumstances, bringing heaven's reality into the natural world.

Living in Expectation: Cultivating a Mindset of Heaven

Manifesting heaven on earth requires cultivating a mindset of expectation. We must believe that God's kingdom is not a distant hope but a present reality that we can experience and release in our lives. This means living with the expectation that God's power is available to us today, and that His love and justice can transform even the most challenging situations.

Philippians 3:20 (TPT) reminds us that "we are a colony of heaven on earth." This means that as believers, we are ambassadors of God's kingdom, carrying His authority and presence wherever we go. Living with this mindset changes the way we approach life. Instead of being overwhelmed by the problems of the world, we see every challenge as an opportunity for God's kingdom to be manifested. Instead of focusing on what is lacking, we live with an expectation that God is able to do "exceedingly abundantly above all that we ask or think" (Ephesians 3:20, TPT).

Visual 25.3 depicts a city transformed by the light of God's presence, with believers walking in hope and expectation, representing the manifestation of heaven on earth.

Visual 25.3: A city transformed by the light of God's presence, with believers walking in hope and expectation, representing the manifestation of heaven on earth.
(**Source:** image of A city transformed by the light of God's presence - Search Images)

Conclusion: The Ongoing Mission of Manifesting Heaven

Manifesting heaven on earth is not a one-time event; it is the ongoing mission of every believer. We are called to be agents of God's kingdom, bringing His love, power, and justice into every sphere of life. This mission requires walking in the power of the Holy Spirit, living with heaven's perspective, and praying with faith and expectation.

As we continue on this journey, we will see God's kingdom breakthrough in remarkable ways. Lives will be transformed, communities will be healed, and the realities of heaven will become visible on earth. This is the heart of our calling as sons and daughters of God— to reveal His glory, extend His kingdom, and bring His will to pass on earth as it is in heaven.

PART 6

Creation Restored

Chapter 26

Creation's Response to Mature Sons

One of the most remarkable truths revealed in the Scriptures is that all of creation is deeply connected to the destiny of humanity, particularly to the maturity of God's sons and daughters. Romans 8:19 (TPT) declares, "The entire universe is standing on tiptoe, yearning to see the unveiling of God's glorious sons and daughters!" Creation itself waits eagerly for the revelation and maturity of the children of God because the fullness of our redemption is intertwined with the restoration of creation. In this chapter, we explore how creation responds to the maturity of God's people, what it means for us to live in harmony with creation, and how the future restoration of all things is linked to our growth as mature sons and daughters of God.

Creation's Groaning: The Effect of the Fall

To understand why creation waits for the maturity of God's sons and daughters, we must first look at the impact of sin on the natural world. When Adam and Eve disobeyed God, their sin did not just affect humanity; it affected all of creation. Genesis 3:17-18 (TPT) reveals that the ground itself was cursed because of sin, resulting in pain, decay, and struggle: "Cursed is the ground because of you; through painful toil you will eat food from it all the days of your life. It will produce thorns and thistles for you."

The fall introduced disorder, corruption, and suffering into the world, not just for humanity but for every part of creation. Romans 8:20-22 (TPT) describes creation as being "subjected to futility" and "groaning as if in the pains of childbirth." This groaning reflects the deep longing for redemption, not only for humanity but for the entire created order. The effects of sin—death, decay, natural disasters, and environmental degradation—are all symptoms of a creation that is waiting for the renewal and restoration promised in Christ.

Yet, amid this groaning, there is hope. Creation's suffering is not permanent; it is temporary, and it is intricately connected to the redemption of humanity. Just as sin brought disorder to the world, the revelation and maturity of God's sons and daughters will bring healing and restoration.

Visual 26.1 depicts creation's groaning, with images of the earth, trees, and animals yearning for restoration, symbolizing their anticipation of the maturity of God's children.

Visual 26.1: Creation groaning—an image of the earth, trees, and animals yearning for restoration, symbolizing their anticipation of the maturity of God's children.
(**Source:** image of Creation groaning—an image of the earth, trees, and animals yearning for restoration - Search Images)

As we examine how creation responds to mature sons and daughters of God, it's helpful to understand the biblical perspective on creation's longing for renewal. The Sidebar explores how creation eagerly awaits the revealing of God's children and the harmony that comes with it.

Sidebar: Creation's Response to the Sons of God

Romans 8:19 describes creation eagerly awaiting the revealing of the mature sons of God. As believers align with God's heart, creation responds positively, reflecting the glory and purpose God intended. Jesus exemplified this maturity, commanding storms to cease, raising the dead, healing the sick, and even guiding fish into nets. In His footsteps, as sons and daughters of God, we are called to bring healing and restoration to creation, stewarding it in alignment with God's will.

This commission to govern creation was originally given to Adam and is now passed to the Church. God does not retract His gifts or callings (Romans 11:29), so this responsibility remains with us. Our role requires maturity and intimacy with God, knowing His heart so that we can act as His representatives, bringing His order and blessing into every part of creation.

However, creation can also respond negatively to human actions. When we collectively engage in pursuits that oppose God's design, creation can suffer—through natural disasters, environmental degradation, and a loss of harmony. This adverse response reflects the consequences of humanity's disconnection from God's purpose, seen in the effects of pollution, resource depletion, and the breakdown of ecosystems.

God invites us into a partnership of restoration, empowering us to shape creation for good. As we grow into our identity as His children, creation will respond in kind, reflecting God's glory, beauty, and order. This divine partnership calls us to engage responsibly with creation, bringing God's life and peace into the world and spreading His goodness everywhere.

Creation's Connection to Humanity: Dominion and Stewardship

From the very beginning, God designed humanity to have a special relationship with creation. In Genesis 1:26-28 (TPT), God gave Adam and Eve dominion over the earth, instructing them to "rule over" the animals and the earth and to "fill the earth and subdue it." This dominion was not about exploitation but about stewardship—caring for creation in a way that reflects God's own love and care for His creation.

However, when sin entered the world, humanity's relationship with creation was fractured. Instead of exercising godly dominion, humanity often exploited and abused the natural world, contributing to its decay and suffering. Environmental destruction, pollution, and ecological imbalance are all symptoms of this broken relationship between humanity and creation.

As sons and daughters of God, we are called to restore this relationship by embracing our role as stewards of creation. Our maturity in Christ includes learning to live in harmony with the earth, caring for it in ways that honor God's original design. This is part of the broader redemptive work that God is doing in the world—restoring not just our spiritual lives but our relationship with creation as well.

Our dominion over creation is a reflection of our maturity as sons and daughters of God. When we walk in our identity as mature children of God, we exercise authority over creation in a way that reflects God's love, wisdom, and order. We are called to be caretakers of the earth, ensuring that its resources are used wisely and that the environment is protected for future generations.

The Unveiling of Mature Sons: A New Era for Creation

Romans 8:21 (TPT) reveals a profound truth: "Creation itself will be liberated from its bondage to decay and brought into the glorious freedom of the children of God." This passage shows that creation's liberation from suffering is directly linked to the maturity and revelation of God's sons and daughters. As we grow into the fullness of who we are in Christ, creation itself will experience freedom and restoration.

The unveiling of mature sons and daughters refers to the moment when believers come into the fullness of their identity and authority in Christ. This is not just a future event but an ongoing process as we grow in spiritual maturity, walking in greater intimacy with God, and exercising our God-given authority on earth. The more we walk in this maturity, the more we will see creation respond to the order, peace, and restoration that comes from God's kingdom.

This unveiling is part of God's grand plan of redemption, which culminates in the new creation. Revelation 21:1 (TPT) speaks of a new heaven and a new earth, where all things are restored to their original beauty and perfection. In this new creation, there will be no more death, decay, or suffering, and humanity will live in perfect harmony with creation. The process of creation's restoration begins now, as we, the sons and daughters of God, partner with Him in bringing His kingdom to earth.

Visual 26.2 shows creation being liberated, depicting a flourishing earth with vibrant colors, animals, and plant life, symbolizing the freedom that comes with the maturity of God's children.

Visual 26.2: Creation being liberated—an image of a flourishing earth with vibrant colors, animals, and plant life, symbolizing the freedom that comes with the maturity of God's children.
(**Source:** image of Creation being liberated—an image of a flourishing earth with vibrant colors, animals, and plant life - Search Images)

Living in Harmony with Creation: A Call to Stewardship

As we grow in our understanding of the connection between our maturity and the restoration of creation, we are called to live in harmony with the natural world. This means adopting a mindset of stewardship, recognizing that the earth is not ours to exploit but God's creation to care for and preserve. Psalm 24:1 (TPT) reminds us, "The earth is the Lord's, and everything in it, the world, and all who live in it."

Living in harmony with creation involves practical steps:

Caring for the Environment: As believers, we should take seriously our responsibility to protect the environment. This might involve reducing waste, conserving natural resources, and supporting efforts to combat climate change and environmental degradation. By doing so, we reflect God's heart for His creation and participate in His redemptive work.

Sustainable Living: We are called to live sustainably, using the earth's resources in a way that honors God and ensures that future generations can enjoy the beauty and abundance of His creation. This might mean adopting sustainable practices in our homes, workplaces, and communities, and encouraging others to do the same.

Advocating for Creation: As stewards of God's creation, we have a responsibility to advocate for policies and practices that protect the environment. This might involve supporting environmental initiatives, speaking out against harmful practices, and educating others about the importance of caring for the earth.

By living in harmony with creation, we become part of the solution to the environmental challenges facing our world. We participate in God's plan to restore all things, beginning with our own relationship with the earth.

Creation's Future Restoration: The New Heaven and New Earth

The Scriptures point to a future where all of creation will be fully restored and made new. Revelation 21:1 (TPT) describes a vision of "a new heaven and a new earth, for the first heaven and the first earth had passed away." This new creation is the fulfilment of God's promise to redeem not only humanity but the entire cosmos.

In this new creation, the effects of sin will be completely erased. There will be no more death, decay, or suffering. The harmony between humanity and creation will be fully restored, and we will live in perfect relationship with God, one another, and the earth. This is the ultimate hope for creation and the final outcome of God's redemptive plan.

While we wait for the full manifestation of the new creation, we are called to be agents of restoration in the here and now. As mature sons and daughters of God, we can bring glimpses of this future restoration into the present by living in harmony with creation and exercising godly stewardship over the earth.

Visual 26.3 depicts the new heaven and new earth—a scene of peace, beauty, and harmony, with humanity and creation flourishing together in the presence of God.

Visual 26.3: New heaven and new earth—a scene of peace, beauty, and harmony, with humanity and creation flourishing together in the presence of God.
(**Source:** image of new heaven and new earth - Search Images)

Conclusion: Partnering with God in Creation's Restoration

The restoration of creation is deeply tied to the maturity of God's sons and daughters. As we grow in our identity as children of God, we are called to exercise dominion over the earth in a way that reflects God's love, wisdom, and care. Creation itself waits eagerly for the revelation of mature sons and daughters, knowing that its own freedom from decay is linked to our growth and maturity in Christ.

As we live in harmony with creation and embrace our role as stewards of the earth, we participate in God's ongoing work of restoration. We are not passive observers of creation's groaning; we are active participants in bringing healing and renewal to the world around us. This is part of the larger story of redemption, a story that culminates in the new heaven and new earth, where all things are made new and creation is fully restored.

The journey toward mature sonship is not only about our personal spiritual growth; it is about joining God in His redemptive plan for the entire cosmos. As we walk in this maturity, we will see creation respond, and we will experience the joy of partnering with God in the restoration of all things.

Chapter 27

New Creation Physics

As believers grow into mature sons and daughters of God, we are invited to explore not only spiritual truths but also the profound realities of the created universe. The restoration of all things in Christ has implications that extend beyond spiritual transformation to include the physical world itself. In this chapter, we delve into the concept of "New Creation Physics," an exploration of how the natural laws and structures of the physical world are influenced by God's overarching plan of redemption and the emergence of the new creation.

The concept of new creation physics challenges us to consider how the very fabric of the universe will be transformed as God's redemptive purposes are fully realized. It is a blending of spiritual and physical realities, where heaven and earth converge, and where the principles that govern the material world align with the power, wisdom, and glory of God's kingdom. In this chapter, we explore how science and faith intersect in the restoration of creation, the role of miracles in revealing new creation principles, and how the future new heaven and new earth will be governed by a new order.

The Intersection of Science and Faith: God as Creator and Sustainer

The Bible affirms that God is both the Creator and Sustainer of the universe. Colossians 1:16-17 (TPT) declares, "For through the Son everything was created, both in the heavenly realm and on the earth, all that is seen and all that is unseen. Every seat of power, realm of government, principality, and authority—it was all created through Him and for His purpose! He existed before anything was made, and now everything finds completion in Him." This passage reveals that all things—both physical and spiritual—were created by God through Christ, and everything continues to be held together by His power.

Science, as a tool for exploring the physical world, provides insights into the laws and structures that govern the universe. These natural laws, such as gravity, electromagnetism, and thermodynamics, reveal the order and precision with which God designed the universe. But these natural laws are not static or independent of God's will; they are subject to His sovereignty. The same God who spoke the universe into existence has the power to transcend or alter these laws according to His purposes.

New creation physics is the idea that, as God's kingdom continues to advance and creation is restored, the physical world will increasingly reflect the order, beauty, and power of heaven. While the current natural order has been affected by the fall—resulting in decay, death, and disorder—God's redemptive plan involves restoring both the spiritual and physical realms to their original design. This will culminate in the new heaven and new earth, where the laws of the universe will be governed by God's perfect will.

Visual 27.1 shows the cosmos with light breaking through, symbolizing the convergence of the spiritual and physical realms under God's sovereign rule.

Visual 27.1: The cosmos with light breaking through, symbolizing the intersection of the spiritual and physical realms under God's sovereign rule.
(**Source:** image of The cosmos with light breaking through - Search Images)

The Role of Miracles: Signs of New Creation Power

Miracles serve as glimpses of the new creation, revealing the ways in which God's kingdom breaks into the natural world, often defying or superseding the laws of physics. Throughout the Bible, we see miracles that demonstrate God's power over the physical realm—Jesus walking on water, healing the sick, calming storms, and raising the dead. These events are not just supernatural interruptions; they are signs of the new creation, showing us how the world will function under the full reign of God's kingdom.

261

In the Gospels, Jesus often performed miracles to reveal the reality of God's kingdom. When He healed the blind, fed the multitudes, or cast out demons, He was demonstrating that the natural order was being restored and realigned with heaven's order. In Matthew 12:28 (TPT), Jesus says, "But if it is by the power of the Spirit of God that I cast out demons, then the kingdom of God has arrived among you!" Miracles, then, are not merely acts of divine intervention; they are manifestations of the new creation breaking into the present.

As mature sons and daughters of God, we are called to participate in this supernatural dimension of new creation physics. Jesus declared in John 14:12 (TPT), "I tell you this timeless truth: The person who follows Me in faith, believing in Me, will do the same mighty miracles that I do—even greater miracles than these because I go to be with My Father!" The ability to operate in supernatural power is part of our inheritance as God's children, revealing the new creation reality through signs, wonders, and miracles.

Visual 27.2 shows Jesus performing miracles, with light radiating from His hands, symbolizing the breakthrough of new creation power into the physical world.

Visual 27.2: Jesus performing miracles, with light radiating from His hands, symbolizing the breakthrough of new creation power into the physical world.
(**Source:** image of Jesus performing miracles, with light radiating from His hands. - Search Images)

The Laws of Physics in the New Heaven and New Earth

As we look forward to the new heaven and new earth described in Revelation 21, we are invited to imagine a world where the current limitations of the physical realm no longer exist. The natural world as we know it, governed by the laws of entropy, decay, and death, will be replaced by a new order where life, light, and harmony prevail.

Revelation 21:4 (TPT) offers a glimpse into this new reality: "He will wipe every tear from their eyes, and eliminate death entirely. No one will mourn or weep any longer. The pain of wounds will no longer exist, for the old order has ceased." This passage points to a profound transformation not only in human experience but in the very fabric of creation. The new heaven and new earth

263

will be free from the effects of sin, and the laws that govern the universe will reflect the eternal, life-giving nature of God.

In the new creation, time and space may function differently than they do in our current reality. The constraints of time—aging, decay, and the inevitable progression toward death—will no longer apply. Instead, we will experience eternal life in perfect harmony with God's presence. The new creation will be characterized by perpetual renewal, where the limitations of the old order are replaced by the limitless possibilities of God's kingdom.

Isaiah 65:17 (TPT) speaks of this new reality: "For I am creating a new heaven and a new earth, and no one will even think about the old ones anymore." This transformation will affect not only the physical earth but the entire cosmos. The stars, planets, and galaxies will be part of the new creation, all aligned with God's perfect order. The laws of physics that govern the new creation will reflect the beauty, harmony, and eternal nature of God's kingdom.

Visual 27.3 depicts the new heaven and new earth, with vibrant light, renewed landscapes, and transformed creation, symbolizing the restoration of the cosmos under God's reign.

Visual 27.3: New heaven and new earth, with vibrant light, new landscapes, and transformed creation, symbolizing the restoration of the cosmos under God's reign.
(**Source:** <u>image of New heaven and new earth, transformed creation, symbolizing the restoration of the cosmos under God's reign. - Search Images</u>)

The new creation introduces principles that surpass our current technology and understanding of physics. The Sidebar explores the concept of divine physics and how it transcends earthly limitations.

Sidebar: Beyond Current Technology - Exploring Divine Physics

In the new creation, God's principles operate beyond the limits of human technology and earthly physics, introducing a dimension where divine power supersedes natural laws. For example, Jesus' miracles—walking on water, multiplying food, passing through crowds, and His resurrection—demonstrate a reality that transcends our physical constraints. These acts reveal a quantum-like interaction where observation and divine intention alter outcomes, much like wave functions collapsing in quantum mechanics.

In John 14:12, Jesus promises that His followers will "do greater works" because of their connection to Him. This suggests that believers will access this divine reality more fully, impacting creation in profound ways. Romans 8:19-21 also speaks of creation eagerly awaiting the revealing of the sons of God, indicating a future in which mature believers influence and restore creation to its original glory.

The "divine physics" of the new creation encompasses the miraculous, reshaping our understanding of possibility and reality. As humanity aligns with God's purpose, we will move from relying solely on human technology to participating in the supernatural order God has established—a realm where all creation responds to the sons and daughters of God.

Scientific Exploration and Revelation: The Role of Believers in New Creation Physics

As believers, we are invited to explore the mysteries of creation through both science and faith. While science seeks to understand the physical world, faith reveals the deeper spiritual realities that govern the universe. These two approaches are not in conflict; rather, they complement each other in helping us understand the full scope of God's creative power.

The pursuit of scientific knowledge, when done with a heart of worship and reverence for God as Creator, can lead to greater awe and wonder at the complexity and beauty of His design. Psalm 19:1 (TPT) declares, "God's splendor is a tale that is told; His testament is written in the stars. Space itself speaks His story through the marvels of the heavens." As we explore the laws of physics, biology, chemistry, and other fields, we uncover the intricate details of God's handiwork.

However, the role of believers in new creation physics goes beyond scientific exploration. We are called to bring the reality of the new creation into the present through prayer, intercession, and supernatural acts of faith. Just as Jesus demonstrated the power of the new creation through miracles, we are called to release God's kingdom into the world around us, transforming both the spiritual and physical realms.

As we grow in spiritual maturity, we gain greater insight into how God's kingdom operates and how we can partner with Him in bringing restoration to the earth. Whether through acts of healing, environmental stewardship, or scientific discovery, we have the privilege of participating in God's redemptive plan for creation.

Conclusion: The Unveiling of New Creation Physics

New creation physics invites us to consider how the natural world will be transformed as God's redemptive purposes are fully realized. While the laws of physics currently govern the universe, they are subject to God's sovereign will, and as His kingdom advances, these laws will increasingly reflect His perfect order. Miracles serve as glimpses of the new creation breaking into the present, revealing the power and beauty of God's kingdom.

As believers, we are called to live in the tension between the now and the not yet, participating in the restoration of creation while awaiting the full unveiling of the new heaven and new earth. Through faith, we can access the resources of heaven and operate in the supernatural power of God, bringing healing, transformation, and renewal to the world around us.

The new creation is not just a future hope; it is a present reality that we are called to manifest in our daily lives. As we grow in spiritual maturity, we gain greater insight into the mysteries of God's kingdom and the ways in which His power is at work in both the spiritual and physical realms. This journey invites us to explore the depths of creation, to engage with the wonders of science, and to live in the expectation of the day when all things will be made new.

Chapter 28

Beyond Current Technology

As we consider the future of creation and the unveiling of God's kingdom, we must also reflect on how technological advancements fit into His grand design. Technology has become a defining feature of modern life, shaping how we interact, communicate, and live. But as we look toward the new creation, the question arises: what lies beyond our current technology? How does God's plan for redemption and restoration influence the trajectory of technological development? This chapter explores the role of technology in light of God's eternal purposes, how advancements in science and innovation might intersect with His kingdom, and how believers are called to steward technology in ways that align with God's values.

While technology can be used for incredible good, advancing human flourishing and solving complex problems, it also raises ethical questions and challenges that require spiritual discernment. As mature sons and daughters of God, we are called not only to engage with technology wisely but also to envision a future where technological advancements align with God's redemptive plan for creation. Ultimately, this chapter challenges us to consider how innovation and faith converge and how technology might be transformed in the new heaven and new earth.

Technology and God's Sovereignty: The Role of Innovation in Creation

Throughout history, human beings have created tools, machines, and systems that allow us to solve problems, enhance productivity, and communicate across great distances. From the invention of the wheel to the rise of artificial intelligence, technology has been a means of exercising the dominion God entrusted to humanity in Genesis 1:26-28 (TPT): "Let them have complete authority over the earth...so they may reign over all the fish of the sea, the birds of the air, the tame beasts, and over all the earth." The development of technology reflects our innate creativity, a gift given by God, and our desire to bring order and solutions to the challenges of life.

However, technology in itself is not neutral. It can be used for good or for harm, for enhancing life or diminishing it. Just as sin distorted humanity's relationship with the earth and one another, it also distorted the way we use technology. In a fallen world, technology can become a tool for exploitation, control, or even destruction. Yet, when aligned with God's purposes, technology can serve as a powerful force for redemption, healing, and restoration.

God is sovereign over all creation, including human innovation and technological development. He is not opposed to progress, but He calls His people to engage with technology in ways that reflect His wisdom and goodness. In Proverbs 3:5-6 (TPT), we are reminded to "trust in the Lord completely, and do not rely on your own opinions. With all your heart rely on Him to guide you, and He will lead you in every decision you make." This call to seek God's guidance applies not only to personal decisions but also to how we develop and use technology.

As we navigate the complexities of technological innovation, we must remember that God's sovereignty extends over every invention, discovery, and advancement. He is the ultimate source of wisdom, and as we seek His will, He can direct our steps, ensuring that our use of technology aligns with His kingdom purposes.

Visual 28.1 illustrates hHumanity standing at the forefront of technological advancement, with light shining down from above, symbolizing divine guidance in the pursuit of innovation.

Visual 28.1: Humanity standing at the forefront of technological advancement, with light shining down from above, symbolizing divine guidance in the pursuit of innovation.
(**Source:** image of Humanity standing at the forefront of technological advancement, with light shining down - Search Images)

The Ethical Dilemmas of Technology: Wisdom for the Digital Age

As technology advances at an unprecedented rate, it presents new ethical dilemmas that require careful discernment. Developments in artificial intelligence, genetic engineering, and biotechnology challenge us to consider not only what we can do but what we should do. While technology offers incredible opportunities for improving healthcare, communication, and the economy, it also brings the potential for misuse, raising questions about privacy, autonomy, and the very nature of life itself.

For example, artificial intelligence (AI) is rapidly transforming industries, offering solutions to complex problems, from healthcare diagnostics to autonomous vehicles. Yet, AI also raises concerns about privacy, surveillance, and the dehumanization of labor. Similarly, advances in genetic engineering hold the promise of curing diseases but also open the door to ethical questions about altering human DNA and "playing God" with the building blocks of life.

As believers, we are called to approach these ethical dilemmas with wisdom, guided by biblical principles and the Holy Spirit. James 1:5 (TPT) offers this promise: "If anyone longs to be wise, ask God for wisdom and He will give it!" Our engagement with technology must be rooted in a commitment to God's values—upholding human dignity, protecting life, promoting justice, and stewarding creation. This means advocating for ethical practices in technological development, questioning practices that violate God's design, and using technology in ways that promote the common good.

One practical way believers can engage with technology ethically is by participating in conversations about its development and use. As Christians, we have a responsibility to influence technological ethics, whether in academic, professional, or community settings. By bringing a kingdom perspective to the table, we can help shape the future of technology in ways that honor God and protect human dignity.

Stewarding Technology: A Call to Responsibility

Technology, like every gift from God, must be stewarded well. In Matthew 25:14-30, Jesus tells the parable of the talents, illustrating the importance of using the resources God gives us wisely and faithfully. This parable applies not only to financial resources but also to the technological innovations that shape our world. As stewards of technology, we are responsible for using it in ways that benefit others, promote justice, and reflect God's love and creativity.

Stewardship of technology involves asking key questions:

How Does This Technology Impact Others? We must consider how our use of technology affects individuals, communities, and even the environment. Does it enhance human flourishing, or does it contribute to inequality, environmental harm, or exploitation?

Does This Technology Align with God's Purposes? Technology can be used to advance God's kingdom by promoting justice, healing, and education, but it can also be used for harm. We must assess whether the tools we use align with God's heart for love, mercy, and justice.

Am I Using Technology Wisely? Technology can easily become a distraction or even an idol in our lives. As believers, we must be mindful of how we use technology—whether for work, entertainment, or communication—and ensure that it does not hinder our relationship with God or others.

Stewardship also extends to how we develop new technologies. As creators and innovators, we are called to create tools and systems that serve others, promote equity, and reflect God's wisdom. Whether we are working in tech development, healthcare, education, or business, we can approach our work as an act of worship, seeking to honor God in every innovation we pursue.

Visual 28.2 depicts a world operating within a quantum reality of limitless possibilities, symbolizing the boundless potential and interconnectedness of creation under God's infinite wisdom and design.

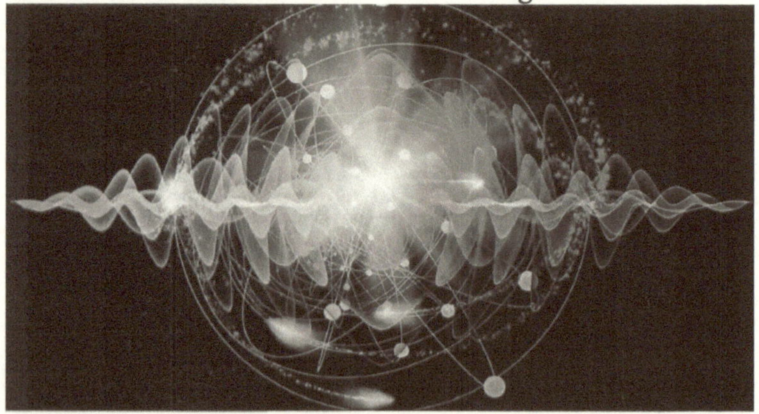

Visual 28.2: World that operates in quantum reality with limitless possibilities.
(**Source:** image of quantum world - Search Images)

Technology in the New Creation: A Vision for the Future

As we look toward the future new heaven and new earth described in Revelation 21, we are invited to imagine a world where technology is perfectly aligned with God's purposes. In the new creation, human creativity will be fully redeemed, and the innovations we develop will reflect God's glory and wisdom without the taint of sin or exploitation.

In the new creation, technology will no longer be a source of division or harm but a means of enhancing life, beauty, and relationship. Revelation 21:24-26 (TPT) describes the nations of the world bringing their glory into the new Jerusalem: "The people of the world will walk by its light, and the kings of the earth will bring their wealth into it. Its gates will never be closed...for there is no night there! People will bring the glory and wealth of the nations into it!" This passage suggests that the achievements of human culture—including technological advancements—will find their fulfilment in the new creation, transformed and redeemed for God's glory.

In this future reality, technology will no longer be a source of environmental destruction or ethical tension but will serve as a tool for bringing God's love, creativity, and order into every aspect of life. It will enhance relationships, promote justice, and reflect the perfect harmony between humanity, creation, and God.

In the realm beyond human understanding, God's heavenly assembly—the Divine Council—plays a vital role in decision-making that shapes creation. The Sidebar explores this council, revealing how God includes spiritual beings in His divine governance.

Sidebar: The Divine Council - God's Heavenly Assembly

Scripture introduces a fascinating concept known as the Divine Council—a heavenly assembly where God gathers with angelic beings, and, on occasion, even humans, to make significant decisions. Psalm 82 and Psalm 89 portray God presiding over this assembly, exercising justice and delegating authority. In Daniel 4, we see that "the decision by the watchers" resulted in Nebuchadnezzar's humbling, indicating that angels may play an active role in guiding the course of events.

1 Kings 22 provides a unique example of this process, where God allows the members of His council to contribute to the outcome of Israel's battle. When asked for suggestions, a spirit steps forward with a plan, and God permits it to be carried out, even though the decision leads to a negative outcome for King Ahab. This instance reflects God's inclusive leadership within the council, allowing His created beings to participate in His purposes, sometimes going along with their choices even if they may not align perfectly with His ideal.

Occasionally, humans are included in this council. Figures like Enoch and, through prophetic visions, prophets such as Isaiah and Ezekiel, are brought into God's presence and invited to witness or contribute to divine decisions. This council model, with God as the ultimate chair, suggests that God values the input and engagement of His creation in governance and extends this authority to His trusted servants.

Through the Divine Council, God not only leads but invites others to share in His decision-making process, reflecting a relationship of trust and participation within His heavenly family. This interaction also foreshadows our own role as believers, called to eventually co-reign with Christ as sons and daughters in God's kingdom.

Bringing Heaven's Technology to Earth: Practical Steps for Today

While we await the full manifestation of the new creation, we are called to bring glimpses of heaven's reality into our present world. This means approaching technology with a kingdom mindset, using it to advance God's purposes and promote justice, healing, and restoration. Here are a few practical steps for believers:

Engage in Ethical Innovation: Whether working in tech, healthcare, education, or business, seek to develop and use technology that benefits humanity, honors God, and promotes the common good.

Promote Digital Justice: Advocate for policies that protect privacy, ensure equitable access to technology, and promote ethical standards in technological development.

Use Technology for Kingdom Purposes: Leverage digital platforms, social media, and other technological tools to spread the gospel, share God's love, and promote justice and mercy in the world.

Pray for Wisdom: As we engage with technology, we must continually seek God's wisdom and discernment, asking Him to guide our decisions and influence in the digital age.

Visual 28.3 depicts the New Jerusalem with advanced technology seamlessly integrated into the city, symbolizing redeemed human innovation in the new creation.

Visual 28.3: New Jerusalem with futuristic technology integrated harmoniously into the city, symbolizing redeemed human innovation in the new creation.
(**Source:** image of New Jerusalem with futuristic technology - Search Images)

Conclusion: A Future Beyond Current Technology

As we consider the future of technology, we are reminded that God's kingdom transcends the limitations of the present world. While current technology offers incredible opportunities for innovation and advancement, it also presents challenges that require wisdom, discernment, and faith. Beyond the current age lies a new creation where technology will be fully aligned with God's purposes—enhancing life, relationships, and creativity in ways we can only begin to imagine.

As believers, we are called to steward technology wisely, using it for the glory of God and the good of others. We are invited to engage with innovation, not with fear or suspicion, but with hope, knowing that God's redemptive purposes extend to every aspect of life, including the tools and systems we create. As we partner with Him, we can bring heaven's reality into our present world, offering glimpses of the future kingdom where all things—including technology—are made new.

Chapter 29

Restoring All Things

One of the most beautiful promises in Scripture is that God will one day restore all things. This includes not only the redemption of humanity but also the renewal of the entire creation. The story of the Bible is a narrative of creation, fall, redemption, and restoration, with the ultimate goal being the full restoration of all that was lost through sin. As we near the end of the story, the restoration of all things points to the culmination of God's redemptive plan, where everything is brought into perfect harmony under His rule. In this chapter, we explore the biblical promise of restoration, what it means for us as believers, and how we are called to participate in this process of restoration even now.

The Promise of Restoration: A New Beginning

The promise of restoration is central to the gospel message. Throughout Scripture, we see God's heart to restore what has been broken, lost, or corrupted by sin. In Acts 3:21 (TPT), Peter speaks of Jesus, saying, "For He must remain in heaven until the restoration of all things has taken place, fulfilling everything that God said long ago through His holy prophets." This verse points to a future event when God will restore everything to its original design, undoing the effects of the fall and bringing all of creation into alignment with His perfect will.

Restoration is more than just fixing what was broken; it is about making all things new. Revelation 21:5 (TPT) declares, "And God-Enthroned spoke to me and said, 'Consider this: I am making everything to be new and fresh.'" This newness signifies the complete transformation and renewal of all things—humanity, creation, relationships, and systems. It is not simply a return to the way things were before the fall but an elevation of creation to its intended glory, free from the stain of sin and death.

This promise of restoration is both cosmic and personal. It includes the renewal of the heavens and the earth, the redemption of human bodies through resurrection, and the healing of relationships. God's plan of restoration encompasses every aspect of life—spiritual, physical, relational, and environmental. It is the ultimate fulfilment of His purpose for creation, where everything will reflect His glory and operate according to His perfect order.

Visual 29.1 depicts creation renewed—a vibrant scene of the earth, animals, and people thriving together in harmony, symbolizing the restoration of all things.

Visual 29.1: Creation being renewed—a vibrant scene of the earth, animals, and people thriving together in harmony, symbolizing the restoration of all things.
(**Source:** image of Creation being renewed—a vibrant scene of the earth, animals, and people thriving together in harmony - Search Images)

Restoring Humanity: Redemption and Resurrection

The restoration of all things begins with the redemption and resurrection of humanity. When sin entered the world through Adam and Eve, it brought spiritual death, separation from God, and physical decay. But through Jesus Christ, the second Adam, God's plan to redeem humanity was set into motion. Romans 5:17 (TPT) proclaims, "Death once held us in its grip, and by the blunder of one man, death reigned as king over humanity. But now, how much more are we held in the grip of grace and continue reigning as kings in life, enjoying our regal freedom through the gift of perfect righteousness in the one and only Jesus, the Messiah!"

The restoration of humanity is rooted in the work of Christ, who came to reverse the effects of the fall and restore us to our original identity as sons and daughters of God. This restoration is both spiritual and physical. Spiritually, we are already restored to right relationship with God through faith in Jesus. 2 Corinthians 5:17 (TPT) affirms, "Now, if anyone is enfolded into Christ, he has become an entirely new creation. All that is related to the old order has vanished. Behold, everything is fresh and new."

But this restoration will also be fully realized in the resurrection of our bodies. 1 Corinthians 15:52-54 (TPT) describes this transformation: "For the dead will be raised never to die again, and we who are alive will be transformed...Death is swallowed up by a triumphant victory!" The resurrection is the ultimate victory over death and decay, as our bodies are restored to their intended glory, free from pain, sickness, and mortality.

The resurrection points to a future where humanity will live in perfect harmony with God and one another, fully reflecting His image and walking in the freedom and joy of eternal life. This is the heart of God's plan for restoring all things—the renewal of humanity as His beloved children, living in His presence forever.

Restoring Creation: The New Heavens and New Earth

God's promise of restoration also includes the renewal of creation itself. The earth, like humanity, was affected by sin and has been subjected to decay, violence, and disorder. Romans 8:20-21 (TPT) explains, "For against its will, the universe itself has had to endure the empty futility resulting from the consequences of human sin.

But now, with eager expectation, all creation longs for freedom from its slavery to decay and to experience with us the wonderful freedom coming to God's children."

This passage reveals that creation is groaning for the day when it will be set free from the curse of sin. The restoration of creation is deeply connected to the restoration of humanity. As God's sons and daughters are revealed and restored, creation itself will experience renewal. This points to the ultimate transformation of the physical world in the new heavens and new earth, where all things will be made new.

Revelation 21:1 (TPT) offers a vision of this future: "Then in a vision I saw a new heaven and a new earth. The first heaven and earth had passed away, and the sea no longer existed." This imagery of the new heaven and new earth speaks to the complete renewal of the cosmos—a world free from pollution, decay, natural disasters, and death. The new creation will be a place of perfect harmony, where humanity and the environment live in peace, reflecting the beauty and order of God's kingdom.

In this new creation, the effects of sin will be entirely erased. There will be no more pain, suffering, or environmental destruction. Everything will flourish according to God's original design, and humanity will fulfil its role as stewards of the earth, caring for creation in ways that reflect God's love and wisdom.

Restoring Relationships: Healing and Reconciliation

The restoration of all things also includes the healing of relationships. Sin not only damaged humanity's relationship with God, but it also fractured relationships between people. Hatred, jealousy, division, and violence are all consequences of the fall, but God's plan of restoration brings healing and reconciliation to broken relationships.

Ephesians 2:14 (TPT) declares, "Our reconciling 'Peace' is Jesus! He has made Jew and non-Jew one in Christ. By dying as our sacrifice, He has broken down every wall of prejudice that separated us and has now made us equal through our union with Christ." This passage highlights the power of Christ's work to reconcile people to one another, breaking down the barriers of hostility, prejudice, and division that exist in the world.

Restoration means the renewal of peace and unity among people. It is a return to the kind of relationships God intended—where love, forgiveness, and understanding flourish. In the new creation, there will be no more conflict or division. Revelation 7:9 (TPT) paints a picture of this restored unity: "I saw an enormous crowd—so huge that no one could count—made up of victorious ones from every nation, tribe, people group, and language. They were all in glistening white robes, standing before the throne and before the Lamb with palm branches in their hands." This image of people from every nation and culture, united in worship before God, speaks to the reconciliation and harmony that will be fully realized in the new creation.

Even now, we are called to participate in this work of reconciliation. 2 Corinthians 5:18 (TPT) states, "And God has made all things new and reconciled us to Himself, and given us the ministry of reconciling others to God." As believers, we are ambassadors of God's reconciliation, called to bring healing to broken relationships and to work toward unity and peace in the world.

Participating in Restoration: Our Role in God's Plan

While the full restoration of all things will be completed when Jesus returns, we are invited to participate in this process even now. As sons and daughters of God, we have a role to play in bringing glimpses of God's kingdom into the present, advancing His work of restoration in the world around us.

This begins with living out the gospel in our daily lives—sharing the message of reconciliation, healing, and hope with those who are lost and broken. It also involves working for justice, caring for creation, and promoting peace and unity in our communities. Micah 6:8 (TPT) calls us to "do what is right, to love mercy, and to walk humbly with your God." This is the heart of our participation in God's plan of restoration—acting as agents of His love and justice in the world.

We are also called to pray for and anticipate the full restoration that is to come. Revelation 22:20 (TPT) records the final prayer of Scripture: "He who testifies to these things says, 'Yes, I am coming quickly.' Amen! Come, Lord Jesus!" This prayer reflects our longing for the day when Jesus will return to restore all things, bringing an end to pain, suffering, and death, and making everything new.

Visual 29.2 shows people working in harmony with creation and with each other, symbolizing our role in God's plan for restoration.

Visual 29.2: Working in harmony with creation and one another, symbolizing our role in God's restoration plan. (**Source:** image of working in harmony with creation - Search Images)

The restoration of all things points to a renewed earth where harmony is fully restored under God's reign. The Sidebar expands on this vision, illustrating how life in the restored earth will reflect God's glory and peace.

Sidebar: The Restored Earth - Life in Harmony

Throughout Scripture, we see visions of a restored earth, where all of creation lives in harmony under God's reign. Isaiah 11:6 describes a time when "the wolf will live with the lamb, the leopard will lie down with the goat," a profound image of peace extending throughout the animal kingdom. This peace reflects changed hearts and renewed relationships, as humanity and creation are restored to their original, God-given purpose.

Isaiah 35:1-2 speaks of "the desert and the parched land" rejoicing, with "the wilderness blossoming like the crocus." God's presence brings life to the barren places, making rivers flow in the desert (Isaiah 35:6), transforming creation so that His glory is displayed everywhere. This vision of restoration also includes Micah 4:3-4, which foretells a time when "swords will be beaten into plowshares" and "no one will make them afraid," as nations live together peacefully.

In this renewed world, God's glory fills the earth (Habakkuk 2:14), and creation itself is liberated from decay and brokenness (Romans 8:21). As sons and daughters of God, we are called to participate in this restoration, spreading His peace and life throughout the world. This promise is not only a future hope but also an invitation for us to begin living out God's vision of harmony, justice, and love here and now.

The restored earth reflects God's heart for wholeness and unity in all things. Through changed hearts and renewed minds, we step into His purpose, engaging with creation and one another in ways that reveal God's love, beauty, and glory. This vision reminds us that we are part of a greater story, one where God's presence renews everything, making earth a place of life, peace, and flourishing for all.

Conclusion: The Hope of Complete Restoration

The restoration of all things is the fulfilment of God's redemptive plan—a plan that encompasses humanity, creation, and relationships. This future restoration is not just a distant hope; it is the heartbeat of the gospel. As we look forward to the day when all things will be made new, we are invited to participate in God's work of restoration even now.

The promise of restoration gives us hope in the face of brokenness, suffering, and decay. It reminds us that no matter how dark the world may seem, God is actively working to restore everything to its original glory. As we live in this tension between the now and the not yet, we carry the message of reconciliation and hope to a world in desperate need of healing.

The restoration of all things will culminate in the new heaven and new earth, where God will dwell with His people, and everything will reflect His glory. In that day, there will be no more pain, no more tears, and no more death. All things will be made new, and creation will flourish in perfect harmony with its Creator. This is the hope we cling to—the hope of complete restoration in Jesus Christ.

Chapter 30

The New Earth Reality

The concept of the "new earth reality" brings into focus the culmination of God's plan for creation—the point at which heaven and earth are united in perfect harmony. This future reality represents the fullness of God's kingdom, where all things are restored, sin and death are no more, and God dwells among His people forever. The new earth is not just a spiritual concept; it is the transformed, renewed creation where we will live in God's presence, experiencing the fullness of life as He intended from the beginning. In this chapter, we will explore the biblical vision of the new earth, the nature of life in this new creation, and how this future reality shapes the way we live today.

The Vision of the New Earth: Heaven and Earth United

The Bible paints a beautiful picture of the new earth, a place where God's original design for creation is fully realized. In Revelation 21:1-3 (TPT), John writes, "Then in a vision I saw a new heaven and a new earth. The first heaven and earth had passed away, and the sea no longer existed. I saw the holy city, the New Jerusalem, descending out of the heavenly realm from the presence of God, like a pleasing bride that had been prepared for her husband, adorned for her wedding. And I heard a thunderous voice from the throne, saying: 'Look! God's tabernacle is with human beings, and from now on He will tabernacle with them as their God.'"

This passage describes the merging of heaven and earth into one unified reality. The "new heaven and new earth" are not two separate realms but a single, integrated creation where God's presence permeates everything. The holy city, the New Jerusalem, symbolizes the union of God's kingdom with the physical world, where God will dwell directly with His people. This is the ultimate fulfillment of God's plan, where the separation between heaven and earth is removed, and all things are brought under His reign.

The phrase "the sea no longer existed" is symbolic in this context, representing the end of chaos, disorder, and evil, which were often symbolized by the sea in biblical literature. In the new earth reality, everything is in perfect harmony, with no trace of the forces of sin, destruction, or rebellion that once marred creation.

The new earth is a place where heaven's realities are fully manifested in the physical world. It is the restored, redeemed creation where life flourishes without the limitations and brokenness caused by the fall. In this new reality, there is no death, pain, suffering, or decay. Revelation 21:4 (TPT) assures us, "He will wipe away every tear from their eyes and eliminate death entirely. No one will mourn or weep any longer. The pain of wounds will no longer exist, for the old order has ceased."

Visual 30.1 shows the New Jerusalem descending onto a renewed, vibrant earth, symbolizing the unity of heaven and earth.

Visual 30.1: New Jerusalem descending onto a renewed, vibrant earth, symbolizing the unity of heaven and earth. (**Source:** image of New Jerusalem descending onto a renewed, vibrant earth, symbolizing the unity of heaven and earth. - Search Images)

The Nature of Life on the New Earth

Life on the new earth will be characterized by fullness, joy, and eternal fellowship with God. The new earth is not a return to Eden; it is something even greater—a transformed, glorified reality where the effects of sin are entirely erased. Here, the curse of death and decay is lifted, and creation will experience unending renewal and flourishing.

1 Corinthians 15:42-44 (TPT) describes the resurrection of our bodies, saying, "The body is 'sown' in corruption but will be raised in incorruption. It is sown in dishonor but will be raised in honor. It is sown in weakness but will be raised in power. It is sown a physical body but will be raised a spiritual body." This passage reveals that, in the new earth, we will have glorified bodies that are no longer subject to the limitations and frailties of

our current physical existence. Our new bodies will be perfectly suited for life in the presence of God, free from sickness, aging, and death.

The new earth will also be a place of peace, justice, and righteousness. Isaiah 65:17-25 (TPT) offers a prophetic glimpse of this future reality: "For I am creating a new heaven and a new earth, and no one will even think about the old ones anymore. Be glad; rejoice forever in My creation!" In this passage, we see a vision of a world where people live in harmony, where work is joyful and fulfilling, and where creation itself is renewed and free from violence. The lion lies down with the lamb, and there is no more fear or danger. It is a world where God's shalom—His peace and wholeness—permeates every aspect of life.

The new earth will be a place of unimaginable beauty and creativity. Revelation 22:1-2 (TPT) describes a river of life flowing from the throne of God and the Lamb, with trees bearing fruit for the healing of the nations. This imagery speaks to the abundance and vitality of life on the new earth. Everything will flourish under God's rule, and humanity will fulfil its original calling to steward creation, bringing out its full potential in harmony with God's purposes.

Visual 30.2 shows a vibrant, peaceful scene of the new earth—lush landscapes, flowing rivers, symbolizing the fullness of life in the presence of God.

Visual 30.2: A vibrant, peaceful scene of the new earth—lush landscapes, flowing rivers, and people in joyful fellowship, symbolizing the fullness of life in the presence of God. (**Source:** image of A vibrant, peaceful scene of the new earth - Search Images)

In the new earth, God's presence will be fully manifest among His people, making us His living temple. The Sidebar explores this concept of God's permanent dwelling, where His glory fills every part of creation.

Sidebar: The Living Temple - God's Permanent Dwelling Place

Throughout Scripture, the concept of God's dwelling place evolved, revealing His deep desire to be present with His people. In the wilderness, Moses' mobile tabernacle was a temporary structure made of materials like skin, hair, and cloth. This tabernacle housed God's presence intermittently, appearing on sacred occasions such as the Day of Atonement. Later, Solomon built a stone temple, providing a more enduring but still conditional dwelling place for God's glory, which filled the temple only at certain times.

During Jesus' earthly ministry, He taught and ministered in the temple, but as His ministry reached its climax, He drove out the money changers who had turned it into a marketplace. This act symbolized a pivotal moment—the departure of God's presence from the physical temple. Jesus then foretold a new kind of temple, saying, "Destroy this temple, and I will raise it again in three days" (John 2:19), referring to His own body as the new, eternal dwelling of God's Spirit.

Despite this, the Jewish people continued their worship in the physical temple, unaware that Jesus had prophesied its imminent destruction. "Not one stone here will be left on another," He warned (Matthew 24:2). This prophecy was fulfilled in AD 70, when the Romans destroyed the temple, bringing an end to the era of worship centered on physical buildings.

Under the new covenant, we are now God's living temples—His permanent, mobile dwelling place on earth. As believers, God's Spirit dwells in us constantly; we are His address on earth, carrying His presence wherever we go. This reality also emphasizes the importance of the redemption of our bodies as part of God's complete work of restoration. Even those who have gone before us, the cloud of witnesses (Hebrews 12:1), await this redemption (Hebrews 11:39-40), where body, soul, and spirit are wholly transformed in His presence.

We are, therefore, not just symbolic temples but living, sacred vessels of His Spirit, designed to reflect His love and embody His purposes on earth. Unlike the temporary tabernacle or stone temple, God's presence resides within us permanently, making each believer a dwelling place of the Most High. This union with God is our true and eternal identity, revealing His glory and purpose to the world.

Eternal Fellowship with God: The Center of the New Earth Reality

At the heart of the new earth reality is our eternal fellowship with God. The greatest joy of the new creation is not the absence of pain or the beauty of the renewed earth, but the fact that we will live in the direct presence of God forever. Revelation 21:22-23 (TPT) declares, "I saw no temple in the city, for its temple is the Lord God, the Almighty, and the Lamb. And the city has no need of the sun or moon, for the glory of God illuminates the city, and the Lamb is its light."

In the new earth, there will be no need for temples, mediators, or barriers between us and God. We will experience His presence continually, with nothing to separate us from His love and glory. The light of God Himself will illuminate the new earth, symbolizing His perfect guidance, truth, and purity. This eternal fellowship with God is the fulfilment of the promise made throughout Scripture—that He will dwell with His people, and they will be His.

The experience of God's presence will be one of unending worship, joy, and communion. Revelation 7:9-

10 (TPT) describes a vast multitude standing before the throne of God, worshiping Him with palm branches in their hands and declaring, "Salvation belongs to our God who sits on the throne, and to the Lamb!" Worship will be the natural response of every heart, as we behold God in all His beauty and majesty.

This eternal fellowship with God also means that our relationship with Him will grow deeper and richer throughout eternity. Even in the new earth, where we are fully restored, we will continue to discover more of God's infinite glory, love, and wisdom. There will always be more to know and experience of Him, and this will fill our eternity with purpose and joy.

The Kingdom Come: Living in Light of the New Earth Today

The vision of the new earth is not just a distant future hope; it shapes how we live today. As believers, we are called to live in the light of this coming reality, allowing the values and truths of God's kingdom to transform the way we engage with the world now. Jesus taught us to pray, "Your kingdom come, Your will be done, on earth as it is in heaven" (Matthew 6:10, TPT), inviting us to bring glimpses of the new earth reality into our present world.

Living in light of the new earth means that we view our work, relationships, and the world around us through the lens of God's kingdom. It means seeking justice, promoting peace, caring for creation, and loving others in ways that reflect the heart of God. Our actions today can be a foretaste of the new creation, as we partner with God in bringing restoration, healing, and reconciliation to a broken world.

It also means living with hope, knowing that the brokenness, pain, and suffering of this world are temporary. 2 Corinthians 4:17-18 (TPT) encourages us, "We view our slight, short-lived troubles in the light of eternity. We see our difficulties as the substance that produces for us an eternal, weighty glory far beyond all comparison, because we don't focus our attention on what is seen but on what is unseen. For what is seen is temporary, but the unseen realm is eternal." The reality of the new earth gives us the strength to endure, knowing that our present struggles are preparing us for the eternal glory to come.

Conclusion: The Eternal Hope of the New Earth Reality

The new earth reality is the culmination of God's redemptive plan—the point where all things are made new, and the fullness of God's kingdom is realized. In this future reality, heaven and earth are united, and God dwells with His people forever. It is a place of unending life, joy, peace, and communion with God, where the effects of sin are entirely erased, and creation flourishes as it was meant to.

For believers, the new earth is our ultimate hope and the source of our joy as we look toward the future. It gives us perspective on the trials and challenges of this life, reminding us that we are part of a much larger story—one that ends with the complete restoration of all things and eternal fellowship with our Creator.

As we live in anticipation of the new earth, we are called to bring the values of God's kingdom into the present, participating in His work of restoration and living in a way that reflects His love, justice, and peace. The new earth reality invites us to live with hope, purpose, and joy, knowing that we are destined for an eternity in the presence of God, where all things will be made new.

PART 7

The Ultimate Glory

Chapter 31

The New Humanity

The concept of the "new humanity" encapsulates the profound transformation that God brings to those who are in Christ. This transformation is not merely an internal change but a complete renewal of who we are—spirit, soul, and body. Through Jesus, we are not just improved versions of our old selves; we become entirely new creations, adopted into God's family, restored to His original design, and empowered to live as His sons and daughters. The new humanity is the fulfilment of God's eternal purpose for humanity, a people who reflect His image, walk in His authority, and live in perfect harmony with one another and with creation.

In this chapter, we explore what it means to be part of the new humanity, how this transformation affects our identity and purpose, and what it looks like to live in the fullness of this new reality. We will also consider the implications of the new humanity for our relationships, communities, and the world at large as we anticipate the day when God's redemptive work is fully realized in the new heaven and new earth.

Becoming New Creations in Christ

The transformation into the new humanity begins with becoming a new creation in Christ. This is the fundamental shift that occurs when we place our faith in Jesus—our old selves, marked by sin and separation from God, are crucified with Christ, and we are raised to new life with Him. 2 Corinthians 5:17 (TPT) captures this beautifully: "Now, if anyone is enfolded into Christ, he has become an entirely new creation. All that is related to the old order has vanished. Behold, everything is fresh and new."

This new creation is not simply a matter of behavior modification or moral improvement; it is a complete change of identity. We are no longer defined by our past, our failures, or our limitations. Instead, we are defined by our relationship with Christ. We are "enfolded into Christ," meaning that our lives are now fully integrated with His life, and we share in His righteousness, authority, and victory. This transformation affects every aspect of who we are—our hearts, minds, desires, and even our bodies are renewed by the power of the Holy Spirit.

This new identity as part of the new humanity also means that we are adopted into God's family. Galatians 4:4-7 (TPT) explains, "But when that era came to an end and the time of fulfilment had come, God sent His Son, born of a woman, born under the written law. Yet all of this was so that He would redeem and set free all those held hostage to the written law so that we would receive our freedom and a full legal adoption as His children." Through Christ, we are not only forgiven and restored, but we are given the status of sons and daughters of God, with all the privileges and responsibilities that come with this position.

Visual 31.1 shows a person being transformed from the old self to a new creation in Christ.

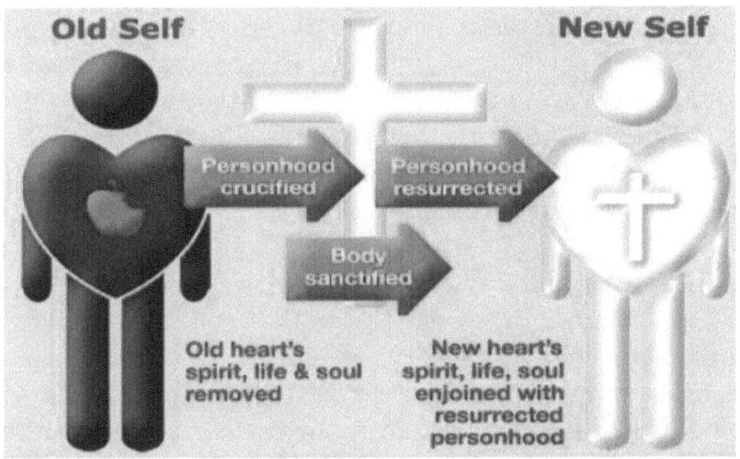

Visual 31.1: A person stepping into a radiant light, symbolizing the transformation from the old self to the new creation in Christ.
(**Source:** image of A person from old self to new self in Christ - Search Images)

The Identity and Purpose of the New Humanity

As part of the new humanity, our identity is no longer rooted in the things of this world—our achievements, status, or possessions. Instead, our identity is grounded in Christ and His finished work on the cross. Ephesians 2:10 (TPT) reminds us, "We have become His poetry, a re-created people that will fulfil the destiny He has given each of us, for we are joined to Jesus, the Anointed One. Even before we were born, God planned in advance our destiny and the good works we would do to fulfil it!"

This passage highlights two important truths about our identity as part of the new humanity: we are God's workmanship, and we have a purpose that was designed for us from the beginning. Our lives are not accidents or random events; they are part of God's eternal plan. He has uniquely crafted each of us to reflect His glory and to fulfil the specific assignments He has given us. These assignments—what Paul refers to as "good works"—are the ways in which we bring God's kingdom into the world, using our gifts, talents, and resources to serve others and advance His purposes.

The new humanity is also characterized by unity and love. In Christ, the divisions that once separated people—whether by race, class, gender, or nationality—are broken down. Galatians 3:28 (TPT) declares, "And we no longer see each other in our former state—Jew or non-Jew, rich or poor, male or female—because we're all one through our union with Jesus Christ." This unity does not erase our differences but brings them into harmony, where diversity is celebrated, and every person is valued as a member of God's family.

As part of the new humanity, we are called to live in a way that reflects God's love and grace to the world. This means treating others with dignity and respect, seeking reconciliation where there is conflict, and working for justice and peace in our communities. Our purpose is to be ambassadors of Christ's kingdom, demonstrating through our lives what it means to live as God's renewed people.

Living in the Power of the Holy Spirit

One of the defining features of the new humanity is the indwelling of the Holy Spirit. The Holy Spirit is the one who enables us to live out our new identity and purpose. Romans 8:9-11 (TPT) explains, "But when the Spirit of Christ empowers your life, you are not dominated by the flesh but by the Spirit. And if you are not joined to the

Spirit of the Anointed One, you are not of Him. Now Christ lives His life in you! And even though your body may be dead because of the effects of sin, His life-giving Spirit imparts life to you, because you are fully accepted by God."

The Holy Spirit empowers us to live in victory over sin, to walk in love, and to fulfill God's purposes. He is our guide, teacher, and source of strength. Through the Spirit, we are able to do things that are impossible in our own strength—whether it's loving our enemies, enduring suffering with hope, or exercising spiritual gifts to build up the body of Christ.

The Spirit also transforms our desires and mindset. As part of the new humanity, we are no longer driven by the desires of the flesh—selfishness, pride, and greed— but by the desires of the Spirit, which lead to love, joy, peace, patience, kindness, goodness, faithfulness, gentleness, and self-control (Galatians 5:22-23, TPT). These are the fruits of a life that is yielded to the Holy Spirit and reflects the character of Jesus.

Visual 31.2 depicts a believer filled with the Holy Spirit, radiating light and love, symbolizing the empowerment of the new humanity through the Spirit.

Visual 31.2: A believer filled with the Holy Spirit, radiating light and love, symbolizing the empowerment of the new humanity through the Spirit.
(**Source:** <u>image of filled with the Holy Spirit - Search Images</u>)

The new humanity reflects God's restored image, embodying His design and character. The Sidebar expands on how, through Christ, we are transformed to reflect God's nature and fulfil our purpose.

Sidebar: The Restored Image of God

God's redemptive plan restores humanity to His image—a likeness that was distorted by the fall but now fully restored in Christ, who is the perfect image of God (Colossians 1:15). When we accept Jesus, we enter into an exchanged life where His righteousness, holiness, and perfection are imparted to us. The risen Jesus is now our life

(Colossians 3:4), and it is His presence in us that the Father sees, which is why we are holy, blameless, perfect, and righteous in His sight. We cannot be otherwise, for we are seen through the lens of Christ's finished work.

Jesus lived a vicarious humanity—a life lived not only for us but as us. Through His death and resurrection, we are included in every stage of His redemptive journey:

- We were co-crucified with Him, symbolizing the end of our old self.
- We were co-buried with Him, signifying that our past life is completely laid to rest.
- We were co-resurrected and co-ascended with Him, and we are now co-seated in the heavenly places, face-to-face with God in the spirit.

Our union with Christ means that we are in Him, and thus, everything He is, we are; everything He has, we possess. This reality establishes our identity as coheirs with Christ (Romans 8:17), where we share in His inheritance and authority. As sons and daughters, we carry His divine nature, fully restored to the image of God, equipped to live out His character, love, and purpose on earth.

In this exchanged life, we are not merely forgiven but transformed. Christ's life within us enables us to reflect God's character and love, preparing us for eternal fellowship with Him. Our restored identity is grounded in the reality of being "in Christ," where we are empowered to live in alignment with God's original design—holy, complete, and beloved.

As Paul affirms, "As He is, so are we in this world" (1 John 4:17). Through Christ's finished work, we are renewed as the image-bearers we were always intended to be.

The New Humanity in Community: Building the Body of Christ

The new humanity is not an individualistic concept; it is deeply rooted in community. We are not transformed in isolation but as part of the body of Christ. Ephesians 4:15-16 (TPT) describes how this new humanity grows together: "But instead, we will remain strong and always sincere in our love as we express the truth. All our direction and ministries will flow from Christ and lead us deeper into Him, the anointed Head of His body, the church. For His 'body' has been formed in His image and is closely joined together and constantly connected as one. And every member has been given divine gifts to contribute to the growth of all."

This passage highlights the importance of community in the life of the new humanity. We are joined together as members of one body, with Christ as the head. Each of us has been given unique gifts and abilities that are meant to serve and build up the body of Christ. As we live in community, we are called to encourage, support, and challenge one another, helping each other grow into the fullness of Christ.

The community of the new humanity is also a witness to the world. Jesus said in John 13:35 (TPT), "For when you demonstrate the same love I have for you by loving one another, everyone will know that you're My true followers." The way we love and care for one another in the body of Christ is a powerful testimony to the world of the transforming power of the gospel.

The New Humanity and the World: Agents of God's Kingdom

As part of the new humanity, we are not only called to live differently within the church but also to impact the world around us. Jesus prayed in John 17:18 (TPT), "I have commissioned them to represent Me just as You commissioned Me to represent You." We are sent into the world as representatives of Christ, carrying the message of His kingdom and demonstrating His love, justice, and truth.

This means that the new humanity is not passive or withdrawn from the world. Instead, we are called to engage with the world, bringing the light of Christ into every sphere of life—our families, workplaces, communities, and nations. We are agents of God's kingdom, working for the restoration and renewal of all things, as we anticipate the day when Jesus will return to fully establish His reign on earth.

Conclusion: Living in the Fullness of the New Humanity

The new humanity represents the fulfilment of God's plan for creation—a people who are restored to His image, filled with His Spirit, and living in perfect relationship with Him and one another. As part of the new humanity, we are called to embrace our new identity, live out our God-given purpose, and participate in the building of Christ's body and the advancement of His kingdom.

This new reality is both a present experience and a future hope. We live now as new creations, empowered by the Holy Spirit, while we look forward to the day when the fullness of the new humanity will be revealed in the new heaven and new earth. Until that day, we are called to live as ambassadors of God's kingdom, reflecting His love, grace, and truth to a world in need of redemption.

The journey of the new humanity is one of ongoing transformation, as we grow deeper in our relationship with Christ, walk in the power of the Spirit, and engage with the world in ways that bring healing, justice, and hope. It is a journey that leads to the ultimate fulfilment of God's purpose for humanity—a people fully united with Him, living in the joy and freedom of His kingdom forever.

Chapter 32

Heaven and Earth United

The culmination of God's redemptive plan is the unification of heaven and earth—a reality where God's presence fully dwells among His people, and the spiritual and physical realms are seamlessly integrated. This unification marks the fulfilment of God's eternal purpose to reconcile all things to Himself through Christ. In this chapter, we explore the biblical vision of heaven and earth becoming one, the implications of this union for creation, and how this glorious future shapes our understanding of eternity and our lives today.

The merging of heaven and earth is not merely a distant, ethereal event; it is the ultimate realization of God's kingdom, where the beauty, love, and order of heaven flood the renewed earth. This chapter will unpack the significance of this unity and how it transforms the future of all creation, from human beings to the cosmos itself.

The New Jerusalem: God Dwelling with Humanity

Revelation 21 presents a vivid picture of the union between heaven and earth. In verses 1-3 (TPT), the apostle John writes, "Then in a vision I saw a new heaven and a new earth. The first heaven and earth had passed away, and the sea no longer existed. I saw the holy city, the New Jerusalem, descending out of the heavenly realm from the presence of God, like a pleasing bride that had been prepared for her husband, adorned for her wedding. And I heard a thunderous voice from the throne, saying: 'Look! God's tabernacle is with human beings, and from now on He will tabernacle with them as their God.'"

The New Jerusalem represents the central point where heaven and earth meet, where the spiritual reality of God's presence is made fully manifest in the physical world. In this city, God's dwelling place is no longer distant or separated from His people; instead, He lives directly among them. This fulfils the deepest longing of humanity, which has always been for communion with God, and restores the intimate relationship that was lost at the fall.

The imagery of the New Jerusalem as a bride adorned for her husband also emphasizes the beauty, purity, and perfection of this union. It speaks to the covenant relationship between God and His people, now fully realized and eternally secure. Just as a bride and groom come together in perfect unity, so too will heaven and earth be united in God's eternal kingdom.

The new heaven and new earth are not simply replacements for the old creation; they represent the complete renewal and transformation of all things. The old order, with its pain, suffering, and sin, will have passed away, and God will make all things new (Revelation 21:5, TPT). This marks the beginning of a new age where heaven's reality becomes fully integrated with the material world.

The Union of Heaven and Earth: Restoring the Original Design

The unification of heaven and earth represents the restoration of God's original design for creation. In the beginning, God created the heavens and the earth as a harmonious, interconnected reality, with humanity serving as the bridge between the spiritual and physical realms. Genesis 1:27-28 (TPT) explains that God created human beings in His image and gave them authority to "be fruitful, multiply, and fill the earth and subdue it." Humanity's role was to exercise dominion over the earth while living in perfect fellowship with God, reflecting His rule and presence throughout creation.

However, the fall disrupted this harmony. Sin brought separation between humanity and God, leading to brokenness in both the spiritual and physical realms. The earth became subject to decay and suffering, and humanity was cut off from the fullness of God's presence. As a result, heaven and earth were no longer in perfect alignment.

But through Jesus Christ, God's plan of redemption is to restore this original design. Colossians 1:20 (TPT) declares, "And by the blood of His cross, everything in heaven and earth is brought back to Himself—back to its original intent, restored to innocence again!" This passage highlights that Jesus' sacrifice on the cross not only reconciles humanity to God but also brings all of creation—both heaven and earth—back into alignment with God's purpose.

The future union of heaven and earth is the final step in this restoration process. It is the moment when all things are brought under the reign of Christ, and the separation between the spiritual and physical realms is eliminated. Ephesians 1:10 (TPT) reveals that God's ultimate plan is "to bring everything together under the authority of Christ—everything in heaven and on earth." This means that the entire cosmos will be united under Christ's lordship, and His kingdom will be established on earth as it is in heaven.

Visual 32.1 depicts the Garden of Eden restored, with humans, animals, and nature flourishing in perfect harmony, symbolizing the original design of creation restored.

Visual 32.1: Garden of Eden restored, with humans, animals, and nature flourishing in perfect harmony, symbolizing the restored original design of creation.
(**Source:** image of Garden of Eden restored, with humans, animals - Search Images)

As heaven and earth are united, harmony fills every aspect of creation, bringing life into perfect alignment with God's will. The Sidebar expands on this vision of a restored earth, where peace and life flourish under God's presence.

Sidebar: The Restored Earth - Life in Harmony

Throughout Scripture, we see visions of a restored earth, where all of creation lives in harmony under God's reign. Isaiah 11:6 describes a time when "the wolf will live with the lamb, the leopard will lie down with the goat," a profound image of peace extending throughout the animal kingdom. This peace reflects changed hearts and renewed relationships, as humanity and creation are restored to their original, God-given purpose.

Isaiah 35:1-2 speaks of "the desert and the parched land" rejoicing, with "the wilderness blossoming like the crocus." God's presence brings life to the barren places, making rivers flow in the desert (Isaiah 35:6), transforming creation so that His glory is displayed everywhere. This vision of restoration also includes Micah 4:3-4, which foretells a time when "swords will be beaten into plowshares" and "no one will make them afraid," as nations live together peacefully.

In this renewed world, God's glory fills the earth (Habakkuk 2:14), and creation itself is liberated from decay and brokenness (Romans 8:21). As sons and daughters of God, we are called to participate in this restoration, spreading His peace and life throughout the world. This promise is not only a future hope but also an invitation for us to begin living out God's vision of harmony, justice, and love here and now.

The restored earth reflects God's heart for wholeness and unity in all things. Through changed hearts and renewed minds, we step into His purpose, engaging with creation and one another in ways that reveal God's love, beauty, and glory. This vision reminds us that we are part of a greater story, one where God's presence renews everything, making earth a place of life, peace, and flourishing for all.

The Implications of Heaven and Earth United

The union of heaven and earth carries profound implications for creation and for humanity's future. First, it means that the physical world will not be discarded or destroyed; rather, it will be redeemed and transformed. The material creation is good—it was created by God and declared "very good" (Genesis 1:31, TPT). The future of creation is not one of abandonment but of renewal, where the earth will be freed from its bondage to decay and restored to its full glory.

Romans 8:19-21 (TPT) describes this cosmic restoration: "The entire universe is standing on tiptoe, yearning to see the unveiling of God's glorious sons and daughters! For against its will, the universe itself has had to endure the empty futility resulting from the consequences of human sin. But now, with eager expectation, all creation longs for freedom from its slavery to decay and to experience with us the wonderful freedom coming to God's children."

In this renewed creation, the curse of sin will be completely lifted. There will be no more death, suffering, or disease. The earth itself will be restored to its original beauty and vitality, and humanity will live in perfect harmony with creation. This is the fulfillment of God's promise to make all things new.

Second, the unification of heaven and earth means that God's presence will no longer be mediated through temples, rituals, or symbols. Instead, His presence will be immediate and tangible, permeating every aspect of life. Revelation 21:22-24 (TPT) states, "I saw no temple in the city, for its temple is the Lord God, the Almighty, and the Lamb. The city has no need for the sun or moon to shine on it, because the glory of God illuminates it and its lamp is the Lamb."

This direct experience of God's presence will bring complete joy, fulfillment, and peace. There will be no more need for sacrifices, intercessions, or intermediaries because we will dwell in perfect communion with God, face to face. Revelation 22:3-4 (TPT) proclaims, "The throne of God and of the Lamb will be in the city, and His servants will serve and worship Him. They will see His face, and His name will be written on their foreheads."

Finally, the union of heaven and earth means that humanity's role as stewards of creation will be fully restored. In the new earth, we will exercise dominion in partnership with God, not through exploitation or harm, but through wisdom, care, and love. Our work will be meaningful and fulfilling, as we cultivate and enjoy the beauty of the renewed creation in perfect harmony with God's will.

Living in Anticipation of Heaven and Earth United

The promise of heaven and earth united shapes the way we live today. While we await the full realization of this future, we are called to live in anticipation of it, bringing glimpses of heaven's reality into the present world. Jesus taught His disciples to pray, "Your kingdom come, Your will be done, on earth as it is in heaven" (Matthew 6:10, TPT), inviting us to participate in the work of advancing God's kingdom now.

As believers, we are called to live as citizens of heaven (Philippians 3:20, TPT) while engaging with the world around us. This means living in a way that reflects the values of God's kingdom—love, justice, mercy, and peace—while also caring for creation, working for the flourishing of our communities, and seeking reconciliation in our relationships.

The union of heaven and earth also gives us hope in the face of suffering and brokenness. The world we live in is marked by pain, injustice, and decay, but we know that this is not the end of the story. The promise of a renewed creation gives us strength to endure, knowing that God will one day make all things right.

Visual 32.2 illustrates the concept of bringing heaven to earth, depicting a scene where divine light touches and transforms the physical world, symbolizing the infusion of God's presence, peace, and righteousness into earthly life.

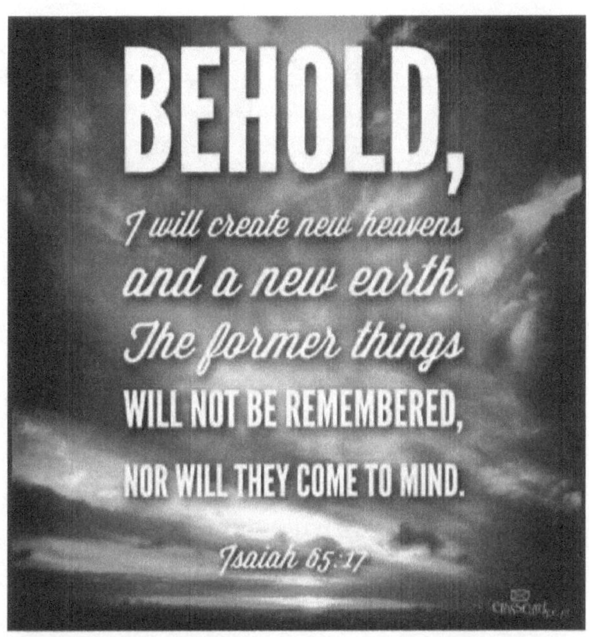

Visual 32.2: Bringing heaven to earth.
(**Source:** <u>image of bringing glimpses of heaven to earth - Search Images</u>)

Conclusion: The Eternal Reality of Heaven and Earth United

The union of heaven and earth is the ultimate fulfilment of God's redemptive plan, where the separation between the spiritual and physical realms is forever removed, and all things are brought into perfect harmony under Christ's rule. This new reality marks the beginning of eternal life in God's presence, where His glory fills the earth, and His people live in unending joy, peace, and communion with Him.

For believers, the promise of heaven and earth united is our greatest hope and the foundation of our faith. It reminds us that God's plan is not just to save individual souls but to redeem and restore all of creation. As we live in anticipation of this future, we are called to participate in God's work of restoration, bringing the values of His kingdom into the present world.

This vision of heaven and earth united invites us to live with purpose, hope, and joy, knowing that the best is yet to come—that one day, we will dwell with God forever in the renewed creation, where heaven and earth are one.

Chapter 33

Love's Final Victory

The story of God's redemptive work culminates in one ultimate, triumphant reality: Love's final victory. From the beginning of time, the essence of God's nature has been love, and this divine love has driven His plan to reconcile, restore, and renew all things. In this chapter, we explore the profound truth that, in the end, love conquers all. Every force that stands in opposition to God—sin, death, evil, and separation—will be vanquished, and the eternal reign of God's love will encompass all creation.

Love's final victory is not merely a sentimental conclusion but the fulfilment of the deepest truths of Scripture. It is the revelation of God's heart and the purpose for which all things were created. As we explore this victory of love, we will see how it transforms eternity and how it speaks to us today, giving us hope, purpose, and a clear understanding of God's character and intentions.

God is Love: The Source of All Things

The Bible repeatedly declares that God is love. This truth is central to our understanding of His nature and His plan for humanity. 1 John 4:8 (TPT) says, "The one who doesn't love has yet to know God, for God is love." This means that everything God does—His creation, redemption, and restoration—is motivated by love.

God's love is not a passive or abstract emotion; it is an active, self-giving force that seeks the good of others. His love is most fully revealed in the person of Jesus Christ, whose life, death, and resurrection demonstrate the lengths to which God will go to bring humanity back into relationship with Him. John 3:16 (TPT) expresses this love beautifully: "For this is how much God loved the world—He gave His one and only, unique Son as a gift. So now everyone who believes in Him will never perish but experience everlasting life."

From the very beginning, God's love has been the foundation of His relationship with humanity. He created us in His image, designed for fellowship and communion with Him. But even when sin entered the world and broke that fellowship, God's love did not waver. He set in motion a plan to redeem and restore all things, culminating in the cross, where Jesus gave His life as the ultimate expression of divine love. Romans 5:8 (TPT) proclaims, "But Christ proved God's passionate love for us by dying in our place while we were still lost and ungodly!"

The final victory of love is the fulfilment of this redemptive plan. It is the moment when everything that opposes love—sin, death, and evil—is finally defeated, and God's love reigns supreme in all creation.

Visual 33.1 shows Jesus on the cross—the passion of Christ, love's ultimate sacrifice—pointing toward the final victory of love.

Visual 33.1: Jesus on the cross, the passion of Christ. (**Source:** image of Jesus on the cross - Search Images)

The Defeat of Sin and Death: Love's Conquest

The central enemies of God's love are sin and death. These forces entered the world through the fall of humanity and have plagued creation ever since. Sin, with its corrupting influence, separates humanity from God, while death is the ultimate consequence of sin, representing the final barrier between God and His people.

But the victory of love is most powerfully demonstrated in Jesus' triumph over both sin and death. Through His death on the cross, Jesus took upon Himself the full weight of sin, offering Himself as a sacrifice to restore humanity's broken relationship with God. His resurrection from the dead three days later is the ultimate declaration of love's victory over death.

1 Corinthians 15:54-57 (TPT) proclaims this victory: "And when that which is mortal puts on immortality, then the Scripture will be fulfilled that says: Death is swallowed up by a triumphant victory! So death, tell me, where is your victory? Tell me, death, where is your sting? It is sin that gives death its sting, and the law that gives sin its power. But we thank God for giving us the victory as conquerors through our Lord Jesus, the Anointed One!"

Through the resurrection, Jesus defeated the power of death, and His victory guarantees the eventual resurrection of all who are in Him. Death, the final enemy, will be destroyed completely. Revelation 20:14 (TPT) foretells this: "Then death and the unseen world were thrown into the lake of fire. This is the second death—the lake of fire." In the new heaven and new earth, death will no longer exist. The victory of God's love will be total and complete, leaving no room for death, decay, or suffering.

Sin, too, will be eradicated. The power of sin to corrupt and separate will be utterly broken in the new creation. As God's love fills every corner of the universe, sin's destructive influence will be a thing of the past. Revelation 21:27 (TPT) assures us that in the New Jerusalem, "Nothing evil will be allowed to enter—no one who practices shameful idolatry and dishonesty— but only those whose names are written in the Lamb's Book of Life."

This defeat of sin and death is not just a theological concept; it is the heart of God's plan for the world. His love is so powerful that it will not stop until every last vestige of sin and death is removed, and His people are fully restored to life and righteousness.

Visual 33.2 shows an empty tomb, symbolizing the resurrection and love's triumph over sin and death.

Visual 33.2: An empty tomb, symbolizing the resurrection and love's victory over sin and death.
(Source: image of An empty tomb, symbolizing the resurrection and love's victory over sin and death. - Search Images)

Evil Overcome: The End of Opposition to Love

Beyond sin and death, God's love will also triumph over all forms of evil. Throughout history, forces of evil have sought to oppose God's purposes, bringing destruction, pain, and suffering to humanity. But the Bible assures us that in the end, all these forces will be vanquished by the power of God's love.

Revelation 20:10 (TPT) describes the ultimate fate of evil: "Then the devil who had deceived them was thrown into the same place with the wild beast and the false prophet—the lake of fire and sulfur—where they will be tormented (refined, purified) day and night forever and ever." This passage reveals that the devil, the originator of evil and rebellion against God, will be permanently defeated. His schemes to destroy, deceive, and oppose God's love will come to an end, and he will no longer have any influence over creation.

The victory of love is also the victory of justice. Every wrong will be made right, every injustice will be addressed, and every tear will be wiped away. Revelation 21:4 (TPT) promises, "He will wipe away every tear from their eyes and eliminate death entirely. No one will mourn or weep any longer. The pain of wounds will no longer exist, for the old order has ceased."

In this new reality, where God's love reigns supreme, there will be no more war, violence, or oppression. Isaiah 2:4 (TPT) gives a glimpse of this future: "He will judge fairly between the nations and settle disputes among many peoples. They will beat their swords into plowshares and their spears into pruning hooks. Nation will not take up sword against nation, nor will they train for war anymore."

Love's final victory means that every force of evil—whether spiritual or human—will be overthrown. The new creation will be a place of perfect peace, righteousness, and justice, where God's love is the governing reality.

Visual 33.3 shows a man beating a sword into a plowshare, symbolizing the end of war and the triumph of love and peace.

Visual 33.3: Beating sword into a plowshare, symbolizing the end of war and the triumph of love and peace.
(**Source:** image of sword being beaten into a plowshare - Search Images)

The final victory of God's love encompasses the restoration and reconciliation of all creation. The Sidebar explores the vast scope of this reconciliation, showing how God's love restores all things to Himself.

Sidebar: Restoring All Things - The Scope of Reconciliation

The Bible speaks of God's all-encompassing love and desire to reconcile all things through Christ. Colossians 1:20 tells us that God has reconciled "all things, whether on earth or in heaven," through Jesus' work on the cross. This includes every created being—humans, as well as spiritual beings. Even though the actions of fallen angels and demonic forces have led to immense suffering, God's forgiveness and reconciliation in Christ encompass everything.

In Jesus, God has forgiven sins—whether great or small, past or future. Jesus said, "As I have forgiven you, you must forgive others" (Matthew 6:14-15), showing that the heart of God's forgiveness knows no bounds. This raises profound questions: If God has forgiven us, can we forgive even those who have caused great harm? Paul writes in 1 Corinthians 6:3, "Do you not know that we will judge angels?" suggesting a future role for believers in discerning and engaging with spiritual beings.

God's restorative judgment isn't about punishment but about healing and bringing beings back to their intended wholeness. Could it be that, as believers judge, they will reflect God's own heart of restoration, even toward fallen angels? The Bible describes God's refining fire (Malachi 3:2, Revelation 20:14-15) as a force that purifies and restores. Might this also extend to beings who, like humans, have gone astray?

If God's goal is to reconcile all of creation, then even spiritual enemies could one day be transformed, becoming allies in the restoration of all things. Romans 8:21 speaks of creation "waiting eagerly for the revelation of the sons of God," suggesting that as we fulfill our roles as coheirs with Christ, we may extend God's redemptive work to every corner of creation—including to the spiritual forces that once opposed God's purposes. This vision of turning foes into friends challenges us to rethink forgiveness, judgment, and the ultimate reach of God's love.

The New Creation: A World of Love

With the final victory of love, the new creation will emerge as a place where God's love is fully realized in every aspect of life. The new heaven and new earth will be marked by the complete absence of sin, death, evil, and suffering. In their place, the perfect love of God will reign, creating an environment of eternal joy, peace, and flourishing.

Revelation 21:1-3 (TPT) gives us a vision of this new creation: "Then in a vision I saw a new heaven and a new earth. The first heaven and earth had passed away, and the sea no longer existed. I saw the holy city, the New Jerusalem, descending out of the heavenly realm from the presence of God, like a pleasing bride that had been prepared for her husband, adorned for her wedding. And I heard a thunderous voice from the throne, saying: 'Look! God's tabernacle is with human beings, and from now on He will tabernacle with them as their God.'"

The new creation will be a place of perfect communion between God and humanity, where love is the defining reality. The unity between heaven and earth will reflect the unity of God's love with His people. This love will not only fill the hearts of individuals but will also shape the culture, environment, and relationships in the new creation.

Every relationship will be characterized by love—love for God and love for one another. There will be no more division, hatred, or jealousy. Instead, the new creation will be a place of perfect harmony, where every person is valued and honored, and where the love of God flows freely through every interaction.

Living in the Light of Love's Victory

Although the final victory of love is a future event, it has profound implications for how we live today. As followers of Christ, we are called to live in the light of this victory, embodying God's love in our daily lives and advancing His kingdom on earth.

Jesus said in John 13:35 (TPT), "For when you demonstrate the same love I have for you by loving one another, everyone will know that you're My true followers." Our lives should be a reflection of the love that will one day reign in all creation. We are called to love our enemies, to seek reconciliation, and to pursue justice, knowing that these actions are a foretaste of the ultimate victory of love.

Moreover, the victory of love gives us hope in the face of suffering and injustice. We know that no matter how dark the world may seem, God's love will prevail. This hope sustains us in difficult times and empowers us to be agents of love and healing in a broken world.

Visual 33.4 shows people loving and serving one another, reflecting the reality of God's love on earth and pointing toward love's final victory.

Visual 33.4: People loving and serving one another, reflecting the reality of God's love on earth, pointing toward love's final victory.
(**Source:** <u>image of believers loving and serving one another -Search Images</u>)

Conclusion: The Eternal Reign of Love

Love's final victory is the heart of God's redemptive plan. It is the triumph of His nature, His will, and His purpose. In the end, every enemy of love—sin, death, evil, and suffering—will be defeated, and God's love will reign forever in the new creation. This victory is the fulfilment of the gospel and the hope that sustains us as we journey through life.

As we look forward to the day when God's love fills every corner of the universe, we are invited to live in that love now. We are called to be carriers of His love, bringing healing, peace, and reconciliation to a world that desperately needs it. And we do so with the assurance that, in the end, love will win.

God's love will have the final word, and His kingdom
will be an eternal kingdom of love, joy, and peace.

Chapter 34

The Eternal Purpose Fulfilled

As we approach the conclusion of God's redemptive story, we see the unfolding of His eternal purpose: the reconciliation of all things to Himself through Christ. The fulfilment of God's plan is more than the restoration of humanity or creation; it is the complete and perfect realization of His divine will, in which His glory fills all things, and His love reigns without end. In this chapter, we explore the final fulfilment of God's eternal purpose, what it means for creation, humanity, and God Himself, and how this ultimate reality invites us to live with purpose and anticipation.

God's eternal purpose is vast, stretching beyond human understanding, encompassing every facet of creation, and uniting all things in Christ. From before the foundation of the world, God's plan has been to create a family, a people who would share in His love, reflect His glory, and participate in His reign. The fulfilment of this purpose brings history to its ultimate conclusion, where God's perfect plan is realized in every way.

God's Eternal Purpose: Uniting All Things in Christ

At the heart of God's eternal purpose is His desire to unite all things in Christ. Ephesians 1:9-10 (TPT) captures this grand vision: "And through the revelation of the Anointed One, He unveiled His secret desires to us—the hidden mystery of His long-range plan, which He was delighted to implement from the very beginning of time. And because of God's unfailing purpose, this detailed plan will reign supreme through every period of time until the fulfilment of all the ages finally reaches its climax—when God makes all things new in all of heaven and earth through Jesus Christ."

God's plan was never just about redeeming individual souls; it has always been about the cosmic reconciliation of all things, both in heaven and on earth. Through Jesus, God is bringing together the spiritual and the physical, the seen and the unseen, into perfect harmony. This unity is not merely a return to the way things were in Eden; it is the consummation of God's original design, now elevated and perfected in Christ.

The purpose of uniting all things in Christ includes restoring broken relationships, healing the physical world, and bringing justice to all creation. Colossians 1:19-20 (TPT) affirms this cosmic scope: "For God is satisfied to have all His fullness dwelling in Christ. And by the blood of His cross, everything in heaven and earth is brought back to Himself—back to its original intent, restored to innocence again!" Christ is the center of this eternal purpose, and in Him, every dimension of creation finds its true meaning and fulfilment.

Visual 34.1: Christ at the center of the universe, symbolizing the uniting of all things in heaven and earth.

Visual 34.1: Christ at the center of the universe, symbolizing the uniting of all things in heaven and earth.
(**Source:** image of Christ at the center of the universe - Search Images)

The Revelation of God's Glory: Filling All Things

The fulfilment of God's eternal purpose also means the full revelation of His glory throughout creation. From the very beginning, God's desire has been to fill the earth with His glory, and the final outcome of His redemptive plan is the complete saturation of all things with His presence, His character, and His love.

Habakkuk 2:14 (TPT) prophesies this glorious reality: "But the time is coming when the earth shall be filled with the knowledge of the glory of the Lord, as the waters cover the sea." This means that every part of creation—every atom, every creature, every human being—will be fully immersed in the beauty and power of God's glory. There will be no place untouched by His presence.

The glory of God is not merely a display of His majesty or power; it is the expression of His nature—His goodness, love, holiness, and truth. In the new heaven and new earth, God's glory will be the atmosphere in which all things exist. Revelation 21:23-24 (TPT) describes this reality: "The city has no need for the sun or moon to shine, for the glory of God is its light, and its lamp is the Lamb! The people will walk by its light and the kings of the earth will bring their wealth into it."

This light of God's glory is not just physical illumination but the spiritual and relational fullness of knowing and experiencing God without any barriers. The fulfilment of God's purpose is, therefore, the revelation of His glory in its entirety, where every person and every part of creation reflects His beauty and love.

Visual 34.2 depicts the new heaven and new earth, with light emanating from God's throne, filling all of creation with His glory.

Visual 34.2: New heaven and new earth, with light emanating from God's throne, filling every part of creation with His glory.
(**Source:** image of new heaven and new earth - Search Images)

The Role of Humanity: Sons and Daughters in the Eternal Kingdom

Part of the fulfilment of God's eternal purpose is the role that redeemed humanity will play in His kingdom. From the beginning, God created humanity in His image, with the intention that we would share in His reign over creation as sons and daughters. This calling is fully realized in the new heaven and new earth, where we will live as co-heirs with Christ, participating in His eternal reign.

Romans 8:29-30 (TPT) reveals God's ultimate goal for humanity: "For He knew all about us before we were born, and He destined us from the beginning to share the likeness of His Son. This means the Son is the oldest among a vast family of brothers and sisters who will become just like Him. Having determined our destiny ahead of time, He called us to Himself and transferred His perfect righteousness to everyone He called."

In the new creation, we will finally be fully conformed to the image of Christ, living in perfect righteousness, holiness, and love. This transformation is not only spiritual but also physical, as we receive glorified bodies, free from sin, decay, and death. 1 Corinthians 15:49 (TPT) promises, "Once we carried the likeness of the man of dust, but now let us carry the likeness of the Man of heaven."

As sons and daughters in God's kingdom, we will reign with Christ. Revelation 22:5 (TPT) declares, "Night will be no more. They will never need the light of the sun or a lamp, because the Lord God will shine on them. And they will reign as kings forever and ever!" This reign is not one of domination or exploitation but of stewardship, love, and service, reflecting the character of God Himself. In the fulfilment of God's purpose, humanity will fulfil its original calling to rule over creation in partnership with God, bringing out the full potential of His creation in harmony with His will.

Visual 34.3 depicts glorified, transfigured humanity reigning with Christ over a restored and flourishing creation, symbolizing the fulfilment of our calling as sons and daughters of God.

Visual 34.3: Glorified humanity, reigning with Christ over a restored and flourishing creation, symbolizing the fulfilment of our calling as sons and daughters of God.
(**Source:** <u>image of transfigured humanity, reigning with Christ - Search Images</u>)

The New Creation: Heaven and Earth United in Perfection

The eternal purpose of God finds its ultimate fulfilment in the new creation, where heaven and earth are united, and God's kingdom is fully established. This new creation is the final realization of God's promise to restore and renew all things. Revelation 21:1-3 (TPT) describes this perfect reality: "Then in a vision I saw a new heaven and a new earth. The first heaven and earth had passed away, and the sea no longer existed. I saw the holy city, the New Jerusalem, descending out of the heavenly realm from the presence of God, like a pleasing bride that had been prepared for her husband, adorned for her wedding."

This new creation is not a return to Eden; it is something greater, where the spiritual and physical realms are united, and God's presence dwells permanently with His people. The "New Jerusalem" symbolizes the perfect relationship between God and humanity, where there is no separation, no sin, and no death. This is the ultimate fulfilment of God's purpose—to dwell among His people, to share His glory, and to reign with them forever.

Revelation 21:4 (TPT) assures us that in this new creation, "He will wipe away every tear from their eyes and eliminate death entirely. No one will mourn or weep any longer. The pain of wounds will no longer exist, for the old order has ceased." The fulfillment of God's eternal purpose brings an end to all suffering, pain, and death, and ushers in an era of eternal joy, peace, and life.

This new creation is also a place of unimaginable beauty, where creation itself is renewed and glorified. Romans 8:21 (TPT) speaks of this transformation: "Creation itself will be set free from its bondage to decay and experience the glorious freedom of God's children." In the new creation, all things—humanity, animals, nature, and the cosmos—will reflect the perfect order, peace, and harmony of God's kingdom.

Living in the Fulfilment of God's Eternal Purpose

As we live in the present, the knowledge of God's eternal purpose shapes the way we view our lives and the world around us. The fulfilment of God's plan is not just a distant future event; it is something that we are invited to participate in today. Through Christ, we are already part of this eternal kingdom, and we are called to live as citizens of this new creation, even in the midst of a fallen world.

Philippians 3:20 (TPT) reminds us, "But we are a colony of heaven on earth as we cling tightly to our life-giver, the Lord Jesus Christ." This means that we are to live out the values of God's kingdom—love, justice, peace, and mercy—here and now, as we anticipate the full realization of His eternal purpose.

Our lives are part of a much larger story, one that stretches from before the foundation of the world to the fulfilment of all things in Christ. As we live with this eternal perspective, we are empowered to face the challenges and struggles of this world with hope, knowing that God's purpose will prevail, and that we have an eternal inheritance in His kingdom.

As God's eternal purpose is fulfilled, we see that separation from Him was never His desire. The Sidebar expands on this union, illustrating how God's purpose brings us into complete oneness with Him.

The idea of separation between God and humanity is a misunderstanding. While sin has caused alienation in humanity's mind (Colossians 1:21, Isaiah 59:2), God has never turned away from us. From the very beginning, when Adam sinned, it was God who sought him out, demonstrating His desire to remain close. This separation exists only in our perception, not in reality.

In John 14 and 17, Jesus describes a profound union, saying, "I am in the Father, and you are in Me, and I am in you." This divine relationship is not one of distance, but of oneness and inclusion. Acts 17:28 affirms this, declaring that "in Him we live, move, and have our being." God is not a distant deity, but One who is fully present within us, sustaining and filling all things.

The apostle Paul expresses this reality in Galatians 1:16, when he says that God "revealed His Son in me," emphasizing the inner presence of Christ. As believers, we are the temple of God; His Spirit dwells in us continually. God is not in some far-off place, waiting for us to reach Him. He is closer than we can imagine, residing in our hearts, fully engaged with our lives here and now.

This intimate union means that God is not a distant future hope, but a present reality. Any belief that God is "not here, not now, not me" is a misconception. God's nearness, as both Creator and Redeemer, assures us that He is always with us, dwelling in us as a source of love, strength, and purpose. The truth of our union with Him means we are never separated, but fully embraced in His presence.

Conclusion: The Eternal Purpose Fulfilled

The fulfilment of God's eternal purpose is the grand conclusion to the story of redemption. It is the realization of His desire to unite all things in Christ, to reveal His glory in all creation, and to establish His eternal kingdom where His people reign with Him in perfect harmony. This is the ultimate destiny of the universe—a new creation where heaven and earth are united, where love, peace, and joy abound, and where God's presence fills all things.

As we look forward to this glorious future, we are invited to live in the light of this purpose, embracing our identity as sons and daughters of God, and participating in His kingdom work today. The fulfilment of God's purpose is not just an end; it is the beginning of an eternal relationship with God, where we will experience His love, His glory, and His joy forever.

This is the hope that sustains us, the vision that guides us, and the purpose that defines us. God's eternal purpose will be fulfilled, and we will share in His glory forever.

Chapter 35

Beyond Glory

In this final chapter, we explore the mystery that lies "beyond glory." After the fulfilment of God's eternal purpose, after the unification of heaven and earth, and after love's final victory, what comes next? The concept of eternity is difficult for the human mind to grasp, and yet Scripture gives us glimpses of what lies beyond—an eternal unfolding of life, love, and fellowship with God. In this chapter, we reflect on the eternal journey that awaits us in the new creation and how it points to a future filled with limitless discovery, joy, and communion with our Creator.

While the Bible provides many details about the new heaven and new earth, the nature of eternity itself is something that is not fully revealed. What we do know is that eternity with God will be an unending experience of His glory, love, and presence. We will explore what this means, drawing from biblical truths and the grand narrative of God's plan, as we look forward to an eternity where God's people will continually grow in their knowledge of Him and where His love and glory will be forever expanding.

The Limitlessness of God: Infinite Discovery

One of the most profound truths about eternity is that it is not a static existence but an ever-deepening journey into the heart of God. God is infinite—His love, His wisdom, and His glory are boundless. Even in the new creation, we will never reach the limits of who God is. Instead, eternity will be a time of continual discovery, where we experience more and more of God's character, His creation, and His purposes.

Ephesians 2:6-7 (TPT) gives us a glimpse of this eternal unfolding: "He raised us up with Christ the exalted One, and we ascended with Him into the glorious perfection and authority of the heavenly realm, for we are now co-seated as one with Christ! Throughout the coming ages we will be the visible display of the infinite riches of His grace and kindness, which was showered upon us in Jesus Christ."

This passage suggests that throughout the "coming ages"—in other words, for all of eternity—God will continue to reveal the "infinite riches of His grace and kindness." This indicates that eternity is not a static state of existence but a dynamic, ongoing revelation of God's goodness and love. Each new moment will bring fresh experiences of His glory, deeper understanding of His ways, and greater joy in His presence.

The idea of infinite discovery also extends to our relationship with creation. The new heaven and new earth will be a place of unending beauty and wonder, where we can explore the vastness of God's renewed universe. As redeemed sons and daughters of God, we will have the privilege of engaging with creation in ways we can only begin to imagine—discovering its mysteries, cultivating its potential, and enjoying its glory, all in perfect harmony with God's purposes.

Visual 35.1 depicts the new creation, symbolizing the eternal unfolding of God's glory.

Visual 35.1: New creation, symbolizing the eternal unfolding of God's glory.
(**Source:** image of new creation reality - Search Images)

Eternal Fellowship with God: Love Without End

At the heart of eternity is our relationship with God. The ultimate reward of eternal life is not merely the absence of suffering or the presence of physical beauty, but the unending fellowship we will have with our Creator. Revelation 22:4-5 (TPT) declares, "They will see His face, and His name will be on their foreheads. Night will be no more, and they will need no light of lamp or sun, for the Lord God will shine on them, and they will reign forever and ever."

To see God's face is the ultimate fulfilment of human longing. Throughout Scripture, the greatest desire of God's people has been to dwell in His presence, to behold

His glory, and to experience His love firsthand. In the new creation, this desire will be fully realized. We will see God face to face, living in unbroken communion with Him for all eternity.

But this eternal fellowship is not a static relationship. Just as God is infinite, our relationship with Him will continually grow and deepen throughout eternity. We will never exhaust the depths of His love or the richness of His character. Instead, we will move from glory to glory, always discovering more of His beauty and more of His heart.

1 Corinthians 13:12 (TPT) gives us a hint of this future reality: "For now we see but a faint reflection of riddles and mysteries, as though reflected in a mirror, but one day we will see face-to-face. My understanding is incomplete now, but one day I will understand everything, just as everything about me has been fully understood."

This verse reminds us that, even in eternity, we will be learning and growing in our understanding of God. Our knowledge of Him will continually expand, and our love for Him will grow deeper with each passing moment. Eternity will be a never-ending journey into the fullness of God's love—a journey that brings unimaginable joy and fulfilment.

The Joy of Perfect Community: Life in Eternal Harmony

Eternity will also be marked by perfect community—both with God and with one another. The new creation is not only a place of individual communion with God but also a place of shared life and fellowship with the entire family of God. Revelation 7:9 (TPT) paints a picture of this eternal community: "After this I looked, and behold, a vast multitude that no one could number, from every nation, from all tribes and peoples and languages, standing before the throne and before the Lamb, clothed in white robes, with palm branches in their hands."

This vision shows people from every tribe, language, and nation united in worship and love before the throne of God. In eternity, all divisions, conflicts, and misunderstandings will be healed. We will live in perfect harmony with one another, enjoying relationships that are free from jealousy, fear, and strife. The love of God will flow through every relationship, creating a community where each person is fully known, fully valued, and fully loved.

This perfect community extends beyond human relationships. The new creation is a place where all of creation is in harmony—where animals, nature, and humans live together in peace. Isaiah 11:6-9 (TPT) describes this harmony: "The wolf will dwell with the lamb, the leopard will lie down with the young goat, and the calf and the lion and the fattened calf together, and a little child will lead them. The cow and the bear shall graze; their young shall lie down together; and the lion shall eat straw like the ox... They shall not hurt or destroy in all My holy mountain."

This vision of peace extends to every part of creation. In eternity, all things will be reconciled and restored, and we will live in a world where love governs every relationship, every action, and every moment.

Visual 35.2 depicts people from every nation and tribe standing together in joyful worship, symbolizing the perfect community of the new creation.

Visual 35.2: People from every nation and tribe standing together in joyful worship, symbolizing the perfect community of the new creation.
(**Source:** people from every nation and tribe standing together in joyful worship - Search Images)

Beyond Glory: Eternal Purpose and Adventure

What lies beyond glory? Eternity with God is not an end; it is a beginning—a journey that stretches beyond time and space, where we will continually discover new aspects of God's character, His creation, and His plans for the universe. The glory of eternity is not a static reward but an ongoing adventure into the limitless possibilities of life with God.

As sons and daughters of God, we will not only dwell in His presence but also participate in His ongoing creative work. 2 Timothy 2:12 (TPT) promises, "If we endure, we will also reign with Him." This reign is not about power or control but about stewardship, creativity, and participation in God's purposes. We will be co-creators with God, exploring the vastness of His renewed universe and bringing forth the full potential of His creation.

What will this look like? Scripture gives us glimpses but not full details. What we do know is that God's purpose for us goes beyond mere existence. We are called to reign with Christ, to cultivate and enjoy His creation, and to explore the infinite possibilities of life in His kingdom. Eternity will be filled with purpose, meaning, and adventure as we continue to grow, create, and discover in partnership with God.

Visual 35.3 depicts glorified humans journeying into the vast expanse of the renewed cosmos.

Visual 35.3: Glorified humans journeying into the vast expanse of the renewed cosmos.
(**Source:** glorified humans journeying into the vast expanse of the renewed cosmos - Search Images)

The promise of resurrection grants believers immortality, allowing us to move beyond earthly limitations into an eternal, glorified state. The Sidebar explores this profound transformation, highlighting the hope of eternal life through resurrection.

Sidebar: Immortality through Resurrection

Through Jesus' death, resurrection, and ascension, believers receive the incredible promise of immortality and transformation. Jesus didn't merely die for us; He died as us, taking on the full consequence of sin. In Him, we were co-crucified (Galatians 2:20), and through this profound union, we also share in His resurrection and ascension, becoming a new creation (2 Corinthians 5:17). This transformation is as radical as the metamorphosis of a caterpillar into a butterfly—where what was once bound by limitations becomes something entirely new and glorious.

- 1 Corinthians 15:53-54 assures us that mortality is exchanged for immortality, where "death is swallowed up in victory." Jesus overcame sin and death, transferring to us His victory, righteousness, and eternal life. In His resurrection, we too have the assurance of a glorified existence, where the hidden glory of Christ in us will one day be fully revealed (Colossians 1:27).

- Romans 6:5 states, "If we have been united with Him in a death like His, we will certainly also be united with Him in a resurrection like His." Jesus' resurrection marks the defeat of death, not as an escape to heaven but as the beginning of a new, eternal quality of life in God's presence. The death of a saint is described as "costly" in Psalm 116:15, not because it is precious in a sentimental sense, but because each life carries immense value and purpose in God's kingdom.

- Jesus' ascension to the Father also becomes ours: "I am ascending to My Father and your Father, to My God and your God" (John 20:17). Through this, we inherit His relationship with the Father, living in union with God as members of His family. Whether part of the cloud of witnesses (Hebrews 12:1) or living on earth, we are united with God, participating in the fullness of His life.

In Colossians 2:15, Paul explains that Jesus "disarmed the powers and authorities" and paraded them in victory, symbolizing the defeat of all enemies. We share in this triumph, as Jesus' victory over death, sin, and every opposing force becomes ours. This promise of immortality and transformation fuels our hope, knowing that our present struggles are temporary, and we await the day when we will fully experience our glorified state.

Just as Jesus' glory was momentarily veiled in His humanity, our true glory is hidden until the day of full transformation. Through Jesus, we are being conformed to His glorious image, destined to live eternally with God in a transformed, victorious state. Death is not an end but a transition, a stepping into the reality of our true, eternal life with Him.

Conclusion: The Eternal Journey Begins

The story of redemption concludes not with an ending, but with the beginning of an eternal journey. Beyond glory lies an unending life of discovery, joy, and communion with God. Eternity is not a distant, far-off reality but the culmination of everything God has planned from the beginning—a reality where His love, wisdom, and glory fill all things, and where His people dwell with Him forever.

As we reflect on this eternal future, we are invited to live with purpose today, knowing that the choices we make, the relationships we build, and the love we share are all part of the eternal story that God is writing. Our lives on earth are the beginning of a journey that will continue for all eternity, a journey that leads us deeper into the heart of God and the fullness of His kingdom.

This is our hope. This is our destiny. Beyond glory lies an eternity of love, joy, and purpose, where we will forever be in the presence of our Creator, discovering more of His beauty, His grace, and His infinite goodness.

www.ingramcontent.com/pod-product-compliance
Lightning Source LLC
Chambersburg PA
CBHW031115160726
47991CB00004B/1390